# FU-GO

*Studies in War, Society, and the Military*

# FU-GO

The Curious History of Japan's
Balloon Bomb Attack on America

**ROSS COEN**

University of Nebraska Press
Lincoln and London

Chapter 5 was originally published in
altered form as "'If One Should Come
Your Way, Shoot It Down': The Alaska
Territorial Guard and the Japanese Balloon
Bomb Attack of World War II," *Alaska
History* 25 no.2 (Fall 2010), 1–19.

Library of Congress
Cataloging-in-Publication Data

Coen, Ross Allen.
Fu-go: the curious history of Japan's balloon
bomb attack on America / Ross Coen.
pages    cm.
(Studies in war, society, and the military)
Includes bibliographical
references and index.
ISBN 978-0-8032-4966-0 (cloth: alk. paper)
ISBN 978-0-8032-5668-2 (epub)
ISBN 978-0-8032-5669-9 (mobi)
ISBN 978-0-8032-5667-5 (pdf)
1. World War, 1939–1945—Aerial
operations, Japanese. 2. World War,
1939–1945—Balloons—West (U.S.)
3. West (U.S.)—History—1890–1945.
4. West (U.S.)—History, Military. I.
Title. II. Title: Curious history of Japan's
balloon bomb attack on America.
D792.J3C63 2014
940.54'28—dc23
2014023332

Set in Ehrhardt by Lindsey Auten.
Designed by N. Putens.

# Contents

# Illustrations

MAPS

TABLES

# Acknowledgments

Many friends and colleagues provided assistance in the writing of this book. I thank Mariko de Freytas for translating Japanese texts and for encouraging me to pursue the project when it was new and I did not yet know where the research trail would lead. I owe Leda Hunter a huge debt of gratitude for helping me understand what happened in Bly. For invaluable research assistance I thank Derek Mueller, Katie Breen, John Haile Cloe, Koichi Yoshino, Shunichi Yamamoto, and my dearest friend, Sanae Ohtsu. Thanks to Monique Dolak and Galen Roger Perras of the University of Ottawa, Saori Tachibana and Eddy Harrison at the University of Washington's East Asia Library, Todd Kepple at Klamath County Museum, Alice Ray and Stevie Ruda at the U.S. Forest Service, Carol Buswell at the National Archives in Seattle, Samira Bozorgi and Vishnu Jani at Stanford University's Hoover Institution, Rose Speranza at the Elmer E. Rasmuson Library at the University of Alaska Fairbanks, Angela Linn and Mareca Guthrie at the University of Alaska Museum of the North, Sarah D'Aurelio at Library and Archives Canada in Ottawa, Steve Henrikson at the Alaska State Museum in Juneau, Mathias Joost at the Canadian National Defence Headquarters' Directorate of History and Heritage, and Jeff Noakes, Carol Reid, and Susan Ross at the Canadian War Museum in Ottawa. At the University of Nebraska Press I thank Bridget Barry, Sabrina Ehmke Sergeant, and the reviewers of the manuscript. I thank Dixon Jones at the University

*Acknowledgments*

of Alaska Fairbanks for producing the terrific maps of Alaska, Canada, and the western United States that appear in the book. For providing me with the opportunity to deliver public lectures on the topic I thank Suellyn Novak at the Alaska Veterans Museum, Barbara Lando and Cynthia Steiner at Osher Lifelong Learning Institute, and the Alaska Historical Society, especially Pat and Frank Roppel, Jo Antonson, and Jim Ducker.

# FU-GO

# *Introduction*

Forest Service 34, a one-lane gravel road known to locals as the Dairy Creek Road, runs north by northeast from the small lumber town of Bly, Oregon, through cattle pasture dotted with juniper trees and outcroppings of basalt rock to the rising slopes of Gearhart Mountain twelve miles away. Straddling the border between Klamath and Lake Counties in south-central Oregon, the volcanic peak features long, sloping ridges at lower elevations and craggy cliffs near its 8,364-foot summit. On a clear day from the top, visitors can see hundreds of miles to other peaks up and down the Cascades. The mountain's dry pine forest features old-growth white fir and ponderosa and lodgepole pines, while open meadows with aspen and wildflowers dot the upper elevations of the peak. Deer, elk, coyote, black bear, and mountain lion, as well as dozens of species of birds, inhabit the mountain. The profusion of rainbow and brook trout in the many streams of the lower slopes make the area a popular destination for fishermen, especially from nearby Bly.

It was to those streams that the Reverend Archie Mitchell, on the bright, sunny morning of Saturday, May 5, 1945, took his wife and five children from his Sunday school class for a picnic lunch and a day of fishing. The tall, lanky, bespectacled Mitchell was the new pastor of the Christian and Missionary Alliance Church in Bly. His wife Elsie was five months pregnant with their first child. Having accepted the pastorate in Bly just two weeks before, the

Mitchells looked forward to introducing themselves to the community. Archie was especially keen to become acquainted with the children in his congregation. Joining the Mitchells that day were Dick Patzke, fourteen, his sister Joan Patzke, thirteen, Jay Gifford, thirteen, Edward Engen, thirteen, and Sherman Shoemaker, eleven. Elsie had baked a chocolate cake for the trip and wondered if she would be able to keep up with the youngsters, the pregnancy often leaving her quite ill.

With Archie at the wheel of his sedan, the group headed up the Dairy Creek Road to the forest on the southern face of Gearhart Mountain. The bright sun and warm springtime temperatures had melted the snow at the mountain's lower elevations, turning the gravel road into a slippery, slushy, pot-holed mess. A few miles up the slope, just short of a muddy stream called Leonard Creek, Mitchell encountered a Forest Service crew extracting a road grader that had become bogged down in the slush and mud the day before. Richard Barnhouse, the crew foreman, cautioned Mitchell against driving any farther up the snow-covered road.

Archie turned the car around and parked at a narrow pullout back down the road. The children immediately jumped out and ran down the slope toward the creek. Elsie, by then feeling a bit carsick and eager to get some fresh air, hurried after to keep an eye on them. Joan Patzke trailed behind the boys, her attention drawn to a large, dull-gray object resting on a knoll above the creek. She called to the others to come have a look.

Archie was by this time collecting the picnic basket and fishing poles from the trunk of the car. He glanced up and saw his wife and the children, some fifty yards away, standing in a tight circle looking down at something on the ground.

"Look what we found," Elsie called out to her husband. "It looks like some kind of balloon." One of the children reached down to pick up the object from the ground. Archie turned to shout a warning.

FIG. I. Archie and Elsie Mitchell. U.S. Forest Service, Fremont-Winema National Forests

He'd only begun to open his mouth when a tremendous explosion tore through the forest.[1]

At that moment Barnhouse was seated atop the road grader preparing to head back down the mountain. The explosion shook the ground, and he looked up to see tree branches, pine needles, and clumps of soil flying through the air. Barnhouse jumped from the grader and ran down the slope. The other members of the crew, George Donathan and John Peterson, trailed a few steps behind.

The men found Mitchell kneeling over his prostrate wife. Her clothes were ablaze and he was trying to beat out the fire with his bare hands. The mangled bodies of five dead or dying children lay scattered around a gaping, smoldering hole in the earth five feet across. All four boys had been killed instantly. Joan Patzke, who had been standing slightly behind the boys as they crowded around the object, remained conscious for only moments before she died. Elsie Mitchell, her husband at her side but unable to do anything about her injuries, died within minutes.

Barnhouse looked around. Debris was scattered everywhere. The force of the blast had embedded shards of metal in the trunks of surrounding trees. Pieces of the device, whatever it was, would later be found as far as four hundred feet away. Immediately adjacent to the smoking crater was a tangle of rope and wires connecting a boxlike frame atop a twisted metal ring roughly the size and shape of a bicycle wheel rim. Curved sections of another smaller ring blown apart by the blast could be seen. Four black and gray cylinders about the size of coffee cans and several white paper or cloth sacks resembling lunch bags also lay nearby. A huge gray canopy of some kind, the object that had first attracted Joan Patzke's attention, lay draped across the snow a short distance away.

While Barnhouse and Donathan drove to Bly to alert authorities, Peterson and Mitchell carefully covered the bodies with spruce boughs. Mitchell, by now in a state of deep shock, stared at his hands and rubbed them compulsively. The picric acid from the explosive device had colored his hands yellow when he attempted to put out the fire on Elsie's clothes. His hands would remain stained for weeks.

Barnhouse and Donathan returned an hour later with the county sheriff, chief forest ranger, and county coroner A. J. Ousley. The men moved the bodies of Joan and Elsie, those farthest from the debris field, but left the boys alone. No one dared get too close to the device or touch anything for fear of setting off another explosion. An ordnance expert from the Naval Air Station in nearby Lakeview was en route. Nothing could be done for the boys now anyway, and the men were content to wait.

Of the many phone calls placed that afternoon by the Lakeview sheriff's office one went to Army Intelligence, "G-2" in military shorthand, at Fort Lewis, Washington. The call was taken by a civilian employee who took down the message and handed it to Lieutenant Colonel Charles F. Bisenius. The note said something about an explosion and a large white balloon. The information meant nothing to anyone in Bly, but Bisenius immediately knew what had happened. He telephoned William Hammond, G-2 assistant chief of staff at the Western Defense Command in San Francisco. In a sense, Hammond had been waiting for this phone call for six months.

Since November the previous year, hundreds of explosive-laden balloons with Japanese markings had turned up across the western United States. The first was fished out of the sea by a U.S. Navy supply boat off San Pedro, California, in early November 1944. Two weeks later, one landed in the ocean off Kailua, Hawaii. In December, balloons were spotted in Thermopolis, Wyoming; Kalispell, Montana; Marshall, Alaska; and Estacada, Oregon. Several more followed in the first week of January, by which time the War Department came to realize the country was under attack from a new type of weapon, ingenious in design but simple in its operation. The balloons were Japanese offensive weapons called *fusen bakudan* ("fire balloons," or more literally "balloon bombs"). The Japanese Imperial Army called them by the code name *fu-go*. Measuring over thirty feet in diameter and filled with hydrogen, the balloons were launched in Japan and carried to North America by the strong, high-altitude westerly winds unnamed then but known today as the jet stream. Each balloon carried four incendiary bombs and one thirty-pound high-explosive bomb, all designed to drop in a timed sequence once the vehicle had completed its transoceanic voyage and was somewhere over the United States. They were free balloons in every sense of the word—uncontrollable once released, their flight path determined only by the ever-fluctuating meteorological conditions in which they traveled. By the end of the war in August 1945, over three hundred had been recovered in North America.[2]

Colonel Hammond of Army Intelligence had been directly involved in the balloon defense from the beginning, though there were many opportunities for him not to be. The FBI assumed investigative jurisdiction over the first balloons to arrive in the United States. Because those initial discoveries contained no bombs, no one suspected they might be weapons of war. An errant weather balloon from a nearby meteorological station, perhaps, or even a new type of barrage balloon that had slipped its mooring somewhere. Once the devices had been positively identified as Japanese in origin, the U.S. Navy's Western Sea Frontier figured the balloons had been launched from enemy submarines that surfaced just off the coast, and accordingly it wrested the investigation from the FBI. The idea that a free balloon could have traveled across the ocean all the way from Japan was initially too preposterous to take seriously. In time, U.S. authorities discovered the balloons had indeed made such a transit. The realization not only made *fu-go* the world's first intercontinental ballistic missile but placed responsibility for the American response with the Western Defense Command. Because Colonel Hammond had taken the first calls about one of the very first balloons, his office became the central point of contact for all balloon reports.

Much about the unusual offensive would remain a mystery to U.S. authorities until after the war. The very name of the aerial weapon was of course unknown—no one in North America knew to call them "fu-go"—thus the WDC referred to the balloons with the code name "Paper," so chosen because the thirty-foot diameter envelope was constructed of a lightweight but durable handmade paper. The exact location of the launch sites remained unknown, as did the number of devices being launched. Most disturbing for Colonel Hammond was that the balloons' true purpose could only be guessed at. The

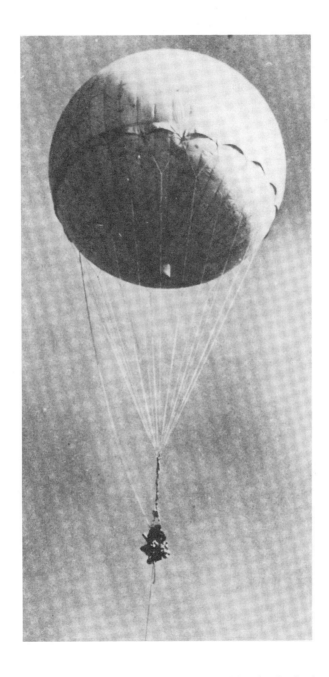

FIG. 2. Fu-go, the Japanese balloon bomb. Smithsonian Institution

presence of incendiary bombs suggested the Japanese hoped to ignite wildfires in the forests and grasslands of the western states, yet the WDC feared the vehicles might also transport enemy saboteurs or harmful bacteriological agents to America.

In time the WDC would reach out to government and civilian agencies, state legislatures, governors, and even elementary school principals and Boy Scout troop leaders in an effort to defend against the menace posed by the bomb-laden balloons. At the time of the Bly incident, however, the War Department had enacted a strict information blackout based on the not altogether misguided belief that keeping word of the balloons out of the newspapers would deny the Japanese the very intelligence they needed to know whether the campaign was successful. The censorship policy worked precisely as designed—with tragic consequences for the Mitchell party in Bly.

Lieutenant H. P. Scott, the bomb disposal officer at Lakeview Naval Station, finally arrived in Bly late in the afternoon. The bodies of the four dead boys still lay on the ground, by now covered with white sheets brought from town a few hours before. The lieutenant found and deactivated four thermite incendiary bombs (the coffee can-sized devices), a demolition charge, a magnesium flash bomb, and several small plugs each containing a small powder charge. He also collected fragments of the bomb that had exploded that morning.

Coroner Ousley then collected the bodies of Dick Patzke, Jay Gifford, Edward Engen, and Sherman Shoemaker and took them to the morgue in Lakeview.

Army officials from Fort Lewis convened a meeting early the next morning at the Forest Service headquarters in Lakeview. They took official statements from Barnhouse, Donathan, and Ousley. (Mitchell had been interviewed the night before.) Lieutenant Scott reported his preliminary findings on the exploded ordnance. As expected, it was a fifteen-kilogram anti-personnel bomb of Japanese make. It was decided that the evidence collected at the scene would be taken to

Fort Lewis for analysis, while the balloon would remain at the naval station in Lakeview.

F. H. Armstrong, the chief forest ranger in Bly, then asked Lieutenant Colonel Bisenius what information he could provide to the press. In anticipation of this question, the lieutenant colonel had already contacted the Office of Censorship in Washington, DC. He'd received clearance to announce only that the six persons had been killed by a blast of unknown origin. That the bomb was Japanese and had been delivered to the United States across the Pacific Ocean by a free balloon was not to be revealed.

Malcolm Epley, managing editor of the Klamath Falls *Herald and News*, protested the censorship policy. By now everyone in the area knew the Mitchell party had found a Japanese weapon, and Epley strongly urged the War Department to allow publication of the full story. Thousands of people who walked into the woods remained at risk, he argued. Who could know how many additional balloons remained in the woods waiting to be discovered by another unknowing group of picnickers? The War Department did not relent. Under the headline "Blast Kills 6," the Monday edition of Epley's newspaper made no mention of a Japanese balloon and stated only that the deceased had been killed by "an explosion of unannounced cause."[3]

That same day, James Ousley, the county coroner, signed the death certificates for all six victims. In each case, per the strict instructions of military officials, he recorded the cause of death as "an explosion from an undetermined source."[4]

# 1

..............

# *Paper*

All eyes were on Lieutenant Colonel James H. "Jimmy" Doolittle as he climbed into the cockpit of his B-25 shortly after 8:00 a.m. on April 18, 1942. His was the first in line of sixteen long-range bombers crowding the deck of the USS *Hornet*, positioned in the Pacific Ocean some 620 miles east of Japan. Doolittle's plane had only 467 feet of deck ahead. The tail of the last B-25 hung out over the ship's fantail. Doolittle steered his plane into position, aligning his left and nose wheels with two white hashmarks the *Hornet's* crew had painted on the deck. Holding to those marks during takeoff would allow the B-25's right wing to clear the ship's superstructure by about six feet.[1]

Before this mission few thought it possible that a land-based plane, fully loaded with thousands of pounds of ordnance, could take off from a carrier at sea. Doolittle, a legendary aviator who had reenlisted in the Army two years before at the age of forty-three after a decade in civilian life, had spent the previous five months studying and training in B-25s for this unusual mission. He stripped the planes of all unnecessary equipment (including the radios) and modified the gas tanks and carburetors for greater fuel efficiency. Doolittle found that on a carrier going full speed into a strong headwind, a B-25 could achieve minimum takeoff speed and be airborne in only a few hundred feet.

The mission that would come to be known as the Doolittle Raid was planned and executed in direct response to the Japanese attack at Pearl Harbor on December 7, 1941. Approval for an offensive air strike on the Japanese mainland came almost immediately from Army Air Force general Henry "Hap" Arnold. On April 2, 1942, the *Hornet* sailed from San Francisco accompanied by four destroyers, two cruisers, and a refueling ship. The force made rendezvous ten days later with the carrier *Enterprise* and her attendant fleet of support vessels. Task Force 16, as the joint armada was now called, fell into cruising formation headed due west across the Pacific. Those crew members not fully informed of the true nature of the top-secret mission could by now make a pretty accurate guess.

The plan called for the *Hornet* to take a position 500 miles from Tokyo on April 19, from which the B-25s would be launched. A day earlier and 120 miles short of the launch zone, however, the fleet spotted a Japanese reconnaissance vessel. Intercepted radio transmissions in Japanese convinced the *Hornet's* officers their position had been compromised. Dive bombers launched from the *Enterprise* attacked and sank the enemy vessel. Doolittle ordered his men to their planes. They were going to take off now.

All the pilots' previous training in short takeoffs had taken place on land at Elgin Field in Florida, where an outline of the *Hornet's* deck had been painted on the runway to simulate the carrier. Persistent mechanical problems and equipment constraints limited the crews to only twenty-five flight hours in the B-25s and not a single practice takeoff from a carrier at sea. Doolittle himself had never before done it. When the deck crew pulled the chocks from his wheels and

Doolittle revved the plane's engines, everyone onboard knew the entire mission was at stake. If Doolittle couldn't take off in 467 feet, it was over. If he could, then each successive plane had that much additional room for takeoff. The sixteenth and last plane would have a clear deck with a more than comfortable 820-foot margin.

Doolittle accelerated just as the *Hornet's* bow began recovering from a plunge into the wind-whipped thirty-foot waves. The deck was still rising when he achieved full speed and took off with room to spare. The crews of the other B-25s breathed sighs of relief. Within exactly one hour all sixteen planes were airborne and flying for Japan. The ships of Task Force 16 turned around immediately and sailed for Hawaii.

At that moment six hundred miles away in Tokyo, civil defense forces initiated a routine air raid drill that had been announced in the newspapers two days before. Planes took to the sky as barrage balloons (large inflatables tethered to cables and held in place high over cities to deter enemy aircraft from approaching overhead) were launched along the waterfront. Firefighters tested their equipment. The city's residents barely noticed, however. There had been no sirens that morning, and the drills were becoming so commonplace as to attract little attention. Few noticed when a twin-engine bomber approached the city from the north just after noon. (Doolittle had maneuvered to come in from that direction figuring the Japanese would concentrate their air defenses for an expected attack from the east.) After dropping its entire bomb payload in an industrial area of the city, the B-25 quickly descended in an S-pattern to rooftop altitude to evade any anti-aircraft fire or Japanese fighters that might be in pursuit (none were).

Joseph C. Grew, the U.S. ambassador to Japan whose repatriation the Japanese would prevent until later that summer, at first believed he was witnessing a training exercise, a mock dogfight among Japanese planes. Even when half a dozen large fires with black, billowing smoke broke out around the city, it hardly seemed possible this was an American attack. Father Bruno Bitter, the rector of Sophia University in Tokyo, would similarly recall that most people thought it was just another drill. But when they realized the sirens were real, he noted, "nobody could hold them back to go outside, to climb the roofs or the chimneys to get a better view." An intense curiosity overcame everyone's better instincts to seek shelter.[2]

Over the course of the hour, the American planes engaged military and industrial targets in five cities in Japan—Tokyo, Yokohama, Osaka, Kobe, and Nagoya—each dropping three 500-pound high explosive demolition bombs and one 500-pound incendiary bomb. None experienced any significant defensive fire from the Japanese. The sixteen planes continued west toward five Allied airfields in China. Deteriorating weather conditions and empty fuel tanks, however, kept every plane from reaching its intended rendezvous point. All either crash-landed short of the airfields or were ditched by their crew. One landed in Russia near Vladivostok.

Doolittle and his crew bailed out over Quzhou and, armed with the one phrase they knew—*Lushu hoo megwa fugi* (I am an American)—received assistance from Chinese civilians and soldiers. Though he survived and was feted by Chiang Kai-Shek, Doolittle knew the bombings had caused little actual damage in Japan. He had lost his entire fleet of B-25s and had no knowledge of the safety or whereabouts of most of his crew. Doolittle wondered whether a court-martial awaited him back in the States. What Doolittle and his fellow airmen received was a hero's welcome. Doolittle received the Medal of Honor, as well as a promotion to the rank of Brigadier General, and all eighty Raiders received the Distinguished Flying Cross. By directly avenging the attack on Pearl Harbor, the Doolittle Raid boosted the morale of Americans and marked a turning point in attitudes about the war. Japanese domination in Asia and the Pacific suddenly appeared vulnerable.

In Japan, the effect was nearly as dramatic.

For a people with an almost spiritual belief their homeland would never be invaded, the Doolittle Raid shook their confidence to its core. The Japanese had absolute faith in the emperor. They believed officials who claimed the nation was invincible. That enemy planes had entered Japan unmolested and dropped bombs in cities across the country belied that notion. What else had the government lied to them about? Besieged for information after the bombing, Japanese military officials first sought to exaggerate the Americans' ruthlessness. They claimed entire fleets of bombers destroyed whole city blocks and killed thousands of civilians, including dozens of children machine-gunned to death in their schoolyard. As embarrassment over the surprise raid set in, however, the government reversed course and began downplaying the attack. Official releases stated the Americans' pathetic strike had caused minimal damage. Newspapers reported nine American planes had been shot down, an obvious lie. For senior officials, allowing the life of the emperor to be put in danger proved the worst humiliation of all. Just six weeks later, Japan sought to expunge the dishonor by attacking Midway Island (from which they suspected the Doolittle Raid had been launched). The disastrous defeat at Midway permanently weakened the Japanese navy and altered the balance of power in the Pacific in favor of the United States.

The Doolittle Raid started in motion still another chain of events in Tokyo. Infuriated that mainland America remained comfortably untouched, the Imperial General Headquarters demanded a retaliatory strike on the United States. The violation of their homeland convinced the Japanese of the need to respond in kind. Even an offensive that caused only minimal damage, no more than the marginally strategic scattering of bombs Doolittle had accomplished, would give Japan a moral boost. Just weeks after the Doolittle bombing, a simple directive went out to scientists and engineers at the Noborito

Institute to devise an offensive strike capability. The order was no more descriptive than that. Find a way to bomb America.

NOBORITO

The Ninth Military Technical Research Institute, more commonly called the Noborito Institute, occupied an expansive compound on a bluff above the Tama River in southwest Tokyo. Founded in 1927 by Captain Ryo Shinoda as part of the Army Science Research Institute, Noborito began as a small research division dedicated to covert warfare. Shinoda, a chemist who had studied at the prestigious Tokyo Imperial University, at first mined spy novels and movies for ideas about intelligence and counterintelligence operations. His staff tinkered with secret inks, miniature cameras, counterfeit foreign currencies, telephone wiretapping devices, and other tools of the espionage trade. Eventually the laboratory moved on to more lethal applications, including poisons and biological agents that could be used to destroy crops and livestock. By the outbreak of World War II, the division had grown to two dozen buildings and nearly one thousand employees. Shinoda himself would achieve the rank of lieutenant general.[3]

In summer 1942 Noborito began investigating ways to fulfill the retaliation directive. One early proposal called for long-range bombers to make one-way sorties from Japan to the U.S. mainland. After dropping the entire payload of high-explosive ordnance on Seattle, San Francisco, Los Angeles, or some other urban center on the West Coast, the crew would use the aircraft itself as a weapon, crashing it into some high-value target. Engineers dreamed up ways a bomber could fly all the way from Tokyo to New York. They'd have to strip the aircraft of all unnecessary equipment and install fuel tanks inside the fuselage, essentially turning the airplane into a flying fuel tank. The plan never advanced beyond a few design drawings, however. A more practical option called for a small bomb-laden aircraft equipped with floats for water landings that could be launched from the deck of a submarine. The proposal was field-tested on September 9, 1942, when Warrant Officer Nobuo Fujita took off in a Yokosuka E14Y floatplane from a submarine that had surfaced off the Oregon coast. Fujita dropped two large incendiary bombs in the Siskiyou National Forest in the hope of starting a forest fire. His plane was spotted from a lookout tower, however, and response crews easily located where the bombs fell and contained the small fires. A recent rainstorm had also made the woods very damp and prevented the fires from spreading any further. Although the sortie was a "success" in that Fujita bombed his target and was safely retrieved after landing the plane alongside the submarine, the Imperial Navy canceled the project.

That same month, Sueki Kusaba, a major general stationed in Manchuria, was recalled to Japan and assigned to Noborito. Like Shinoda and nearly all other top scientists at the institute, Kusaba was a graduate of Tokyo Imperial University, the nation's premier institute of higher learning, where he had studied applied physics. Upon arriving at Noborito he was placed in charge of a unit then experimenting with free balloons. Technicians were modifying weather balloons and barrage balloons to see whether a free balloon could transport ordnance great distances. Engineers at Noborito had first studied the concept of a balloon bomb in the early 1930s, when Lieutenant General Reikichi Tada led a program that designed a four-meter balloon capable of delivering explosives up to seventy miles. The device featured a time-fuse that could be calibrated depending on wind speed and the distance the balloon needed to travel to reach enemy lines.[4]

The small balloon designed by General Tada was one of many unique weapons under development at Noborito, then still in its spy movie phase. Other devices included a small unmanned tank, rocket-propelled explosives, and the "death ray," a concentrated burst of electricity that it was hoped would obliterate any enemy soldier in its path. Each prototype was assigned a code name with the ending *-go*

FIG. 3. Major General Sueki Kusaba, head of the Fu-go program. Bert Webber Papers, Box 2, Hoover Institution Archives, Stanford University

(a numbering suffix in Japanese). The tank was the *I-go*, the rocket the *Ro-go*. Tada's balloon project took the name *fu-go* from the first character of *fusen*, the Japanese word for "balloon."

General Kusaba, who had served under Tada in the 1930s in the original balloon program, now revived the *fu-go* project. Using the very prototypes that had been in storage for a decade, Kusaba began modifying the design for longer flights. After nearly a year of research and testing, his team came up with a design capable of remaining aloft for thirty hours at an altitude of 25,000 feet. Tests demonstrated the balloon could easily travel several hundred miles, though General Kusaba believed a range as great as two thousand miles was possible under optimum wind conditions. According to the proposal then under development, the six-meter balloon was to be inflated on the deck of a submarine and released at night within six hundred miles of the coast of the United States, a distance the balloon could cover in about ten hours. Launching the balloons in the cool nighttime temperatures would keep internal pressure fluctuations to a minimum and offered the best prospect for relatively constant altitude. Looking ahead to the program's operational phase, the Noborito technicians planned to install a time-control device on each balloon that would release a five-kilogram incendiary bomb once the vehicle had completed its flight.

By summer 1943 two submarines had been outfitted with launching equipment, and Kusaba's team had initiated the manufacture of several hundred balloons. Despite this progress, the project was canceled that August. The escalating war in the Pacific required every vessel in the Japanese fleet, and the Imperial Navy proved unwilling to dispatch any submarines on balloon missions that would only scatter minor ordnance on American soil. The finished balloons were warehoused at Noborito.

Could a balloon launched directly from Japan reach the United States? A trans-Pacific flight required a balloon with a range of at least six thousand miles. Engineers at Noborito faced two immediate problems. First, experience with the submarine balloons suggested that such a flight would take several days, meaning the balloon would undergo severe pressure fluctuations over the course of its journey. A fixed volume of gas inside a sealed balloon would expand during the daytime as temperatures rose. The envelope would almost certainly burst unless some means for venting the gas could be devised. At night, cooling temperatures would result in contraction of the gas and loss of altitude. The balloons might fall into the ocean their first night out.

The second problem engineers identified was whether the westerly winds crossing Japan were even capable of carrying a balloon across the ocean. For answers they consulted Hidetoshi Arakawa at the Central Meteorological Observatory in Tokyo. Arakawa and his colleagues had long known of the existence of high-altitude westerlies directly above Japan. They believed these winds continued into the Western Hemisphere, though their probable flow patterns remained a mystery. In attempting to diagram the possible trajectory of winds across the Pacific, Arakawa drew on decades-old research from a pioneer of Japanese meteorology, Wasaburo Ooishi.

As a young atmospheric physicist in the 1910s, Ooishi visited universities and meteorological institutes throughout the United States and Europe, including the Lindenberg Aerological Observatory in Berlin. His travels typified the Japanese practice of the time where promising young scientists were sent abroad to learn Western scientific methods and then brought back home to prestigious university posts. Despite having his travels interrupted by World War I, Ooishi spent several years observing leading scientists who pioneered techniques for studying the upper atmosphere. He brought cases of instruments back to Japan in 1920, intent on researching upper-air wind currents.[5]

Over several days in early December 1924, under brilliantly clear skies with seemingly no limit to upper-air visibility, Ooishi launched a sequence of one-meter balloons from the Tateno Observatory, a small weather station northeast of Tokyo he had established immediately following his return from the West. The balloons reached 30,000 feet in about half an hour. Tracking the balloons' lateral movement with a theodolite, Ooishi calculated the wind speed at 140 knots at altitude.

This and other observations led Ooishi to a simple yet ground-breaking discovery. He had recorded comparable wind speeds before, yet they seemed to vary from week to week and month to month. Wind speeds recorded in summer, for example, rarely exceeded twenty knots, leading Ooishi to theorize that the strong winter winds were unpredictable anomalies. The Western scientific papers available to Ooishi, including the definitive study at the time by Nobel laureate Robert Millikan, all offered the same explanation—strong substratospheric winds were not uncommon but also not persistent. With his long-term observations over multiple seasons, however, Ooishi had discovered definite patterns in the relationship between upper-air features and the passage of weather fronts. From March 1923 to February 1925 he recorded 1,288 observations. Plotting seasonal wind speed and direction using these data points, he found that winter winds were markedly stronger at every altitude (especially above 25,000 feet) than during the other seasons. Far from being anomalies, the westerly winds of the upper atmosphere had great seasonal predictability.[6]

Ooishi published his findings, not in Japanese, but in Esperanto, an auxiliary language invented to allow people of different nations and native tongues to communicate. Regardless, his paper was essentially ignored by the world meteorological community. Though no one realized it at the time, Ooishi had helped lay the foundation for study of what would come to be called the jet stream, a phenomenon Western scientists would not fully understand or appreciate until after World War II.

In late 1943, after Ooishi had received the Order of Sacred Treasure and retired from the Central Meteorological Observatory, Hidetoshi Arakawa used his predecessor's charts of wind flow over Tokyo in an attempt to extrapolate wind speed and direction to the east across the Pacific. He coupled Ooishi's data on surface temperature and wind (relative to conditions at higher altitudes) with surface data from over the ocean. Following a well-established methodology that assumed a decrease in both temperature and pressure at higher altitudes, Arakawa mapped out approximate flow patterns for the different seasons. He estimated a balloon released in winter from Japan that was able to maintain an altitude of between 30,000 and 35,000 feet could reach the North American continent in thirty to one hundred hours. The strongest winds blew from November to March at speeds approaching two hundred miles per hour. Balloons released at other times of year would experience longer flight times, if they were able to cross the ocean at all. Arakawa next obtained data from weather stations in Sendai, Niigata, Wajima, Yonago, Fukuoka, Shio-no-Misaka, and Oshima, which he used to map possible transoceanic flow patterns. This information would later prove useful to Noborito in selecting launch sites for the balloons.[7]

Encouraged by Arakawa's findings, General Kusaba ordered the six-meter submarine balloons taken out of storage and outfitted with radiosondes, small devices capable of recording and transmitting data on basic atmospheric conditions. Originally designed as offensive weapons, they would now be used as weather balloons. Over a period of several months in the winter of 1943–44, a joint task force consisting of officials from Noborito and the Central Meteorological Observatory released two hundred balloons from sites up and down the east coast of Honshu, Japan's main island. Although none came close to reaching North America, many balloons remained aloft for up to thirty-six hours and sent back information that both corroborated Arakawa's findings and facilitated the creation of even more

FIG. 4. Research team from Noborito conducting launch tests at Ichinomiya in 1943. "Nishida Group," Bert Webber Papers, Box 10, Hoover Institution Archives, Stanford University

detailed wind charts. Engineers at Noborito now firmly believed that a transoceanic balloon flight was possible.

## OUR RED BLOOD BURNS

Students at the Yamaguchi Girls High School gathered in the shade of a large ginko tree in the schoolyard on a hot summer day in 1944. The girls, all in their mid- to late teens, had been summoned to the yard to receive a visitor from the nearby Kokura Arsenal, an industrial weapons production compound. Like students all over Japan, the girls at Yamaguchi had already been supporting the war effort for some time. From the start of the war, classes decreased in number and eventually ceased altogether as the girls went to work sewing uniforms for soldiers stationed at a nearby infantry regiment.

As more and more men from the village left for military service, the girls filled in by working the rice fields and mining charcoal from the mountains. They undertook these strenuous labors willingly. The militaristic nature of their schools had prepared them for total allegiance to the emperor and the war. "Sacrifice yourself to serve" was a principle taught to every class.[8]

The Kokura Arsenal officer had come to Yamaguchi to recruit the girls for a special mission. They would be making a "secret weapon," he told them, one that would fly across the ocean all the way to America.[9] While the officer spoke, troops began setting up wooden stands in rows up and down the schoolyard, each supporting a drying board the size of a *tatami* mat (three by six feet). Told they'd be making paper, the girls had no idea what exactly that meant or how their labor would result in a flying weapon. As each student took her place at one of the drying boards, a soldier took out a saw and began cutting down the ginko tree. Its shade would hinder the drying process, the officer explained.

The conscription of the girls to the *fu-go* program followed a series of strategic decisions made by General Kusaba and the Noborito engineers. From the moment he assumed command of the balloon program, the general had grappled with the operational limitations of using balloons as intercontinental weapons. Targeted bombing of American military installations, factories, or urban areas would prove next to impossible since the balloons could not be controlled once released. Even launching them at close range from submarines would only open the vessels to immediate counterattack. Manned balloon flights were briefly considered, but quickly dismissed as impractical. The random nature of balloon flights precluded the selection of specific targets and instead forced Kusaba to consider the meager net effect of isolated attacks that in all statistical probability would occur in sparsely populated rural areas of the western United States.

The Yokosuka floatplane attack over Oregon achieved no strategic objective, only the starting of a few small, easily extinguished fires. Yet the mission demonstrated that if large-scale forest fires could be ignited the Americans would have to fight the blazes by diverting resources that otherwise might be used in the war effort. The nuisance factor alone might be worth the effort, regardless of whatever damage the balloon bombs actually caused. A single incendiary bomb, containing just a few pounds of thermite and dropped on a dry forest, could conceivably ignite a raging fire that would scorch thousands of acres. So what about a hundred incendiary bombs? A thousand? The effect of ten thousand balloons each dropping several incendiary bombs might be devastating, even if only a fraction of those bombs actually started a wildfire. "One match-stick may cause a conflagration," wrote one Noborito technician.[10]

The Imperial Army estimated that only 10 percent of balloons released from Japan would reach America, with an unknown number of those conceivably failing to detonate their bombs. An effective campaign would therefore require tens of thousands of balloons, yet procuring construction materials represented a challenge for resource-poor Japan. Technical Major Teiji Takada, a procurement officer on the *fu-go* project, grasped the large number of fuses, electric components, and other hardware the program would require. He began identifying critical components with respect to whether and how they could be made from cheaper substitute materials.[11] For the envelope, no cheaper substance could be found than that used for every other balloon to date in the *fu-go* program — thin layers of tissue paper.

*Kozo*, a member of the mulberry family, is a deciduous tree native to eastern Asia with bark composed of exceptionally strong fibers. *Washi*, or Japanese paper, can be made from *kozo*, first by scraping, washing, and boiling the bark in a solution of lye. Once washed to remove all traces of lye and other impurities, the fibers are rolled into balls and pounded. The resulting pulp is mixed with water, scooped onto a frame, and finally pressed and dried to form sheets of lightweight yet uniformly strong paper.

The advantages of making balloon envelopes out of *washi* occurred to Noborito engineers from the very beginning of the *fu-go* program. It was cheap, easy to make, lightweight, and durable, and *kozo* trees grew in abundance all over Japan. Large sheets of handmade *washi* obtained from commercial paper companies across the country were brought to Noborito for testing. The samples varied in thickness and quality of construction, even among sheets made by the same company, which convinced the army that the eventual mass production of balloons would require standardized methods. Engineers determined that four or five layers of thin tissue paper pressed and laminated together offered the strongest composition for the balloon envelopes. After experimenting with many different glues and sealants, it was discovered that a hydrocellulose paste made from *konnyaku*, a type of Japanese potato, provided a strong, gas-proof seal between the individual sheets.

One of the Yamaguchi students, fifteen-year old Tetsuko Tanaka, described the schoolyard paper factory forty years later in a memoir of schoolgirls who worked on the project:

> We covered the board with a thin layer of paste made from the *konnyaku* plant and then laid down two sheets of Japanese paper and brushed out any bubbles. When dry, a thicker layer of paste, with a slightly bluish hue, a little like the color of the sky, was evenly applied to it. That process was repeated five times. We really believed we were doing secret work, so I didn't talk about this even at home, but my clothes were covered with paste, so my family must have been able to figure out something.[12]

The army mobilized thousands of teenage girls at schools across the country when it became apparent the commercial paper factories

FIG. 5. Japanese schoolgirls at paper drying boards. "Cutting balloon paper to size," Bert Webber Papers, Box 10, Hoover Institution Archives, Stanford University

would not meet Noborito's order for ten thousand balloons in time for autumn and the start of the windy season. For months, the Nippon Kakokin Company, Mitsubishi Saishi, and Kokuka Rubber Company had been producing paper using standardized steel frames instead of the traditional wooden ones. The army instituted the industrial approach in order to secure paper of uniform size, thickness, and composition. Production hit a bottleneck in the time-consuming step of laminating and gluing the sheets, so the companies began shipping raw paper to schools across Japan.[13]

With the start of the autumn rains the entire operation at Yamaguchi High School had to be moved into the gymnasium, where the drying of the sheets proceeded much more slowly. Eventually the girls tried lighting charcoal in a large hibachi in a futile effort to get the paste to dry. The attempt only succeeded in making several girls sick from carbon monoxide poisoning and very nearly burning down the school. All across Japan, the wet autumn season and coming winter caused the army to reconsider its paper-making operation. Everything had to be moved indoors. The army consolidated its efforts by moving production facilities, including the young female laborers, to factories across Japan.

On January 2, 1945, a day after celebrating the sacred New Year's holiday with their families, the 150 members of the Yamaguchi senior class joined hundreds more from schools around the prefecture at the paper factory at Kokura Arsenal. They had boarded the train for Kokura that morning after a brief visit to a Shinto shrine and a farewell ceremony at the station where their parents and teachers waved goodbye. "You must behave like the daughter of a warrior family," one student was instructed by her grandmother.[14] Fully aware the weapons compound might be targeted for bombing by American planes, the school principal had for a time resisted sending the girls to Kokura. After the students of nearby Nakamura High School were sent away in December 1944, the Yamaguchi students begged to go as well. One girl fetched a razor so they could write the principal a petition in blood.

Upon arriving in Kokura, the girls caught sight of a completed balloon, its billowing canopy much larger than they had imagined. "This was what we'd been making! It fired our determination," Tetsuko Tanaka recalled. The students lined up in formation in the blowing snow of the factory yard along with scores of male army recruits. Each girl wore a white *hatchimaki* (headband) with the school emblem and the words "Student Special Attack Force." They were proud to stand next to the handsome men in uniform and know they too were serving their country. An army officer, so young that he reminded the girls of their older brothers, led them in a pledge of allegiance to the emperor and announced he would receive the spring of their nineteenth year. They would shed their youth, in other words, and pass to womanhood at the factory. Standing side by side in the snow,

FIG. 6. "Plant of utter darkness": Kokura Arsenal where Japanese schoolgirls manufactured paper, 1944-45. Koichi Yoshino

the young men and women proudly sang a war song called "Our Red Blood Burns."[15]

The sight that greeted the girls when they walked into the Kokura factory for the first time put to rest any notion of their sunny schoolyard back home. The entire first floor was filled with countless metal drying boards and dozens of steam-drying machines that operated at temperatures approaching 160 degrees Fahrenheit. Girls operated two boards at a time, shuffling back and forth between gluing one set while the other dried. Condensation dripped continuously from the ceiling above, while the floor was covered with paste that had spilled from the boards. Prohibited from wearing shoes to prevent accidentally tearing the paper with a misstep, the girls worked ankle deep in the muck wearing only thin socks. Fungal infections were common. Long black drapes had been hung over the windows to maintain absolute secrecy, giving the room a gloomy, cavernous feel. The students called it the "plant of utter darkness."[16]

The girls worked twelve-hour shifts in the sauna-like factory, with no breaks except to use the toilet, then trundled back to their unheated dormitory where they peeled dried *konnyaku* paste from their clothes before collapsing of exhaustion. Deprived of a lunch break during the shift, it was not uncommon for girls to slip away to the second floor, where the paste was made in large wooden barrels, and quickly sneak a bite of the powdered *konnyaku*. Dinner usually consisted of two rice balls, the occasional wilted vegetable, and miso soup. Despite the privations, the students also tried to be ordinary teenage girls. They began to loosen their headbands little by little so their hair would fall down as they walked by soldiers in the yard. They tried using toothpaste as make-up and extracted juice from *hechima*, a type of large gourd, to use as skin lotion. Lipstick was a precious commodity obtained from girls who lived near the plant.[17]

The sheets the girls produced, five layers of paper set with their fibers in alternating directions for added strength, were inspected for flaws by being placed atop a large light box. Small tears or areas where the sealant had been insufficiently applied showed clearly as glowing spots on the paper and were subsequently patched. After washing the paper in soda ash, water, and glycerine in order to make it pliable and prevent cracking, girls in the assembly room measured and cut the sheets into long trapezoidal panels, some six hundred of which were required for each balloon. The panels for each hemisphere were arranged over a form and taped and sewn together at the seams. Girls who worked in the assembly room were required to have closely trimmed fingernails and could not wear hairpins.

Once the two halves had been joined with a reinforced waistband seam, the completed balloon was covered with a waterproofing lacquer. For the final step, a scalloped skirt with attach points for the nineteen shroud lines was glued around the balloon just beneath the equator. The final assembly usually occurred, not at the factory, but in large buildings around Tokyo such as the Nichigeki Music Hall and Kokugikan sumo arena. Testing of the balloons by inflating them to their full capacity required such roomy indoor spaces. The army also wished to assemble the envelopes as close as possible to the launch sites on the east coast. Transporting the balloons in their assembled state long distances only increased the risk they would be damaged in transit.[18] The schoolgirls who assembled the balloons, including the students of Yamaguchi High School, greeted every successful test with cries of "Bonzai!" They knew nothing of the stratospheric winds, incendiary bombs, or even whether their creations were actually going to reach the United States. Said Tetsuko Tanaka, "We just pasted paper."[19]

The Imperial General Headquarters placed such importance on the *fu-go* project that it directed the navy to begin its own balloon program in parallel with that of the army/Noborito campaign. Technical Lieutenant Commander Kiyoshi Tanaka headed the navy effort that experimented with a nine-meter envelope made of rubberized silk, what would come to be called the B-Type balloon (the army's balloon received the designation of A-Type).[20]

The Naval Meteorological Service analyzed data from weather balloon flights over the Pacific Ocean and concluded air temperatures at 30,000 feet would vary between 80 degrees Fahrenheit during the day and -60 degrees at night. For a hydrogen-filled balloon to survive the corresponding pressure fluctuations would require either some means for regulating its internal pressure or an envelope of exceptional strength and flexibility. The navy chose the latter approach and developed a fully sealed balloon designed to withstand more than double its expected internal maximum pressure.

Layers of lightweight *habutai* silk were pressed together and then impregnated with a thin layer of rubber. The sheets were cut into panels and pasted together with rubber cement to form a perfect sphere. The rubberized material made the B-Type balloons strong, but also quite heavy. The initial round of tests in early 1944 showed that partially inflated balloons had almost zero lift at ground level. Even fully inflated balloons tended to bounce along the ground several times before rising, in the process risking damage to the payload or to the envelope itself. Eventually the navy refined the design so that the B-Type balloons achieved an altitude of 30,000 feet and entered the currents of strongest wind about two or three hours after launch, still a particularly slow ascent.

Transporting a full payload of bombs appeared beyond the capacity of the B-Type balloons, so the navy focused its program on gathering meteorological data from the far reaches of the eastern Pacific. Radiosondes identical to those previously used on the six-meter balloons were installed on the carriage, while another meter specially designed by the navy measured pressure inside the balloon.

Six B-Type balloons were released from Ichinomiya, a small oceanfront town in Chiba prefecture near Tokyo, in August 1944. Radiosonde transmissions from three of them terminated after only two hours, suggesting the balloons burst immediately after reaching altitude. The navy sent its remaining stock of balloons to the Fujikura Rubber Company, where technicians discovered the failure occurred at the rubber-cemented seams that began splitting apart at high internal pressures. Lieutenant Tanaka ordered all further tests suspended until the seams could be reinforced. The navy also decided to install a simple venting mechanism, a circular, spring-loaded relief valve, to meter off small volumes of gas as the balloon ascended.

By this time the navy program was close to being shut down. Imperial Headquarters had recommended the A- and B-Type programs be consolidated under army control. The supreme naval commander, Admiral Shigetaro Shimada, then under fire for a series of devastating losses including the fall of Saipan in July, was in no position to oppose the move. Not only had the B-Type program not produced any substantive advances, but the availability of materials for the rubberized balloons had dropped off sharply as Japan's resources dwindled. With its paper-production efforts fully ramped up, Noborito assumed formal leadership of the B–Type program. Although army General Kusaba left day-to-day operational control to Lieutenant Tanaka and his original navy team, development and testing of the B–Type balloons continued for several more months without significant results.

Noborito's paper balloon measured ten meters in diameter but weighed just 152 pounds. Constructing the envelope entirely of lightweight paper meant that the device's buoyancy would not be unduly compromised by the bulk of the apparatus itself. With a volume of 19,000 cubic feet of gas, the ten-meter balloon had a lifting capacity of a thousand pounds at sea level and approximately three hundred pounds at altitude. The army engineered the balloon's dimensions based on its degree of buoyancy measured against the combined weight of the altimeters, batteries, bombs, and an altitude-control ballast system then under development that the balloon would carry.

Working with the ten-meter prototype, engineers confronted the penultimate challenge of the entire project: how to regulate internal pressure for the duration of the flight. While the navy's initial approach basically bypassed the problem by dint of the strongest possible envelope, the army sought to finesse a solution with two metal discs and a spring.

Engineers designed a pressure-relief valve to be installed on the inflation stem at the bottom of the envelope. A thin rubber gasket was glued to a steel disk seventeen inches across. A small metal tripod held in place an axial bolt and compression spring that pressed the gasket against the other metal disk and created an airtight seal. The valve's two disks burped open and permitted small volumes of gas to escape when the internal pressure of the envelope exceeded the setting of the compression spring. Not only did the design prevent the

FIG. 7. Pressure relief valve recovered in Alaska, date and location unknown. Untitled photograph, Box 43, Japanese Balloon Sightings, Record Group 499, Western Defense Command, NARA

envelope from bursting when it swelled under the constant daytime solar radiation of the upper atmosphere, but the periodic venting of the gas also kept the balloon from rising above 40,000 feet and exiting the narrow channels of strongest winds that existed at that altitude.[21]

The opposite problem occurred during nighttime when cooler temperatures would cause the balloon to descend below 30,000 feet and drop out of the wind currents. The problem would be exacerbated each successive day of the balloon's journey as more and more unrecoverable gas was released during the daytime. A system of ballast weights that could be jettisoned whenever the balloon dropped below preset minimum altitudes represented the best possible solution.

A team of engineers designed a sophisticated altitude-control mechanism. The device not only represented the bulk of the balloon's entire payload but also included the release mechanism for the bombs themselves. Thirty-two bags of sand, each weighing between three and seven pounds, hung around the perimeter of a cast aluminum four-spoke wheel twenty-four inches in diameter. The wheel had seventy-two evenly spaced holes drilled horizontally around its outer rim, into which an equal number of blowout plugs, each containing a black powder charge, were inserted. Each sandbag was suspended by a small T-shaped flat iron bar, which in turn was held in place by a pair of adjacent blowout plugs, one under each arm of the T. A series of fuses connected all thirty-six pairs of blowout plugs (four for the incendiary bombs and the rest for sandbags) to four aneroid-barometer altimeters housed in a one-foot square box bolted atop the wheel.

An activating fuse, several feet in length and coiled around the aneroid box, was ignited at the time of the balloon's launch. The ballast mechanism would only be activated once the fuse burned through to its end and triggered a pair of spring-loaded contacts that completed the electrical circuit between the aneroids and a small 2.3-volt battery. The fuse took nearly an hour to burn, giving the balloon ample time to ascend above the aneroids' minimum threshold. The delay was necessary to avoid any accidental release of either ballast or bombs before the balloon reached altitude. Engineers worried not about the bombs falling on Japan right after takeoff (the launching facilities would be in rural areas next to the ocean) but that an early release of ballast would compromise the mission's chances, while an inadvertent release of bombs would render the entire contraption worthless.

The aneroids operated by responding to changes in atmospheric pressure. A thin disk made of a flexible, corrugated metal lay flat against a moveable bar. The disk gradually flattened out under increasing air pressure and regained its original shape with decreasing

FIG. 8. Balloon chandelier with sandbags and high-explosive bomb attached, recovered near Coal Harbour, British Columbia, on 12 March 1945. "Coal Harbour," Library and Archives Canada, Department of National Defence fonds, PA-203227

pressure, moving the bar up and down accordingly. When the balloon dropped below a certain preset altitude, the corresponding air pressure would move the bar in such a way that it made contact with an electric lead. The circuit was now closed, causing the first pair of plugs to blow and release its sandbag. The T-bar assembly was designed so that if one blowout plug failed to detonate, the firing of the other would still release the ballast.

The blowing of the plugs also ignited a two-minute fuse that led to a set of jack switches on the direct opposite side of the wheel. The triggering of these switches armed the second pair of blowout plugs. If the balloon hadn't gained enough altitude in the two minutes since the first sandbag dropped, the still-closed aneroid would blow this next set of plugs and release the second sandbag. The process would repeat, alternating from one side of the wheel to the other, until the balloon had lost enough ballast and ascended to an altitude where the aneroid opened and broke the circuit.

The technicians who assembled the mechanism set the first aneroid at between 25,000 and 27,000 feet depending on wind projections.[22] Also called the central aneroid, it featured two pressure elements operating in tandem for greater accuracy. The next two aneroids were usually calibrated to the same altitude to act as backups in case the first failed for any reason. On some balloons the second and third aneroids were set at progressively lower altitudes. The three were always wired parallel with each other, however, so that any one of them could close the circuit when a preset minimum altitude was reached.

Wired on a separate circuit and set to between 13,000 and 20,000 feet, the fourth aneroid acted as the master control of the bomb payload. The circuit remained inoperable during the firing sequence of blowout plug sets 1 through 8. A separate fuse ignited by the firing of the number 9 set activated the fourth aneroid and armed the blowout plugs supporting each of the bombs. Regardless of whether blowout plug sets 10 through 36 fired, the entire system was now armed and capable of dropping bombs in a timed sequence as soon as the master aneroid closed. If every set of blowout plugs fired as intended, the four incendiary bombs (sets 33 through 36) could also be dropped in sequence at any altitude in the same manner as the ballast. The last remaining projectile, an anti-personnel bomb hanging in the center of the main wheel, would be dropped when the fourth aneroid closed at its preset altitude.

At 7:29 a.m. on August 29, 1944, one of the first balloons to include the prototype ballast mechanism was released on a test flight from Ichinomiya. It did not carry bombs. The balloon instead carried a radiosonde specially designed by the Army Weather Bureau. Previous devices had alternately failed in the extreme cold of the upper atmosphere or lacked the transmitting power to consistently send signals from the farthest reaches of the Pacific. The Weather Bureau devised numerous radiosondes with dual two-watt batteries capable of transmitting for up to eighty hours in stratospheric conditions. Three radio stations operated by the army's Fifth Technical Research Institute tracked the signals.[23]

The balloon ascended 20,000 feet in just half an hour and then leveled off at 26,000 feet as it entered the prevailing westerly winds. "Into the observation room, persons slipped one by one," noted Teiji Takada of Noborito Institute. Having worked toward this goal for over two years, everyone was desperate to follow the balloon's flight. Between nine and twelve hours later, just as the sun was setting, the ballast mechanism underwent three separate cycles of sandbag drops. The last cycle sent the balloon above 30,000 feet where it remained until the following evening when another four cycles commenced. Radio contact was lost for ten hours but then reestablished on the flight's third morning. Wrote Takada,

> Two track observers read the degrees of the dial with their bloodshot eyes and plotted the readings on the graph to extend the

tracking curve on it. . . . Everybody fixed their eyes upon the fingers of observers on the handle of [the] dial, without moving nor whispering. In the absolute silence prevailing there, a weak boom of the radio receiver waved up and down in tone as an only sound to be heard, keeping everybody in emotional silence.[24]

By the time radio signals ceased after just over fifty-eight total hours of flight, the balloon had jettisoned twenty-five of its thirty-six sandbags. Based on the number of bags dropped per hour of flying time, engineers believed the balloon remained aloft for another two days.

Officials at Noborito were thrilled. It was only August, well before the strongest winds of autumn and winter, and numerous test balloons released that month kept sending signals for up to eighty hours. Although their precise distance and trajectory could be monitored for only the first ten to thirty hours, that the radio signals continued for so long indicated the balloons remained in flight and were certainly capable of reaching North America.

The engineers behind the successful ballast device next designed a self-destruct mechanism. The dropping of the last bomb ignited two final fuses, one to a demolition charge on the main carriage and the other to a flash bomb cemented to the envelope above. The demolition charge, a two-pound block of picric acid encased in tin, contained a three-minute fuse and was placed atop the aneroid box. If the system worked as designed, the charge would obliterate the carriage shortly after the release of the last bomb. The balloon, now freed of its entire payload, would ascend rapidly to the upper atmosphere where the flash bomb, a simple paper pouch filled with 250 grams of magnesium powder on an eighty-two-minute fuse, would ignite the hydrogen and destroy the envelope. Just as the Doolittle Raid had shocked the Japanese by appearing seemingly from nowhere, the balloon team at Noborito was enthralled by the prospect that

FIG. 9. Japanese launch crew training with inflated balloon, February 1944. Bert Webber Papers, Box 11, Hoover Institution Archives, Stanford University

bombs would rain down on the Americans, who would have no idea where they had come from.

Selection of the launch sites for the balloon bombs, a task that fell to the Special Balloon Regiment, an operational unit of the *fu-go* program, had to be done carefully with a few key criteria in mind. The sites had to be on the coast in the sparsely populated countryside, both for the sake of secrecy and to minimize the risk that a wayward balloon would damage infrastructure in Japan, yet they had to be easily accessible by rail to facilitate transport of the materials. The Special Balloon Regiment also consulted wind charts prepared by various meteorological agencies to determine where in the upper atmosphere the strongest currents passed over Japan.

Ichinomiya was the obvious first choice. The oceanfront village had been used extensively for testing since the revival of the balloon program in 1942, and it already featured a wireless station capable of tracking airborne radiosondes. A battalion of seven hundred men was dispatched to Ichinomiya to set up facilities for six launching stations. The regiment selected two additional adjacent launch sites on the coast north of Tokyo. Nakoso in Fukushima prefecture had another six launching stations and six hundred men. Otsu in nearby Ibaraki prefecture was the largest of the three launch sites with nine stations, a weather unit, and fifteen hundred troops. The Otsu site also featured its own hydrogen plant, while the other two depended on tank delivery from chemical factories near Tokyo. The Special Balloon Regiment also identified potential launch sites in northern Honshu and Hokkaido, Japan's northernmost island, which were ruled out due to their proximity to Kamchatka. Imperial Headquarters wished to avoid any accidental balloon landings in the Soviet Union, a country with which Japan was not at war at the time.

Each launching pad consisted of nineteen anchor screws drilled into the ground and arranged in a circle the same diameter as the balloons. After laying out the deflated envelope within the circle and anchoring its skirt to the screws, technicians connected two high-pressure inflation hoses to the valve stem and pumped in eight thousand cubic feet of hydrogen. The envelopes were intentionally underinflated to allow room for the gas to expand at high altitudes. Men holding buckets of sand stood next to the valve ready to extinguish any flame that might (and occasionally did) occur. The steel relief valve was installed on the stem immediately following inflation.

With the ballast mechanism and bombs hanging on a nearby wooden stand, several crewmen threaded guide ropes through the hooks of the skirt, untethered the envelope from the anchor screws, and allowed the balloon to rise about forty feet off the ground. While other crewmen fastened the shroud lines to the chandelier, technicians performed a final check of the equipment. One by one, and at points directly opposite one another, the guide ropes were carefully detached from the skirt until only a few remained. The activating fuse was ignited as the final step before launch. The remaining guide ropes, looped through the skirt with one end attached to the ground, were then released simultaneously. Any rope that tangled and failed to slide free of the hook as the balloon ascended was quickly cut at the ground and allowed to escape with the balloon.

The entire process took between thirty minutes and an hour, depending on the presence of surface winds that made releasing the balloons more difficult. Early mornings and the period just after sunset were typically the calmest and proved the best time for launching. Even a light breeze forced the crewmen to hold the envelope much closer to the ground while others readied the carriage. In one disastrous launch test in August 1944, a sudden gust forced the inflated envelope to the ground and violently pulled the guide ropes from the hands of all who were present. An engineer visiting from Noborito described the scene:

> The balloon, freed from detention in this way, left the ground swinging the flight equipment like a pendulum of a clock, after dragging it in a smoke of sand on the ground even for some tens of meters. . . . The balloon flattened and then elongated, bulged at the top and then at the bottom, continuously changing its feature.[25]

One of the launch crew was unlucky enough to be shot and seriously wounded by a blowplug that fired when the carriage impacted the ground. The distressing episode caused launch technicians to develop an alternate procedure to be used whenever light winds were present. For this method, guide ropes slightly shorter than the shroud lines were attached to small, breakaway paper bags at the envelope's skirt. A moment after the balloon's release from ground level, the guide ropes snapped taut (while the shroud lines still had a bit of slack) and tore apart the paper bags. The momentary hitch in the balloon's ascent resulted in a gentler liftoff of the 250-pound carriage and avoided the sudden jolt that may have snapped the lines, ripped the skirt from the balloon, or otherwise damaged some part of the apparatus.

For six weeks starting in late September, with the Navy's B-Type program still nominally active, a few final rubberized balloons were outfitted with radiosondes and released from Ichinomiya on data-gathering missions. Following the successful testing of the A-Type's ballast system, a rudimentary version of the mechanism was installed on the navy balloons. Technicians also recemented the defective seams that had caused some of the first B-Types to burst. With these improvements in place, the balloons outperformed any to date. One remained aloft for a then-record eighty-seven hours. One of this final group, B-32, was launched on the afternoon of November 2. Transmission ceased after only five hours, and radio operators assumed the balloon had somehow failed. Unbeknownst to the Japanese, however, B-32 continued flying east for nearly three days before settling gently in the Pacific some sixty-six miles off the coast of southern California.[26]

Sailors aboard U.S.S. LCI (L) 778, an American auxiliary ship operating in those waters, observed a large, dull gray object floating in the water. Closer inspection revealed it to be a balloon, about two-thirds inflated, bobbing at an angle with lines extending down to some weight beneath the surface. In attempting to haul it aboard, the crew found it necessary to fully deflate the balloon—which they noted produced "a cooling effect" as the gas escaped—and also cut several of the suspension cords. Although the sailors would later report they believed some of the gear was lost in this process, they did manage to recover an aneroid barometer and a two-tube radio transmitter housed in a small wooden box.

"Balloon at first thought to be merely some special type of meteorological equip[ment]," noted a confidential telegram from the Eleventh Naval District in San Diego to the director of Naval Intelligence.[27] A check with the U.S. Weather Bureau provided no clues as to the possible origin of the balloon. A preliminary examination revealed the radio transmitter had been manufactured in Tokyo, and a small patch inside the rubber envelope contained faded, illegible Japanese characters written in pencil. The salvaged materials were crated up and shipped to the Naval Research Laboratory in Anacostia, just outside Washington, DC, where they remained unnoticed on a shelf for the next five weeks.

The San Pedro balloon (named for the nearest community to the recovery location) was the latest in a series of mysterious incidents over the previous several months. During a B-29 bombing raid of Fukuoka on August 20, pilots observed eight white, silver, or gray balloons, approximately forty to one hundred feet in diameter, at an altitude of 26,000 feet. For three days in mid-October, numerous balloons "with tails" were spotted over Okayama. One report of a sighting near Taiwan noted a "square box" hanging from ropes under the balloon. The Army Air Forces Pacific Ocean Area (AAFPOA) theorized the balloons might be anti-aircraft flak bursts, despite the fact that none that large had ever been observed before. An AAFPOA intelligence officer noted, "It is possible that high altitude balloons that have been seen are an attempt on the part of the Japanese to obtain more accurate meteorological data at high altitudes."[28]

A few days after the recovery of the San Pedro balloon, Army Air Force interrogators questioned a Japanese officer who had been captured in the Battle of Guam earlier that summer. The prisoner of war, unnamed in the official report, was a nineteen-year veteran of the Japanese Naval Meteorological Service and once studied physics and meteorology at Tokyo Imperial University under Sakuhei Fujiwara, head of the Japanese Weather Bureau. After Pearl Harbor, he served as chief weather officer at Truk, Saipan, and finally Guam. The prisoner told interrogators the Japanese used balloons equipped with radiosondes to monitor the position and conditions of the equatorial front with respect to both cyclones and high-velocity winds of the upper atmosphere. They also subscribed to the Polar Front Theory of weather analysis with techniques gleaned from available Norwegian literature (a probable holdover of the Wasaburo Ooishi era). Unstated in the Army Air Force report, but certainly known to the Japanese officer, was that the huge temperature contrast between cold polar air and warmer subtropical air—in other words, the boundary between the polar and equatorial fronts—is what causes the currents of high-altitude winds and their seasonal variability.[29]

That very same week U.S. Coast Guard personnel at Kailua, Hawaii, observed an airborne object descend into the ocean five miles out. The men dispatched to retrieve the object returned with a fragment of paper from a large balloon and an assembly of switches, fuses, and barometric contactors. The partially inflated envelope had split open as they attempted to pull it aboard, resulting in the loss of most of the envelope and damage to the payload. Weather and signal officers believed the device could be a weather balloon, though it contained no writing or markings that might identify its origin. Like its San Pedro counterpart, the Kailua balloon was shipped to Anacostia, where it aroused little attention or concern.[30]

## BALLOONS AWAY

In the predawn hours of November 3, 1944—the birthday of Japan's former ruler, the Meiji Emperor—crewmen at Ichinomiya readied several paper balloons for launch. The chandeliers that hung nearby contained, for the first time, a complete payload of incendiary and anti-personnel bombs. Numerous radiosonde tests the month before had not only proven the operational success of the ballast mechanism but also detected the start of the strong autumn winds. With several hundred completed balloons in stock at the three launch sites and thousands more on the way in the coming weeks, the army was ready to begin the balloon bomb offensive.

The first bomb-laden paper balloon was released at 5:00 a.m.

FIG. 10. *Fu-go* launch, date and location unknown. Koichi Yoshino

Soon the sky was filled with half a dozen more, the silence of their ascent broken only by the faint rustle of paper in the light morning breeze. With ropes dangling from the underinflated concave envelopes, observers compared the balloons to huge jellyfish swimming through the pale blue sky.[31] The tranquility of the balloons' ascent belied their ultimate purpose—to infiltrate the United States, spreading fire throughout its forests and panic among its people.

# 2

............

## *Thermopolis*

Three men working at the Hi-Line Coal Mine thirteen miles north-west of Thermopolis, Wyoming, stepped out of a mine tunnel in the early evening twilight of Wednesday, December 6, 1944, and heard what sounded like a shotgun report far away to the southwest.[1] The sound raised no concern for John Hoagland, Byron Goe, and Jack Boyce as gunfire was a common occurrence in the rural area. Hoagland and Goe started for a small shed that housed a gas-powered electrical generator, while Boyce, the mine's on-site caretaker, entered a nearby house he shared with his wife, Doris. Barely a minute later Hoagland and Goe heard a loud whistling sound over their heads, followed by a tremendous explosion on a ridge about a mile to the northeast. Boyce, thinking the mine's powder magazine had exploded, bolted from his house but stopped short when he observed a faraway cloud of dust and smoke rising a thousand feet in the sky. He joined his coworkers on the brink of a knoll in the direction of the cloud. Hoagland and Goe believed an airplane must have crashed. Boyce disagreed, noting the sharp report of the blast suggested a bomb of some kind. The men stood on the knoll for a few minutes and watched the dust settle. Boyce then turned and noticed a bright object high in the clear evening sky.

It first appeared to be a star, but as it descended the outlines of a parachute came into focus. Boyce guessed its color to be white, though the last rays of the setting sun gradually gave it a deep reddish hue. As it drifted lower the men noticed a dark object hanging underneath the canopy. A red light on the object then flashed three times. Hoagland believed it was a man who had jumped from the crashed plane and supposed the lights, which he later said flashed about as quickly as he could snap his fingers, to be signal lights for landing purposes. The men watched the parachute for several minutes as it drifted to the southeast—in the direction of Thermopolis—before it faded from view in the darkening sky.

At that moment two and a half miles to the east, Louis Hartman, a sheepherder at the nearby Stoddard Ranch, was climbing into his wagon after bedding down his flock on a hilltop clearing. A dull, rumbling bang from across the valley caught his attention. A few moments later, a loud explosion shook the ground and sent the sheep scurrying down the hill, their bells clanging as they ran. Hartman swung down from the wagon and while calling after them noticed a falling object he guessed was about the size of an oil drum in the sky to the south. It was shaped like an egg, he noticed, with the wide end falling first and the tapered end at the top. With dusk coming on, he momentarily lost sight of the object as it neared the ground, but a moment later a bright red flame shot into the sky and illuminated the countryside for several seconds. By the time he rounded up the sheep it was too dark to investigate the blast, so the following morning he walked a mile from his camp to the spot where he guessed the object fell. There he found a two-foot circle of blackened rock. A strong odor of burnt gunpowder still lingered in the air.

FIG. 11. Sheepherder (possibly Louis Hartman) and FBI agent investigating location of mysterious explosion. The original caption of this FBI photograph reads "Approximate point of red glowing light." "Thermopolis, Wyo.," Acc. 16-5, Box 33, Japanese Balloons, Record Group 499, Western Defense Command, NARA

Morris Stoddard, Hartman's employer and the owner of the Stoddard Ranch, was watering livestock near his house that evening when he heard two blasts within minutes of each other, both of which caused a nearby nide of pheasants to take flight. Later in the evening he looked to the west and noticed a bright, grayish glow atop Owl Creek Mountain. The light lasted for at least an hour and, despite being over twenty-five miles away, was clearly identifiable as a flame of some kind. It looked like a bale of hay had been set on fire, Stoddard later commented. Peter Rice also noticed the fire. As foreman for the nearby Sanford Ranch, Rice often traveled on horseback from one sheep camp to another. He heard a dull thud around 6:30 p.m. while having supper with a sheepherder in the backcountry. Riding home half an hour later he noticed a bright light high up on the mountain. When questioned later, both Stoddard and Rice expressed bewilderment at the fire's origins. No one lived in that area in the wintertime, and the mountaintop had been snow covered for weeks.

Jesse Perkins, a rancher who lived about four miles south of the Hi-Line Mine, had just finished dinner that evening when a loud explosion shook his log house. He first thought a storage tank at the Hamilton Dome Oil Field nine miles away had blown up. Perkins walked to the window to look for flames from that direction. His wife took a few steps out the front door. Three smaller explosions, what the Perkinses took to be smaller oil tanks going off as a result of the larger blast, subsequently occurred in two-minute intervals. They saw no fires, but the fact that the blast had shaken their house suggested something big had happened.

The Perkinses headed into Thermopolis to report the incident—only to discover the town was already abuzz with word of a plane crash near the Hi-Line Mine. John Hoagland and Byron Goe, after stopping every couple of miles on Highway 120 to scan the horizon and call out for the parachutist, had arrived in town with the news a short while earlier. The men positively identified the location of the blast, putting an end to Perkins's hunch of an oil tank fire. Unable to find Kem Moyer, the sheriff of Hot Springs County, Hoagland left messages at his office and with townspeople up and down Broadway. Goe's father was the operator of the Hi-Line Mine, and Hoagland stopped to inform him of the incident. The three men returned to the mine and, joined again by Jack Boyce, set off with flashlights for the crash site. Sheriff Moyer had been investigating an auto accident near Thermopolis that afternoon and, upon his return to town, received Hoagland's summons from the desk clerk at the Emery Hotel. The sheriff then arrived at the mine with another Hi-Line employee. They followed the flickering beams of the flashlights in the distance and joined the search until past midnight. No trace of the plane could be found.

The search resumed at dawn the next morning on a rough slope marked by ravines and dry washes across the valley from the mine. Hoagland recognized a distinctly shaped scrub pine he had observed the night before while looking at the dust cloud, and he headed that direction. While walking across a gulch toward the tree he came upon a sandstone ledge, three to four feet high, the lip of which had been smashed and revealed a wide cut several feet across. Shattered, blackened rocks and dozens of metal shards, some as large as his hand and others no bigger than a coin, lay scattered down the slope for several feet.

Sheriff Moyer had earlier summoned an aircraft from the army base in nearby Casper to perform an aerial search for the downed parachutist. When the pilot arrived that afternoon the sheriff explained he now believed they were dealing with a bomb. He showed the pilot the pieces of metal recovered that morning—circular bands that had apparently been riveted around a cylindrical object, shards with threaded ends, and flat pieces clearly identifiable as tail fins. The sheriff hadn't discounted the missing plane for which he planned to continue his search, but the metal fragments and apparent bomb crater discovered by Hoagland added a new dimension to the mystery. The army pilot flew over the Hi-Line Mine and surrounding area for a few hours without seeing anything unusual. He then returned to Casper with the remnants of the suspected bomb, intending to pass them along to an ordnance expert at the base.

A snowstorm on Friday, December 8, temporarily halted the search efforts. Moyer spent the day visiting the many ranches in the vicinity to see whether anyone had additional information. When the weather cleared the next day he accompanied Shorty Murray, a Sanford Ranch camp tender, on a fruitless search of an area where someone reported seeing an object fall to the earth. Another search party of eight men failed to turn up any bit of evidence. Jesse Perkins reported to the sheriff that he and a ranch hand inspected his property and found nothing unusual, only a shattered rock ledge he believed had been caused by a lightning strike some time before. An aerial search of snowcapped Owl Creek Mountain revealed no trace of a fire. Even the burned rocks first discovered by Louis Hartman the morning after he spotted the falling egg-shaped object had been scrubbed clean by the snow and a flock of sheep that had tramped through the valley.

Just as perplexing as the failure to locate the crashed plane was the fate of the parachutist. Byron Goe claimed to be quite familiar with parachutes as he had seen a number of exhibition jumps at air shows, and both he and John Hoagland were adamant the object they saw hanging from the parachute that night was a man. Based on the miners' guess that the parachute had come down between two and six miles away in the direction of town, search and rescue teams from Casper flew over the area multiple times, though the fresh cover of snow minimized the likelihood of spying anything on the ground.

Throughout the weekend, numerous residents continued to visit the sheriff's office to report unusual events from the previous Wednesday evening. A state game warden, seemingly every sheepherder in the county, and even a nine-year-old child who had been playing outside that night all reported hearing explosions or seeing fires. The large number of eyewitnesses might have seemed surprising considering how sparsely populated the area was. In taking statements from the informants, the sheriff asked each one whether they had seen or heard an airplane either before or after the explosions. Not a single person had. Even Byron Goe, though he still insisted the airborne object was a man, granted the sky was quiet all that day and that the whistling sound just before the blast didn't really sound like an airplane. As time went on, Sheriff Moyer must have realized he was searching for an airplane nobody had seen, a parachutist who had apparently vanished, and the source of several large fires that had simultaneously broken out at distant points all over the county—and the only evidence in his possession was a handful of metal shards and a few blackened, pulverized rocks.

## KALISPELL

On the morning of Monday, December 11, five days after the puzzling events in Wyoming, O. B. Hill and his son Owen drove their truck up a logging road outside Kalispell, Montana, to a small shack known as the Christmas Tree Cabin.[2] The two men worked as woodcutters in the forests of Flathead County and were visiting that location for the first time in over a year. As the men climbed down from the cab of the truck, they saw what looked like a parachute on the ground sixty yards off the road. They paid little attention and instead went about cutting and stacking logs in the back of the truck.

The Hills drove back to Kalispell at 4:00 p.m. and called on Sheriff Duncan McCarthy to report what they had seen. Returning to the site the next day, the three men found a large, deflated balloon stretched out on the ground in a clearing in the woods, its suspension ropes snagged and pulled taut on a three-foot stump. No carriage, harness, or any type of payload could be found. Just the balloon and its lines. The sheriff noticed a long fuse with a singed end indicating it had been ignited at some point. The fuse, later measured at seventy feet in length, led to a small paper cylinder filled with black powder that was attached to the side of the balloon just above the suspension skirt. McCarthy cut the fuse at both ends and removed the charge. A light dusting of snow and frost covered the balloon's exposed surface. Several inches of snow lay underneath. There were no tracks leading from the balloon, nor any indication that anyone had been in the area in the recent past. In order to move the balloon, the men had to cut open the fabric and dump out several gallons of slushy, yellowish water they later reported caused a slight irritation to the skin and eyes. The sheriff rolled up the balloon and stuffed it into the trunk of his car.

William Guy Bannister, an FBI agent in charge of the bureau's Butte field office, took custody of the balloon a few days later and assumed control of the investigation. Interviews with other loggers revealed none had seen the balloon, either in flight or after it had landed, even though one claimed to have recently worked the area where it was discovered. Weather reports indicated the first snowfall in the Kalispell area, nearly six inches, occurred on November 11. Clear sunlight and warmer temperatures over the next two weeks steadily melted the snow until almost none remained. Based on the presence of snow under the balloon but just a light dusting on top, the FBI concluded it had landed in the area sometime after November 11 but before the next snowfall that occurred on November 25.

An examination of the envelope revealed Japanese writing on a six-inch square of paper pasted near the top. Bannister and McCarthy took the patch first to Jiro Masuoka, a forty-year resident of Kalispell who was born in Tokyo and emigrated to the United States as a young man, and later to Yoshi Sakahara, a U.S. citizen of Japanese ancestry who lived in the nearby town of Whitefish. Both men identified the paper as some kind of factory tag that listed production data for the balloon. It was a "No. 2" envelope of "best quality" that had been inspected on October 10, 1944, and completed on October 31. Several characters on the tag that appeared to indicate the balloon's place of manufacture were unfortunately too smeared to be legible.[3]

The revelation that the device was of Japanese origin brought a new level of urgency to Bannister's investigation. The FBI contacted the Army Ninth Service Command, which dispatched a G-2 (Intelligence) officer, Captain W. B. Stannard, to Kalispell. Bannister and Stannard took the balloon back to Butte, where they performed a thorough inspection. The envelope measured over thirty feet in diameter and was constructed of a varnished, cream-colored paper. The seams had been glued with some type of blue-green adhesive. A circular relief valve made of pressed steel was affixed to the bottom of the envelope. The suspension rigging consisted of nineteen three-strand manila ropes that hooked into a catenary band made of the same material as the envelope. The band was located sixty-eight inches below the equator. The lower ends of the ropes came together forty feet beneath the balloon, where they were knotted and looped into a two-foot rubber cable that apparently acted as a shock absorber. Hooked at the bottom end of the rubber cable were coarse manila ropes with frayed ends, the likely fastening points for whatever cargo the balloon once carried.

Two balloon experts, one each from the army and navy, arrived in Butte to examine the device. The men could not positively identify the balloon as Japanese but confirmed it did not in any way resemble those employed by U.S. forces. The specialist from the navy noted his station in Oregon released tan- or white-colored weather balloons twice daily, one at five in the morning, the other at six in the evening, but those measured just four feet in diameter, considerably smaller than the Kalispell device. A check with the Canadian Armed Forces in Edmonton confirmed no commands north of the border employed such large balloons for any purpose, nor had any eyewitness reports of the balloon in flight been made. The crude construction and nondurable material of the Kalispell balloon suggested it was meant for a one-time job only. Operating under the assumption the device was of Japanese origin but was neither a barrage nor weather balloon, the investigators surmised it had been sent aloft for one of three purposes: to carry espionage agents or saboteurs into the United States, to engage in aerial bombardment, or to drop incendiary bombs that might set fire to the forests of the western states. The investigators further believed the balloon had been launched from a Japanese submarine or surface vessel somewhere in the eastern Pacific. A free balloon making the trip all the way from Japan they deemed "an impossibility."[4]

The army's balloon expert calculated a hydrogen balloon that size would have a lifting capacity of at least a thousand pounds, enough to carry five or six men great distances. The theory raised a few questions, however. A manned balloon would likely feature some type of release mechanism between the carriage and its lines, but this balloon had none. At the very least one would expect to find evidence the ropes had been cut with a knife, yet these displayed frayed ends and showed signs of extreme friction. Furthermore, if personnel were to be flown into the country, why did their vehicle lack any apparent means for controlling its flight? A manually operated valve would provide a simple method for regulating altitude—so why did the balloon feature only a pressure relief valve with no external controls? Investigators also ruled out the incendiary bomb theory due to the impracticality of attempting to start a forest fire in the winter months. That left only aerial bombardment, which Army Intelligence cited as the most probable purpose, even though the method provided almost zero degree of accuracy. One G-2 officer called the balloon "some sort of a new device, probably the Japanese counterpart of the [V-2] rocket."[5]

A bomb disposal officer from Fort Lewis, Washington, arrived a few days later to inspect the powder charge. He identified it as an aluminum-powder flash bomb with a fuse that burned at ninety seconds per foot. In its preliminary report, G-2 theorized the flash bomb was designed to destroy the envelope and send the entire payload of bombs crashing to earth:

> It is within the realm of possibility that the enemy could inflate these balloons a short distance off the west coast, attaching an automatic device which would . . . set off the fuse on the [flash bomb] in any given time. Knowing the weather it would be possible to compute the direction and possible speed of the balloon, thus theoretically allowing the bomb to fall within a given area.[6]

This theory failed to explain how and why the Kalispell balloon had jettisoned its payload even though the flash bomb did not explode. G-2 officials also noted the apparent lack of a ballast mechanism, which suggested the balloon had traveled only a relatively short distance from a Japanese ship or submarine. Any flight lasting more than a single day and night would require such an altitude-control device, yet the balloon's crude construction suggested nothing that ingenious was used. "That thing was obviously released from a Jap submarine or surface craft," stated an intelligence officer in a telephone report to G-2's Presidio headquarters. "There's no question about it, it's a free balloon. It couldn't have come from Japan."[7]

On December 20, the balloon was shipped under guard to the Naval Research Laboratory in Anacostia for more comprehensive study. Because investigators believed the balloon had been launched from a submarine or surface craft, the navy's Western Sea Frontier assumed jurisdiction. That its intended target was on land, however, necessitated the participation of the army's Western Defense Command, and the two branches agreed to a joint command. In so doing they wrested the investigation from the FBI (what one navy captain disparagingly referred to as "a bunch of lawyers and accountants, more or less"[8]). Technicians at Anacostia hoped to re-inflate the balloon in order to perform flight tests, but they discovered it had been sliced open at least once and torn in several places from being handled too roughly. They also found places where souvenir hunters had cut numerous swatches from the envelope.

The NRL agreed with G-2's initial finding that the balloon did not transport personnel. Load tests of the rubber shock cord showed it would be ineffective for payloads over 150 pounds and would likely snap over prolonged use if supporting more than 200 pounds. Why include the cord if the presence of even a single passenger would render it useless? The balloon's large size, if not meant to transport a heavy load, must have been necessary to reach considerable altitude. The presence of the relief valve supported this hypothesis as the venting of gas would be unnecessary for low-altitude flights. But the Anacostia analysts then wondered why a balloon launched from a submarine just off the coast would be expected to achieve an altitude of 30,000 feet. A smaller balloon could not only carry the same payload the same distance at lower altitudes but would be far easier to inflate and launch at sea. Such large volumes of hydrogen in particular would be dangerous to handle on the deck of a surfaced submarine.[9]

Lacking any reasonable explanation for why bombs had to travel through the upper atmosphere, the NRL tentatively concluded the device was a meteorological balloon, fused to prevent detection and launched from either a ship in the Pacific or Japan proper, or perhaps an anti-aircraft barrage balloon released in Japan that somehow managed to reach Montana. Though poorly understood, the existence of strong westerly winds over Japan was known to the analysts, and they could not rule out the possibility of a transoceanic flight.

Were the Thermopolis and Kalispell incidents connected? The possibility occurred to the Western Defense Command almost immediately. Within days of the latter discovery, officers from the respective service commands were in contact to share information. FBI agents and G-2 officers shuttled back and forth between locations. The idea that the Thermopolis parachute and the Kalispell balloon were the *same* device was easily disproven. The timeline failed to match up for one thing, as the Kalispell balloon was believed to have landed on the ground at least eleven days before the Thermopolis aerial sighting. A check with the U.S. Weather Bureau confirmed the light, prevailing winds to the south and east during that time period made a balloon flight northwest from Wyoming to Montana impossible. These were clearly two separate incidents—but were they related? Although the Kalispell balloon was confirmed to be Japanese, the provenance of the Thermopolis device was still unknown. On December 20, in response to inquiries from the War Department's Office of Censorship about what information could be released to the press, Colonel William Hammond of Army Intelligence expressed his view that the two incidents were unrelated and that the Thermopolis bomb was an "isolated incident [or] might even turn out to be friendly." Colonel Hammond recommended the Office of Censorship make no connection between the two events and reject any press claims that did.

Unbeknownst to Hammond, however, a definitive link had been established that very day when an ordnance specialist concluded his examination of the metal fragments recovered in Thermopolis. He compared the fragments to diagrams of known enemy bombs and believed the device was a fifteen-kilogram Japanese combat bomb. The fins in particular featured a peculiar arrangement of struts common to bombs of Japanese make. The specialist also noted the device had been painted black, a known trait of Japanese ordnance. A subsequent study by the army's Bomb Disposal Center in Aberdeen, Maryland, confirmed the findings.

The following week on the day after Christmas, a naval intelligence officer who had reviewed the Thermopolis and Kalispell reports visited Anacostia and asked about the rubber balloon that had been found six weeks before in the waters off San Pedro, California. More or less ignored until that moment, the device was retrieved from a warehouse and subjected to a thorough investigation. The preliminary inspection performed in San Diego a few days after the discovery had found Japanese markings on both the envelope and radio transmitter. Now investigators discovered in the envelope a rubber thread that was "strikingly similar" to those used in the shock cord of the Kalispell balloon.

Most significantly, investigators found a bellows and ratchet contact device believed to be part of a ballast release mechanism. A brass, spring-loaded disk featured contact points and ratchet teeth that allowed it to rotate only one direction. Changes in air pressure between 18,000 and 21,000 feet would activate a sealed bellows that moved the disk from one contact point to the next. Each successive turn completed an electrical circuit that investigators believed released ballast. Six of the seven contact points had been tripped, indicating the device had dropped ballast six times, which suggested a long-distance, high-altitude flight lasting several days. "It seems a fairly reasonable conclusion," wrote lead investigator R. H. Bullard, "that the balloon was sent aloft in or near Japan and that it crossed the Pacific. . . . It was probably sent up as an experiment to see what sort of a flight would result and to provide information on how, why and where it came down to serve as a guide to future experiments."[10]

Bullard next retrieved the paper balloon that had come down in the ocean off Kailua, Hawaii, on November 14. He discovered it was by far the most complete device recovered to date. The chandelier, though damaged during its recovery from the ocean, contained its entire complement of fuses, switches, and aneroids. Bullard examined the aluminum wheel with its seventy-two laterally drilled holes. He then diagramed the intricate web of fuses that led from one side of the wheel to the other in a progressively spiral fashion. Noting that each fuse took two minutes and sixteen seconds to burn through to the next set of switches, Bullard believed the device released ballast on a time delay to facilitate altitude recovery:

> It has been concluded that this balloon was a paper one virtually identical with [the Kalispell balloon]. This balloon, and probably the other . . . carried an ingenious ballast release mechanism for maintaining an altitude in excess of 20,000 feet. This would permit a flight of considerable duration and thus increases the possibility that they were sent aloft in Japan rather than from a submarine.[11]

FIG. 12. Underside of altitude-control mechanism showing intricate fuse assembly for the sequential release of ballast. This device was recovered at Fort Simpson in Canada's Northwest Territories on 19 January 1945. "Plain view," Library and Archives Canada, Department of National Defence fonds, PA-203215

Unfortunately none of the ballast objects had been recovered, so Bullard could only speculate on whether they were inert weights or some type of bomb. Either, he noted in his report, was possible.

SEBASTOPOL

Three more balloon incidents occurred in late December and early January, which collectively buttressed the notion that the United States was under attack from long-range Japanese bombardment. On New Year's Eve a rancher found a balloon hanging in a tree seventy feet off the ground in a forest ten miles southeast of Estacada, Oregon. After felling the tree and examining the balloon, G-2 officials determined it was identical to that discovered in Kalispell three weeks earlier. Apart from a square metal frame measuring just over a foot on each side, no object hung from the bottom end of the rubber shock cord. An extensive ground search by FBI agents and soldiers from Fort Lewis, Washington, found no additional evidence.

On January 4, two farmers working in an alfalfa field one mile south of Medford, Oregon, heard a whistling sound followed by a thud a short distance away. A red flame shot thirty feet into the air a moment later. The blast resulted in a smoldering, twelve-inch hole in the ground, at the bottom of which lay a burned metal casing similar to a thermite grenade. The field had recently been plowed and was composed of loose soil, and FBI agents and G-2 personnel found fragments of the device, including a short chain and pieces of molten metal, a full three feet beneath the surface of the ground.[12] (Several other balloon incidents occurred in December 1944 but went unreported to authorities for weeks. A fragment of paper was discovered on December 19 in Manderson, Wyoming, which is approximately fifty air miles northeast of Thermopolis. Since the Thermopolis balloon was never recovered, it seemed likely the Manderson fragment was part of that device. Other incidents not immediately known to authorities during this time included a fragment of paper found in northern Saskatchewan, Canada, and two balloons in Alaska believed to have landed in late December but not recovered until mid-January.)

From a military intelligence perspective the most significant of the three incidents occurred in F. T. Alberegi's apple orchard outside Sebastopol, California, on the early evening of January 4. The farmer and his two sons were standing outside at 6:15 p.m. when from over their heads they heard a loud whistle accompanied by a fluttering sound. Alberegi looked up just in time to see a large object three hundred feet off the ground falling at a terrific rate of speed. The object crashed into his orchard, breaking off a few limbs from one of the trees just a hundred yards from where he stood. He observed no flame or explosion, but as he approached the crashed object he detected a strong odor of burnt gunpowder.[13]

Upon hearing of the incident the next day, Colonel Hammond got on the phone with a fellow G-2 colonel who had just arrived in Sebastopol. "I wish you would [examine the balloon] as soon as you can," he informed his colleague, "because I think that with the information we have here I think we can wrap up something in a hurry in a preliminary way."[14] Hammond asked for an immediate report on the balloon material—he guessed it was paper—and the number and type of shroud lines. Thinking the design of the shock cord was the key to figuring out what sort of payload the balloons carried, Hammond described for the colonel the cord from the Kalispell device and asked for a comparison with Sebastopol.

Of the balloon's envelope only the skirt and a few shredded paper panels remained. The envelope had apparently burst while in flight (though not from the flash bomb, which was recovered intact) sending the chandelier crashing to the ground, the paper fragments and shroud lines flapping behind. (The remainder of the tattered envelope was recovered that same day in Napa, about twenty-five miles away.) Although damaged in the fall, the undercarriage featured more equipment than any other balloon recovered thus far. In addition to the aluminum wheel and web of fuses identical to those found on the Kailua balloon, the carriage included a wooden box with a clear plastic top. Inside was a sealed wet battery and about a quart of slushy liquid with a peculiar chemical odor. Attached to the outside of the wooden box was a small metal container with what looked like a detonator. The fuse leading to this device had worn through a few inches from its connection point, perhaps explaining why the detonator failed to function. The aluminum wheel still contained several unfired blowout plugs, the first such specimens available for inspection. Most significantly, investigators recovered four damaged incendiary bombs still attached to the wheel.

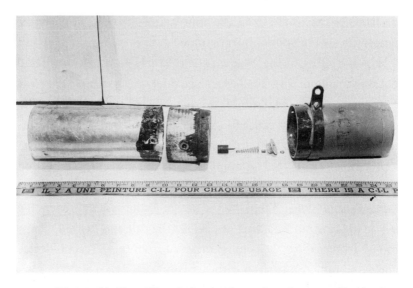

FIG. 13. Disassembled incendiary device showing spring, plunger, and impact fuse assembly designed to ignite the thermite payload upon contact with the ground. CWM-19910238-445-16, Canadian War Museum

"That mechanism is not a weather apparatus," the G-2 colonel dryly informed Hammond.[15]

The Presidio's intelligence unit convinced the FBI to hand over the Sebastopol device so that it could be examined by R. H. Bullard, the naval research technician who was quickly establishing himself as the expert on the Japanese balloons and who would indeed act as lead technical investigator on all subsequent recoveries. He issued his most definitive conclusion to date: "It is now presumable that the Japanese have succeeded in designing a balloon which can be produced in large numbers at low cost and which is capable of reaching the United States and Canada from the western Pacific carrying incendiaries or other devices."[16] Bullard noted the presence of two self-destructive devices—the previously known flash bomb on the envelope and the newly discovered demolition block on the carriage—and concluded that in all likelihood only a small percentage of the total number of balloons had landed intact. Of these only a few would likely be discovered in the wide-open country of the western United States. That the FBI, army, and navy had already discovered half a dozen balloons could only mean the Japanese were launching a considerably higher number—hundreds, if not thousands—which argued against the idea they were being released from submarines. Bullard further concluded the automatic ballast mechanism not only made a sustained flight possible, but the fact that both recovered systems (Kailua and now Sebastopol) were exhausted indicated they had flown a considerable distance indeed.

The design of the battery also suggested a long flight. The clear plastic top of the wooden box likely took advantage of solar radiation for maintaining battery life, while the slushy liquid, determined to be an antifreeze solution, would help forestall battery failure in the subzero nighttime temperatures of the upper atmosphere. Previous theories about the balloons could now be debunked. For one, these were not anti-aircraft barrage balloons, which would have no need for a ballast mechanism. That the system was automated also ruled out the possibility of manned flights—why include altimeters, batteries, fuses, and blowout plugs when onboard personnel could simply toss weight over the side when necessary? Radiosonde flights also seemed unlikely due to the large number of balloons likely being launched.

"We're getting a little clearer picture of it now," stated Colonel Hammond in a telephone conversation with a fellow G-2 officer. "I'm hazarding a few tentative conclusions . . . because we've established now some very definite similarities. I don't think that there is any doubt but that the three paper balloons we've found carry the same type of devices."[17] Hammond wasn't prepared to speculate on the exact nature of the "devices," only that the Sebastopol balloon could have accommodated the weight of several small bombs with pounds to spare.

Of the four incendiary devices recovered in Sebastopol, two had been pulverized too badly to be of any real use for research purposes. The remaining two, however, provided military officials with insight into their design and probable purpose. Both consisted of a cylindrical, pressed steel container almost four inches in diameter. One was seven inches in length, the other nine. A mass of fused metal inside the containers indicated they had been subjected to intense heat. One device contained an impact fuse and plunger, leading investigators to conclude it contained a powder charge that would be ignited upon impact with the ground. The idea the balloon bombs were designed to start forest fires in the western U.S. had been discredited since the Kalispell incident. Now Bullard reintroduced the possibility: "It is to be expected that the number [of balloons] will increase and that when the dry season arrives considerable damage will result unless effective countermeasures are developed."[18]

# 3

...............

## *Alturas*

The first newspaper to get the scoop on the balloon story was not the *New York Times*, *Washington Post*, or some other established daily with an international reputation, but the *Western News*, a weekly published in Libby, Montana. On December 14, just three days after the discovery in Kalispell, the paper ran a front-page story under the headline "Jap Balloon Found in Timber." A rural mailman whose route included the area where the woodcutters made their discovery brought word to Libby of a strange paper balloon large enough to carry up to eight Japanese soldiers. While technically true—the balloon's lifting capacity could accommodate the weight of several men—other parts of the story had become embellished, such as the presence of Japanese war flags that were reportedly attached to the envelope.[1] (The *Northern Wyoming Daily News* actually beat all others to the story with an article on the plane crash at the Hi-Line Mine. Headlined "Phantom Plane Is Being Sought near Thermopolis," the article did not mention a balloon or any possible connection to Japan, however, as it was unknown at the time.[2])

The Kalispell story turned up in a radio news broadcast a few days later, followed by a clearance request from United Press to the War Department's Office of Censorship. The request was granted, perhaps because the FBI had already released information to the press. Articles about the Montana balloon then appeared in the January 1, 1945, editions of both *Time* and *Newsweek*. "Had the balloon carried any passengers?" the *Newsweek* article asked. "If so, where were they? . . . Had the big bag come from an enemy sub operating off the west coast or had it been flown all the way from the Jap homeland?"[3] *Time* posed the same questions: "[T]he balloon had presumably been launched from an offshore submarine. But why? If it had carried men, where had they parachuted to earth?"[4]

"What's the matter with the goddamn fools?" thundered a G-2 colonel when he saw the press coverage. "That's just like giving Tokyo a Christmas present."[5] Both the *Time* and *Newsweek* articles named the FBI as the source for the information, infuriating Army Intelligence whose business it was to keep secrets, not reveal them to reporters. G-2 feared the information would find its way back to Japan and assist its balloon launching strategy.

When a front page article turned up in the January 2 edition of the *Portland Oregonian*—with a photograph of troops searching the woods for balloon parts, no less—the Western Defense Command finally decided to end the press coverage. That same day, on orders from Brigadier General William H. Wilbur, the WDC chief of staff, intelligence officers contacted nine news outlets, including the wire services United Press, Associated Press, and International News Service, and requested they indefinitely hold all details of the balloon landings. The AP and UP indicated they would consider the request but still planned to contact the Office of Censorship in Washington for confirmation.

"The Office of Censorship said they had a national policy against asking a 'kill' on a story of this type that had already had local dissemination," William Hammond noted after taking a call from Byron Price, head of the censorship department.[6] He appealed to Price to change the policy, but the director refused.

Just two days later, however, Price reversed his decision and sent a note to newspaper editors and TV and radio broadcasters. He marked the note "Confidential" and wrote it was "not for publication or broadcast":

> Any balloons approaching the United States from outside its borders can be enemy attacks against the nation. Such attacks involve military security. Information that the balloons have reached this country and particularly what section they have reached is information of value to the enemy. The War Department is appropriate authority for such information. Please do not aid the enemy by publishing or broadcasting such information without appropriate authority.[7]

By the first week of January balloons had been sighted or recovered in half a dozen western states, two territories, one Canadian province, and the Pacific Ocean. Price apparently had come to the same realization as Hammond: the Japanese were certain to launch many more balloons in the coming weeks and months, and the Americans did themselves no favors by publicizing where they were landing. The best defense might be silence. G-2 personnel held meetings with media directors in San Francisco, Seattle, Portland, Salt Lake City, Los Angeles, and San Diego, and spent the better part of a week on the telephone with newspaper editors and radio station managers in eight western states.[8]

At 1:10 p.m. on January 10, 1945, a radio operator at the civilian airfield in Eugene, Oregon, looked up at the partly overcast sky and spotted a balloon just underneath the cloud ceiling. About that same time a state policeman radioed his dispatch officer to report the same balloon in the sky twelve miles north of Eugene. The patrolman got in his car and followed the balloon as directly as the backcountry roads would allow. He maintained visual contact for over an hour as the balloon drifted south by southeast toward Crater Lake.[9]

The Naval Air Station in Klamath Falls was the next to spot the balloon, and at 4:24 p.m. a JRB Twin-Beechcraft took flight and began pursuit. An F6F Hellcat took off forty-one minutes later and made contact in clear skies at 2,000 feet. The Hellcat pilot reported the balloon as gray in color, twenty-five to thirty feet in diameter, with a "black package" hanging twenty feet below the shrouds. Once the JRB took several aerial photographs of the balloon, now slowly descending and crossing into northern California, the pilot of the Hellcat was ordered to shoot it down. His guns jammed unexpectedly (but fortuitously, it would turn out), and rather than destroy the balloon he made repeated passes and forced it to the ground with the slipstream of his aircraft. The balloon landed softly on a tree-covered mountainside southwest of Alturas, California. The G-2 office in San Francisco ordered the balloon be recovered intact and handled with utmost care.

"I've seen a picture of it," Colonel Bisenius told the G-2 headquarters, referring to the grounded balloon. "Although you couldn't see much of the details in the pictures it looks pretty good."[10]

When the Alturas balloon arrived at Moffett Air Base a few days later, officials discovered it was a near pristine specimen with no significant damage. The envelope had no tears, the skirt and shroud lines appeared intact, and the carriage still contained its full complement of fuses, switches, and aneroids. Several of the blowout plugs had fired and both ballast and bombs were missing, but otherwise the device was complete. The Alturas balloon differed in some ways from those previously recovered, however. There was no shock cord between the shroud lines and the chandelier, and the pressure-relief valve on the bottom of the envelope was affixed to a two-foot paper neck, not flush with the surface of the bag.

Personnel at Moffett secured the envelope to the ground with half a dozen guy-wires, then reinflated it with helium, and sent it aloft. A photograph of the tethered balloon would appear in almost every confidential report the War Department produced on the topic for the duration of the war. Following a preliminary inspection of the envelope and carriage, Moffett shipped the deflated Alturas balloon to Lakehurst Naval Air Station in New Jersey to be used in ongoing radar visibility tests.

From the arrival of the first balloons in late 1944, navy technicians wondered whether the devices contained enough reflective material to be detected by radar. Most of the early recoveries had been damaged too severely to be reinflated, and later specimens proved barely adequate. In the first test conducted in mid-February 1945, Lakehurst engineers attempted to inflate a previously recovered balloon—reports of the test do not cite which envelope was used—but found it was badly mildewed and torn in several places. Laying the envelope flat to dry caused the panels to separate at the seams. The men patched the holes and sealed the panels with glue, then tethered the envelope to a dual coil of nylon line and steel cable and filled it with 10,000 cubic feet of helium. The operation allowed the envelope to reach 1,000 feet and hold that altitude for about an hour before enough gas escaped the degraded and increasingly porous envelope that the balloon descended quickly. A second flight followed, this time untethered, in which the free balloon reached 4,500 feet and traveled five and a half miles from the launch point before landing gently in a grove of trees. (An uncontrolled flight was deemed nonhazardous due to the removal of the balloon's carriage and the fact its lifting agent was not explosive hydrogen, but helium, an inert gas. Nevertheless, a navy escort aircraft followed the balloon with orders to shoot it down if it approached any populated area.)

FIG. 14. The Alturas balloon tethered and reinflated at Moffett Field in San Francisco. Untitled photograph, Box 43, Japanese Balloon Sightings, Record Group 499, Western Defense Command, NARA

The brief, low-altitude flights failed to provide a sufficient research platform to test radar visibility, so Lakehurst engineers now hoped the intact Alturas balloon would result in a successful test.[11] While they awaited delivery of the device from California, another team of radar operators at the Anacostia laboratory conducted simulated tests with weather and barrage balloons. They first attached actual Japanese pressure-relief valves to navy zKM barrage balloons and flew them from small powerboats in Chesapeake Bay. To simulate the *fu-go* carriage (but at a fraction of its weight) they wrapped aluminum foil around a cardboard replica the same size and shape and then sent it aloft suspended beneath a small weather balloon.

With the objects airborne, the navy tested various shore- and ship-based radar systems across a range of frequencies. The results were not promising. "None of the present radar equipments will give entirely satisfactory area coverage due to the weakness of the signal involved," Anacostia concluded.[12] While some bands could detect the balloons at ranges up to twenty-five miles, the sheer length of coastline to be defended would require a vast array of radar stations at considerable expense. The navy suggested tight local coverage around cities on the West Coast might be feasible, but nothing more.

When the Alturas balloon arrived at Lakehurst in late February and was sent aloft, radar operators discovered an S-band frequency ably detected not the metal of the carriage but the gas-filled envelope itself. On February 28, Lakehurst released an intact, fully inflated balloon on a free flight over the Atlantic. (It is not clear from records whether the specimen used for this test was the Alturas balloon or another envelope.) A twenty-pound sandbag tied to the bottom of the envelope slowed its ascent. A navy plane again took flight and circled the balloon, mostly to provide a comparative radar target. The pilot lost visual contact with the balloon ten miles from shore when it was traveling due east at seventy knots airspeed. Lakehurst presumed the balloon went down at sea at some considerable distance, probably at nightfall when cooler temperatures contracted the gas and caused a precipitous loss in altitude. The test no doubt made the device the only Japanese balloon to land in the Atlantic.

As before in Chesapeake Bay, radar visibility results proved inconclusive. A joint army-navy report on balloon detection techniques was blunt in its conclusion: "The naked eye offers the best hope of visual detection of balloons in space."[13] Even then, the report noted, detection would only be possible when the balloon descended under 30,000 feet and was almost directly above, not on the far horizon. The Alturas balloon, for example, had been detected while in flight only because it happened to drift directly over a civilian airfield and naval air station, both populated with personnel trained to look up at the sky. The official report of an incident at Burwell, Nebraska, in mid-February likely caused some bemusement at G-2 headquarters. The balloon was first noticed by a flock of turkeys. Only when the birds froze in unison and looked skyward did a farmer glance up and observe a dot high in the clouds.[14]

The naval air station at Anacostia next initiated a thorough study of all numbers, stamps, or other identifying marks that appeared on the devices recovered to date. It had already been determined that a production tag often appeared somewhere on each envelope with the date of manufacture written in pencil. Investigators now paid attention to the numbers on the envelope's valve assembly as well. The Alturas balloon had the number "3060" hand-painted in white on the large valve plate. A balloon recovered in Marshall, Alaska, about the same time featured a pressure-relief valve with the number "93" painted in two places, the number "26" written in chalk, and the number "2569" die-stamped in half-inch numerals on the valve spring support. A reexamination of the valve from the Estacada balloon revealed the number "2647" in the same position, evidently stamped with the same press. Anacostia suspected the four-digit numbers were serial numbers—perhaps indicating a production total in the thousands—while

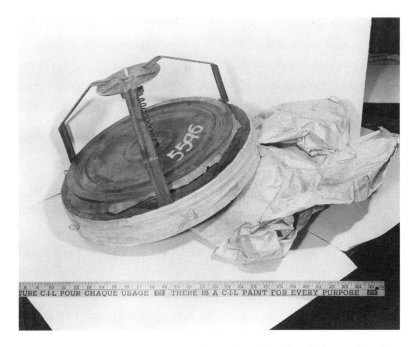

FIG. 15. Pressure relief valve with number written in white chalk on valve plate. Each valve also featured a four- or five-digit serial number die-stamped on one of the three spring supports. CWM-19910238-445-4, Canadian War Museum

the numbers scrawled in paint or chalk might identify workmen, launch personnel, daily production records, or some similar use.[15]

In response to the discovery of these markings, Army Intelligence began keeping meticulous records of the numbers that appeared on recovered valve plates and springs. As dozens and eventually hundreds of balloons turned up throughout the spring of 1945, analysts discerned some definitive patterns in the serial numbers. Four-digit numbers that began with even thousands (i.e., 2000, 4000, 6000) appeared on what they called "A-type" valves, those with flat valve braces and a ribbed valve plate. Other balloons featured valves with slightly bent braces and ridged, not ribbed, valve plates. These "B-type" valves had numbers beginning in the odd thousands.

Analysts then attempted to correlate the order of manufacture of both the envelopes and valves, but the numbers failed to match up. An envelope whose factory tag indicated it was completed on January 10, 1945, for example, had valve number 9678, while an envelope dated three weeks later had valve number 9052. Comparing the valve numbers with the dates of landing in North America also suggested an out-of-sequence assembly. Sebastopol landed on January 4 with valve number 4590, Alturas six days later with valve number 3060, and a balloon in Lame Deer, Montana, came down two days after that with valve number 2621. "If valves were attached to balloons and released in sequence shortly after manufacture, serial numbers and dates of landing would offer a fairly reliable indication of production rates," G-2 concluded. That the valves were not being released in sequence had potentially dire implications: "Apparently considerable stockpiles of valves exist. . . . [A]ny given group of balloons seems to contain a more or less random sampling of valves manufactured before the date of release."[16] The high range of numbers—one valve recovered on February 1 was numbered 13821—indicated Japan was capable of producing valves at a rate of up to 4,800 per month. The presumed stockpiling of many thousands of valves suggested plans for an equal number of balloon launches.

G-2 tempered its dire assessment by noting the production of valves almost certainly outpaced manufacture of other balloon components, including the envelopes. It believed the random sequence of valve numbers indicated that only one of every four valves produced was actually used, and that the stockpile may have resulted from a bottleneck in some other phase of balloon production. Analysts further observed that regardless of each valve's thousands-series, the frequency of the 7, 8, and 9 hundreds was remarkably low. Only one balloon had been recovered with a 7 in the hundreds column, just two balloons with an 8 in the hundreds column, and not a single one had a valve number with a 9 in the hundreds column. The probability of so few 7, 8, and 9 hundreds, if valves had been selected in a truly random distribution, was calculated at less than half of one percent, leading G-2 to suppose the valve manufacturer in Japan had allocated serial numbers in blocks of thousands but that the sequence had rarely if ever been exhausted. The reason so few 7, 8, and 9 hundreds appeared, in other words, was that few 7, 8, and 9 hundreds had been manufactured, which in turn suggested the total number of stockpiled valves was in all likelihood considerably lower than U.S. authorities initially feared. Finally, G-2 noted the entire exercise might be nothing more than an act of numerical deceit, that the four- and five-digit serial numbers had been invented and stamped for no reason other than to disguise the true number of balloons being manufactured.

By the time of the Alturas recovery still another clue had revealed itself to investigators. Many of the blowout plug casings on the first balloons appeared to have been tooled by hand or fabricated individually of machined steel. Later casings were composed of cast aluminum, a method of mass production. Anacostia engineers surmised the early devices were prototypes and that the Japanese had tinkered with components until they found the optimum design for each. At that point automated production commenced. First the stockpile of valves and now the industrial manufacture of blowout plug casings demonstrated that large numbers of balloons were likely being produced at a rapid pace.

About this time Army Intelligence assigned a code name to the Japanese balloons. The word "balloon" could still be used in confidential memos and reports, but all nonsecure communications were to use the code name "Paper."[17]

CONFERENCE

Major General H. C. Pratt stood before dozens of officials from eleven civilian and military defense agencies in a large conference room at the Western Defense Command's Presidio headquarters on the morning of January 17, 1945. Numerous personnel from the WDC's three sector commands, an admiral and half a dozen captains from the Western Sea Command, officers from the army and air force, two representatives from the state of California, two chemical warfare officers, and an FBI agent all crowded into the room. Each participant received a packet of information—stamped "SECRET" naturally—with the officious title "Conference of Interested Commands and Agencies relative to Balloon Borne Attacks Against the West Coast."[18]

"Gentlemen, it is my privilege to welcome you to the Western Defense Command Headquarters," Major General Pratt began. "What we are going to discuss today concerns all defense agencies."[19]

From the moment of discovery of the Kalispell balloon the previous December, the army and navy had assumed a joint command of the balloon investigation. The FBI had agreed to a secondary role, in which it participated in the "full and free exchange of information," according to a memorandum signed by the bureau's director, J. Edgar Hoover. Under the terms spelled out in the agreement, any balloon reports coming first to the attention of the FBI were to be transmitted promptly to the respective army and navy commands in the area. By the opening of the WDC conference on January 17, the number of balloon incidents had surpassed a dozen and was perhaps twice that number, considering the delay with which some incidents were reported. No more than a few days now passed between explosions, sightings, or recoveries somewhere on the West Coast, and the WDC felt compelled to convene the conference to disseminate information on what was certain to be a continuing problem.

Pratt reminded attendees of the sensitive nature of the information they were about to receive—"discuss it only with such individuals as you may consider necessary, and as few as possible," he noted[20]—and stressed the intent of the meeting was only to clarify and evaluate the balloons, how they operated, and the threat they posed to the American mainland. Eventual development of defense procedures would of course be crucial, but Pratt asked participants to not get ahead of themselves and start tinkering with defense plans until they fully understood the nature of the attack. Although the War Department possessed clear and definitive evidence regarding many aspects of the balloon offensive, some particulars remained unknown, and Pratt felt a cautious, deliberative process to be the most prudent.

Colonel William Hammond, the G-2 officer who over the past month had established himself as the point man on balloon intelligence, took the podium and gave attendees a rundown on the sightings, landings, and recoveries to date, from the first at San Pedro the previous November up to the most recent at Lame Deer, Montana, just four days earlier. He described the design and composition of the balloons in precise detail and explained how the pressure relief valves and automated ballast mechanism regulated their transoceanic flight. Although he mentioned the incendiary and high-explosive bombs, Hammond did not dwell on their design and function. This was a military audience after all, and they presumably needed no elaboration to comprehend the threat.

Because the WDC still considered itself to be in the intelligence-gathering phase, Hammond outlined the three-pronged mission: surveillance, recovery, and analysis. Although no direct procedures had been officially approved as yet, Hammond stated his belief that future recoveries should be performed by bomb disposal experts and personnel trained to secure and preserve the evidence for later analysis. The colonel also gave voice to what WDC believed to be the most extreme possible threat: "Japan has sufficient technical personnel, raw materials, and manufacturing capacity to wage bacteriological warfare."[21]

Hammond inserted several caveats into his explanations, such as when he stated the "origin and purpose of these balloons has not yet been determined and probably will not be until more data is collected."[22] He claimed they could have been released from submarines,

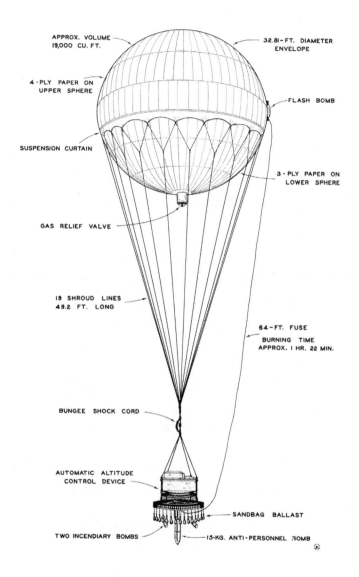

APPROX. VOLUME
19,000 CU. FT.

32.81-FT. DIAMETER
ENVELOPE

4-PLY PAPER ON
UPPER SPHERE

FLASH BOMB

SUSPENSION CURTAIN

3-PLY PAPER ON
LOWER SPHERE

GAS RELIEF VALVE

19 SHROUD LINES
49.2 FT. LONG

64-FT. FUSE
BURNING TIME
APPROX. I HR. 22 MIN.

BUNGEE SHOCK CORD

AUTOMATIC ALTITUDE
CONTROL DEVICE

SANDBAG BALLAST

TWO INCENDIARY BOMBS

I5-KG. ANTI-PERSONNEL BOMB

FIG. 16. Diagram of Japanese balloon bomb. Smithsonian Institution

even though that theory had been almost completely discredited by that date, and named "landing of agents or commandos" as a possible balloon function. (The Army Air Force later calculated that a balloon envelope at least sixty-two feet in diameter with a lifting capacity of nearly two thousand pounds at altitude would be required to ferry a person and all necessary survival equipment from Japan to North America.) The discussion then focused on G-2's plans for developing an "active defense" against enemy saboteurs and trained secret agents already in the United States. With threat assessment as the stated goal of the conference, Hammond may have included these debunked theories in his presentations so as to stimulate open and wide-ranging discussions among the attendees. Informing them of what the balloons were *not* might prejudice their thought process, limit the conversation, and unintentionally exclude input that might prove insightful.

Although he could not have known it at the time, Hammond proved remarkably prescient in his assessment of the campaign to date:

> It appears unlikely that the balloons found so far in themselves constitute an attempted attack on the West Coast. It is possible, however, that they prelude an airborne attack of some sort employing free floating objects in such large numbers that even a very small percentage of 'hits' will produce the desired result.[23]

For all the perfectly justified concern within the War Department, Hammond was correct that the dozen or so balloon landings over the previous two months could hardly be called an "attack." Should Japan launch thousands or even tens of thousands of balloons in the coming months, however, which is precisely what G-2 was expecting to happen, American defense agencies would need to be prepared. Major General Pratt agreed that while the danger posed by a few hydrogen balloons might seem overstated, time spent evaluating the danger and planning for a possible future phase of the Japanese attack was not time wasted.

With the floor now open for questions and discussions, one attendee expressed doubt that any sort of aerial defense against the balloons was even possible. He noted the extreme difficulty of advance detection and that the sheer randomness of a balloon dropping a bomb from as high as 30,000 feet precluded any effective preventative measures. "Therefore, I think that a redisposition of our anti-aircraft defense to cope with these balloons and throwing away everything else that we are defending would not be justified."[24] According to the skeptical army officer, troops in the WDC's northwest sector had been "chasing spooks" for weeks, driving jeeps all over the region in response to every star and blinking light in the night sky. Any reorientation of personnel might only add even more chaos to an already manpower-intensive operation. He also disputed the enemy saboteur theory, doubting a Japanese soldier could survive a balloon flight. "It takes a week to get here. He is going up to 25,000 or 30,000 feet. He will have to have a lot of oxygen, rations, and other things, and dropping one Jap out here, maybe on the top of Mount Rainier, would not be a paying proposition. . . . I do not see any particular use in chasing after a new red wagon."

A rear admiral with the Western Sea Frontier agreed. He placed no credence in the commando theory and expressed little concern over the high-explosive bombs, which he said would likely fall in unpopulated areas. He also saw no need to orient anti-aircraft measures toward shooting down the airborne balloons, as such an operation would send the payload of bombs crashing to earth just the same. The admiral instead listed two primary concerns: the large forest fires the incendiary devices might start throughout the western states and the possibility of biological warfare. "It seems to me the most important thing for us to do right now is to get the bacteriological experts and the Forest Service working on some kind of a plan for counteracting those two threats."[25]

At the close of the conference, the G-2 distributed a written summary of present defense plans and requested all participating agencies and personnel conduct a thorough assessment of how defenses might be improved in their respective regions and areas of responsibility. These surveys were to be completed and submitted to WDC within two weeks so as to enable the command to coordinate its overall defense strategy. "I hope you have gotten something worthwhile out of this meeting," General Pratt stated just before adjourning the conference. "Whether the balloon is a menace or not, maybe it is not, we appreciate your attention, we are glad you came, and we hope that the cooperation we are asking from you will be forthcoming."[26]

## PROPAGANDA

On December 18, 1944, while the Americans still puzzled over the mysterious events in Thermopolis and Kalispell, authorities in Japan obtained a Chinese newspaper, *Takungpao*, that had picked up a story about a mysterious balloon discovered in the mountains of Montana. At the Kokura Arsenal, where hundreds of schoolgirls still toiled long hours turning out sheets of hand-made paper, officials reacted to the news by visiting a shrine to Japanese soldiers killed in the war to let them know their deaths were being avenged.[27]

Confirmation that this one balloon had reached North America demonstrated the operational success of the design and suggested that many other balloons had made and would make a complete ocean crossing as well. Engineers at Noborito were hungry for news of additional landings so as to better coordinate launches for optimum meteorological conditions, but the propaganda machine needed no further details to conduct its work. Domei Tsushinsha, an international news bureau with offices and reporters stationed outside Japan, announced via a radio broadcast that a secret weapon code named "Fireflies" had shattered the Americans' feeling of security:

> Ten thousand people have been killed. One of our weapons caused great fires and damage at Kalispell, Montana. For months residents of the western United States have seen huge objects floating eastward in the sky at night. Each of our secret-type balloons can carry several persons, and the day is not far distant when we will land several million Japanese troops on American soil.[28]

The level of propaganda did not stop there. Long after aeronautical engineers at Noborito had abandoned plans to send huge bomb-laden aircraft on one-way suicide missions to the United States, radio broadcasts in the Japan-occupied Philippines stated, again in English: "A definite plan to shower bombs on New York and to reduce its skyscrapers to ashes has been publicized. . . . With the stratospheric flying plane, now being constructed in Japan, we can reach New York in twenty to twenty-four hours." The report went on to explain the aircraft would be pushed along by the westerly winds of the upper atmosphere, a meteorological advantage that would fortuitously prevent American planes from responding in kind. (One broadcast made mention of *kamikaze*, or "divine winds," a word that would take on new meaning by the end of the Pacific war.) If the winds proved strong enough, the Japanese planes might even cross the Atlantic and land in Berlin. "We will choose the bombs of the largest caliber, say tons or more," the announcer continued, "and bomb New York and Washington at least twice a day."[29]

A British report on Japanese propaganda written in 1944 concluded the disinformation campaigns served "to spur the people on to greater effort, to fortify their belief in the justice of the country's cause, to consolidate their trust in the Government, combat war-time evils, and fight rumors, alarm, and despondency."[30] In the occupied countries of Southeast Asia, the Japanese utilized radio broadcasts to establish total information control. Delivered in English, the primary common language in all non-Japanese speaking areas, the broadcasts featured news and commentary on the empire's dramatic victories over the Allied forces. When defeats received mention on the airwaves they served to illustrate both the courage of deceased soldiers who refused to surrender and the ruthlessness of the enemy. The British report notes the Japanese use the phrase "Thought War" in lieu of the word "propaganda," a semantic distinction that bespeaks a commitment to forced indoctrination.

Colonel Hammond, the G-2 officer at the Presidio for whom keeping track of the Japanese balloons had become an all-encompassing task, received a report in mid-February 1945 that was most unusual, even by the standards of the balloon campaign to date. A radio broadcast throughout Southeast Asia featured Dr. Hideki Yukawa, professor at Kyoto Imperial University, describing a recent dream:

> In a cave halfway up a certain mountain on the Japanese mainland, something like a large chunk of iron can be seen. A narrow streak of cloud coming out of the cave extends way out toward the east and crossing the Pacific is falling on Washington. Suddenly a terrific pillar of flames shot up into the sky. Together with the terrific explosion, the town of Washington was blown up into small pieces. What looked like a streak of cloud might perhaps be a deadly ray.[31]

If such fanciful public pronouncements proved easy to dismiss, more troubling were the intercepted private words of a Japanese diplomat in Buenos Aires. In spring 1945 the man was overheard discussing the *fu-go* campaign. An article in a local newspaper had recently mentioned the offensive, to which Juichi Shinizu responded that the balloons "are nothing more than the prelude to something big. . . . I assure you that this is only a test and that this weapon will be improved to give the maximum efficiency and precision." Shinizu did not elaborate further, according to the confidential cable the U.S. military attaché submitted to Washington, only that future plans for bombing the American mainland would "surprise the United States and arouse the admiration of the world."[32]

# 4

.............

## *BW*

Doctor Charles Mitchell, an animal pathologist with the Animal Diseases Research Institute in Hull, Quebec, received a summons on January 13, 1945, to proceed to Regina, Saskatchewan, and recover a sample of an unknown substance that may or may not have been a weapon of biological/bacteriological warfare, known in military shorthand as "BW."

One day earlier a large white balloon was observed drifting at ground level near Minton, a small town ninety miles south of Regina on the U.S.-Canada border. The balloon's carriage struck the ground with some force, according to witnesses, in the process dislodging one large explosive device, two incendiaries (one burned, one intact), four sandbags, and a clear plastic box filled with some type of slushy liquid. After dropping this cargo, the balloon ascended and drifted away, not to be recovered.

The plastic box contained a block of ice and small, round glob-ules that resembled fish eggs. The discovery convinced authorities

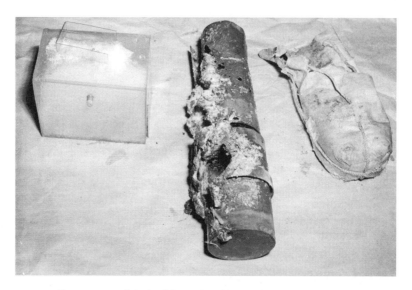

FIG. 17. Components dislodged from the Minton, Saskatchewan, balloon on 12 January 1945. The slushy liquid inside the clear plastic battery case was tested for biological agents. Photograph E011061654, Record Group 24, Volume 5195, Library and Archives Canada

in Regina to treat the device as a possible biological weapon. Sand recovered from the ballast weights contained small leaves and twigs, which caused additional concern that a harmful organic agent might be present. Dr. Mitchell retrieved the evidence and sent samples of the frozen liquid and sand from all four sandbags to three laboratories: his own back in Quebec, the Canadian Directorate of Chemical Warfare in Ottawa, and Connaught Laboratories in Dufferin, Ontario. Noting the samples were secure and in competent hands, the U.S. War Department did not request the evidence to be sent to a laboratory in the United States.

Canada's chemical and biological warfare research was then coordinated by Dr. Otto Maass, a particularly capable and aggressive administrator from Montreal's McGill University who not only established research programs and institutes in his home country but also recognized the advantages of close collaboration with the U.S. War Department and its suite of complementary agencies. Maass served as official liaison on the United States–Canadian Chemical Warfare Advisory Committee established in 1943 and the Biological Warfare Committee formed a year later. The professional ties he forged with his American counterparts, especially General William Porter of the U.S. Army Chemical Warfare Service, indicated that Maass recognized his nation's neighbor to the south possessed superior research facilities and expertise. Much of his research agenda was accordingly set as much by Washington as Ottawa.[1] Canada's chemical warfare capabilities at the start of the war were all but nonexistent, yet Maass quickly established laboratories in Ottawa and Suffield, Alberta, where both offensive and defensive preparations were made in case of attack by Germany or Japan. Maass recruited top scientists from across Canada for a secret research committee code named C-1000.[2] Dr. Mitchell, who served on the committee, dutifully involved his colleagues in the examination of the Minton balloon.

Dr. G. N. Reed of the chemical warfare office inventoried the Minton evidence when it arrived on January 22, a week and a half after the landing. The box, thought to be part of the device's battery enclosure, measured six-by-six-by-eight inches and was made of a thin transparent plastic material. A small rubber stopper closed the only opening. The block of porous ice occupied roughly half of the inside space. The doctor noted that a small crack on one side of the box could have allowed snow or water from the landing site to contaminate the contents. Reed thawed the frozen substance and boiled a sample for several minutes. The liquid was water clear and produced no odor. Microscopic examination of both untreated and centrifuged samples showed a small number of bacterial spores and rod-shaped bacteria. The doctor then introduced a sample of the undiluted fluid into the skin, veins, brain, or nasal passages of white mice and guinea pigs, between one-half and one cubic centimeter per animal host.[3]

That same day at Connaught Laboratories, Dr. James Craigie, another member of the c-1000 committee, ran his liquid sample through a centrifuge for one hour and noted the presence of small clumps of brownish material and oily globules of the type found in stagnant pond water. He observed a number of organisms of varied bacterial morphology, but none in quantities to suggest they had been prepared and assembled for any particular purpose. After diluting the sample with pH-neutral saline and glycerol in a number of different concentrations, Craigie, like Reed in his Ottawa lab, injected the solutions into mice and guinea pigs.

"No evidence has been obtained to date of the presence of virus pathogenic for mice or guinea pigs in any of the specimens," Craigie wrote in his report.[4] The animals seemed to be doing fine. "The specimens of fluid do not have the characteristics of crude virus preparations . . . nor do they appear to be fluids designed to preserve the infectivity of any mammalian virus." The biochemist did record the deaths of a few mice, but in postmortem examinations he discovered no signs of infection or illness.

After watching the inoculated but healthy animals in his lab for two weeks, Reed came to the same conclusions. "None of the animals, mice or guinea pigs, have shown any symptoms of any description," he wrote.[5] Reed then took samples of sand from each of the four bags in his possession and shook them with an infusion broth for thirty minutes. After allowing the sand to settle, he extracted cultures of the supernatant broth and injected it into mice and guinea pigs. Again, none showed any deleterious effects. "The great variety of bacteria in these sand samples, the lack of pathogenicity of the gross washings of the sand and of selected pure cultures suggests that this material does not carry pathogenic bacteria in significant numbers," the doctor reported.[6]

Next to arrive at Reed's laboratory were two samples of fluid from a sealed plastic box on a balloon recovered at Fort Simpson, a small community at the confluence of the Mackenzie and Liard Rivers in the Northwest Territories. Both samples, one a clear fluid and the other containing gray-white particulate matter, gave off an ester-like odor. Mice injected in the body cavity with 1 cubic centimeter of the undiluted clear fluid died within minutes. Those with an equal amount injected just under the skin perished after two to three hours. Reed began diluting the solution and discovered that at 0.1 cubic centimeter the mice, after surviving the initial shock of the toxic injection, recovered and showed no symptoms after fifteen days.

Reed determined the clear fluid was an ethyl acetate and water mixture with low concentrations of an alkaline substance. Although its exact purpose was not determined, the doctors conducting the studies did not believe it was meant to function as a biological weapon. Despite being highly toxic to the mice, the substance contained no bacteriological agents and was incapable of spreading infectious material. The plastic box almost certainly housed the balloon's battery. Previously recovered devices showed this arrangement, and the alkaline substance found in the solution could easily have leaked from the battery itself. In that case the organic fluid might have served some preservative function for sustained battery life.

Charles Mitchell, the doctor who first collected the Minton samples and was coordinating the investigation between the three laboratories, noted that while the Minton and Fort Simpson devices did not appear to be biological weapons themselves, the balloons had great potential as delivery vehicles. "An obvious means has been found of disseminating this type of material and every precaution should be exercised," he wrote. "Moreover, it should not be assumed that the method which is being followed now will not be modified in the near future to spread the material in which we have been interested."[7]

The Minton and Fort Simpson investigations took place at the same time the Western Defense Command convened its Presidio

conference for civilian and defense agencies. Lieutenant Colonel
Oram C. Woolpert of the Chemical Warfare Service (cws) took the
floor at that conference to describe the bw threat as he saw it: "Merely
dropping glass containers or paper sacks might be an effective way to
bring [biological agents] over here and start something which would
be considerably annoying."[8] Woolpert noted the bombs carried and
dropped by the balloons might prove ineffectual as they would be
likely to land in unpopulated areas, but that a biological weapon could
introduce a particularly virulent strain of bacteria capable of being
distributed widely by any number of vectors, including humans, animals, vegetation, and even the wind. In addition, the high altitude and
corresponding low temperatures of the balloons' flight paths could
be exploited by employing organisms suited to such environmental
conditions. When queried on which bacterial agents might be sent
over, Woolpert named foot and mouth disease, Japanese B (a type of
encephalitis), anthrax, and various fungi and plant parasites unknown
in the United States.

To this point in the conference attendees had discussed the need
for bomb disposal officers to be present at each balloon recovery.
Woolpert stated his view that a bacteriologist or someone with similar training should also attend each incident. The wdc instructed
Woolpert's cws to begin drafting response plans. In fact, just a day
earlier Woolpert had visited the U.S. Navy Medical Research Unit
in Berkeley to devise procedures for chemical and bacteriological
investigations. "Since the positive detection of a bw agent employed
by the enemy will have far-reaching consequences with respect to
policy, every suspected instance must have the benefit of thorough
investigation," the research team wrote in one of the first memoranda
on the subject.[9] Whether intended or not, those words made for an
inclusive policy in which nearly every balloon would be subject to
rigorous examination. All could be "suspected" of bw, after all, and
thus none could be excluded.

Woolpert recommended the Berkeley lab serve as the central point of investigation, with CWS specialists on both human and animal pathogens assigned to temporary duty for as long as needed. That same week at a conference of coordination between the navy, army, and administrators from military medical facilities throughout the West, attendees produced a bulletin that would serve as the foundation for all BW defense plans that followed. Bacteriologists and bomb disposal officers were to work in concert to secure the landing site, but only after donning protective gear, approaching from upwind, and spraying the area with insect repellents. Once onsite, the men were to record all pertinent details of the area and collect any specimens, including samples of earth, in sterile jars. A courier from the nearest military facility would then transport the samples to Berkeley for analysis. The memo was brief and lacking in details, but the general principles of BW response had been set.[10]

### HAYFORK

Ray Beals, the district forest ranger for the Shasta and Trinity National Forests in northern California, took a telephone call at his Hayfork office at 6:20 p.m. on February 1, 1945. The caller informed Beals that he and his neighbor were at that very moment watching a large balloon drifting directly over their homes. He described it as white, twenty feet in diameter, with a cylindrical object hanging underneath. A strong and constant wind from the southwest steadily pushed the balloon toward the rugged hills northwest of town. The caller told Beals the balloon was heading roughly in the direction of his ranger station, and all he had to do was look up and he'd see it. The ranger grabbed his field glasses, stepped outside, and observed the balloon four thousand feet in the sky but descending quickly. The neighbor phoned a few minutes later to report the balloon had settled in some trees near her house.[11]

Beals dispatched two of his deputies to locate and guard the balloon until he could inform the county sheriff. The men found the balloon hung up only slightly between two trees, its carriage swaying in the air as the envelope heaved and pulled with the steady breeze. A crowd of half a dozen onlookers had gathered beneath the trees, and the deputies moved everyone back thirty feet. After forty minutes or so the balloon worked itself free from the trees and sailed to the far side of the canyon where it exploded in a puff of white smoke. A second explosion moments later produce reddish-blue smoke and was described by a witness as sounding like two sticks of dynamite.

When G-2 officials from the WDC Northern Sector arrived the next evening, they found the envelope destroyed by the flash bomb (the likely source of white smoke the witnesses observed) and a largely intact chandelier with seven sandbags and three incendiary devices. A fourth unexploded incendiary was found on the ground nearby. A tripped arming wire in the center of the chandelier's bottom ring indicated a missing fifth bomb, perhaps the device that produced the reddish-blue smoke. A torn piece of paper attached to one of the incendiaries had Japanese characters that, when translated, made little sense: "Tiny / state of chemical / compound particle / the way to form / becoming sudden repetition / to adopt the way to."[12] It does not appear G-2 ever made sense of the cryptic message.

The Hayfork incident occurred just two weeks after the Presidio BW conference. Accordingly, the WDC seized the opportunity to field-test its biological warfare response then under development. Although initial reports from Hayfork indicated the balloon "showed no presumptive evidence" of BW agents, the circumstances of its recovery seemed perfect for such a drill. The device had been continuously guarded by the county sheriff and trained G-2 personnel, making for an intact chain of custody that ensured all evidence would be free of any significant contamination. And since Hayfork was only a couple hundred miles north of the WDC's San Francisco headquarters, the

evidence could be transported with little difficulty. The W D C immediately contacted the navy's Medical Research Unit and secured
laboratory space at its facility in Berkeley.

A bacteriologist at the W D C Office of the Surgeon took possession of the Hayfork device when it arrived. He had one of the seven
sandbags packed in dry ice and shipped to the Anacostia laboratory,
while he examined the other six. He then waited while a bomb disposal officer dismantled the incendiary devices, which appeared to be
packed only with thermite. "The conclusion . . . is that the Hayfork
balloon did not contain evidence of the presence of biological warfare
material," he wrote.[13]

The negative test results were but one small part of the W D C
report on the incident. "Certain general and practical observations
have been made relative to the proper function of biological warfare
officers in the field," it continued. The W D C noted the transport of
balloon materials to certified laboratories required the cooperation
of G-2 field staff B W specialists, bomb disposal personnel, the commanding officer and motor pool at nearby bases, and whatever local
law enforcement might also be involved. In the Hayfork case this
joint response went smoothly, but other recoveries seemed to have
been slowed down by miscommunication and misunderstandings. In
one unfortunate episode described in the report, a driver assigned to
deliver a B W officer from a balloon landing site back to base decided
to streamline his work detail by making several other routine deliv-
eries along the way, thereby delaying the officer several hours from
his time-sensitive mission. The bacteriologist who investigated the
Hayfork balloon also noted the as yet unmet need for specimen containers, protective clothing, masks, and decontaminating supplies at
each designated response station in the western states. The report
made clear the W D C had some way to go before its B W plan could
be considered adequate.

JULIAN

Exactly one month later, on March 1, 1945, a rancher named Everett Campbell walked along a fence on his property near Julian, California, sixty miles northeast of San Diego, and saw a gelding inside the enclosure fighting and biting the other horses. Campbell jumped the fence and quickly corralled the animal. The gelding seemed to settle down after a couple of hours, and the rancher released it back to the herd. The next morning he found the animal had died in some agony during the night. Veins stood out on the face and neck, and the horse's eyes protruded from their sockets.[14]

Two and a half weeks after that, Campbell discovered two steers from an adjoining ranch running with his cattle, both foaming at the mouth. One steer turned and charged Campbell, but he was able to mount his horse and ride away without incident. The next day a steer from the Campbell herd broke away and attacked another rancher in the same valley. Two other cattle in the area died with rabies-like symptoms, and one apparently rabid coyote had to be shot when it attacked a man camping outside and attempted to enter another camper's tent. The canine was buried in the desert before it could be tested for the disease.

The strange happenings might have been attributed to just another sweep of rabies through the rural area—a local veterinarian claimed such things happened from year to year and that cattle disease rates were not abnormal at that time—but for the Japanese balloon that a few weeks earlier had drifted over the very field where Campbell's animals took sick.

On January 31 Campbell and one of his ranch hands observed a pear-shaped balloon descend and land atop a mountain that separated their ranch from an adjacent valley. The two men scaled the peak and discovered a badly smashed carriage and a debris trail pointing back in the direction the balloon had traveled. Campbell severed a

burning fuse connected to a small pouch on the side of the envelope. He then cut the shroud lines and lugged the device back down
to his car, placing it in the trunk. The next day Campbell's wife
delivered the apparatus to the county sheriff, who called the FBI
in San Diego, who in turn called the suite of agencies listed on the
dispatch sheet for just such an occurrence, including the G-2 office
in San Francisco.[15] A response team from Fort MacArthur in Los
Angeles arrived two days later, the landing site having been guarded
continuously by sheriff's deputies since the landing. After the bomb
disposal officer determined the area was safe, a bacteriologist from
nearby Camp Haan inspected the envelope carefully and found no
infectious material. He recovered an empty box lying on the ground
fifty feet from the landing site and, uncertain whether it belonged to
the balloon, arranged to have it delivered to a chemical laboratory at
the University of California. The scientist also scraped what he called
"suspicious dust particles" and a few strands of human hair from the
envelope's valve. These he sent to the same laboratory in Berkeley
where the Hayfork balloon was then undergoing tests. As with that
device, all evidence from Julian proved inert and uncontaminated
with any bacterial agents.

The mostly improvised Hayfork and Julian recoveries informed
the specimen collection procedures later formalized by the surgeon
general and adopted by the WDC. "All specimens which do not appear
to have a known function should be collected," stated the list of
approved procedures.[16] The WDC did not mean to encourage responders to collect extraneous and useless material, but it also did not
want them to overlook unusual media that might have an unknown
purpose. Special attention was to be paid to fluids, powders, abrasives,
kernels of grain, bits of cloth or cotton, and all sandbags attached
to the bottom ring of the altitude control mechanism. Responding
officials were further instructed to don protective gear, approach the

site from upwind, document as thoroughly as possible the condition of the landing site and the evidence before handling it, and use the full range of supplies in the forthcoming detection kits—glass containers of various sizes, test tubes, pipettes, scalpel, scraper, forceps, scissors, tape, labels, and sterile gloves—to secure as pure a sample as possible.

There is little evidence the surgeon general's procedures were ever followed, strictly or otherwise, or that the detection kits were actually assembled and delivered to service commands in the western states. The War Department's press censorship policy that had remained in effect since early January meant very few Americans knew about the Japanese balloons and the danger they posed, thus when a large paper balloon descended to earth unknowing locals typically responded by examining the device themselves, only contacting a county sheriff or other local lawman later if at all. The Minton balloon that was the subject of such intense study for bacteriological agents, for example, was recovered only after a group of boys had thoroughly handled the incendiary and high-explosive bombs. Later examination revealed the boys had twisted the arming plug on one to within a centimeter of its detonation point. A balloon landing in Desdemona, Texas, had a similar reception. Intelligence officers (not bacteriologists) from the nearest service command arrived on the scene to find souvenir hunters had already ripped the envelope open and removed large swatches of paper. The deflated balloon gave off a strong odor similar to rotten eggs, according to witnesses, but there was little in the way of chemical evidence for the agents to recover.

One recovery that did conform to the WDC protocol occurred in early April in a wheat field in Turner, Montana, where three dead mice were found under a deflated envelope that evidently had been on the ground for several weeks. The BW officer at the nearest military hospital packed the mice in a sterile container, but only after carefully recording the placement and condition of the envelope and environmental and weather conditions at the site. He noted the presence

FIG. 18. Residents of Bigelow, Kansas, captured and tied balloon to fence post, 23 February 1945. Untitled photograph, Box 42, Japanese Balloon Sightings, Record Group 499, Western Defense Command, NARA

of fecal material on the envelope and holes in the paper where it appeared the mice had gnawed through it. The conscientious officer secured samples of the paper, fecal material, soil from beneath the envelope, and wheat from the field in which the envelope was found, all of which he sent to Lieutenant Colonel H. I. Cole of the Chemical Warfare Service in Washington. He also sent two living mice he managed to catch, though his letter to Cole did not specify whether provisions had been made to keep them alive while in transit.[17]

In developing defense procedures against a possible BW attack, the WDC explored the possibility of using wind charts and meteorological forecasts to predict, on a day-by-day basis, where any balloons then airborne over the Pacific might come down. A lead-time of even a few hours might allow authorities to locate and secure any balloons before unknowing civilians stumbled across one. The first attempt was made by the weather office of the Fourth Air Force in San Francisco.

Recognizing that the Medford and Sebastopol balloons had landed within hours of each other on January 4, meteorologists theorized the two devices had been launched from the same beach at the same time and had crossed the ocean together. They collected weather data for the period from 1500 hours, December 31, to 1750 hours, January 4 (the approximate time of the Sebastopol sighting). Assuming a constant flight at 10,000 feet, a limitation forced upon them by the incompleteness of the data, the weather office plotted the course of each balloon backward from Medford and Sebastopol and found a convergence of their flight paths several hundred miles out over the Pacific. The single trajectory then followed a winding path north of Hawaii to a point on Honshu just southeast of Tokyo. The men admitted their conclusions were wildly speculative. The hour-by-hour flight path they drew contained so many assumptions and educated guesswork they knew it would prove almost useless as a field tool. Even supposing one had the capacity to collect and integrate enough meteorological data points to give a daily prediction on balloon landings, being off by just a hundred miles might mean a dozen balloons could easily slip through unnoticed. The meteorologists also back-mapped the flight path of a balloon recovered in Marshall, Alaska, finding that the periodic presence of north-south meridional winds might allow them to warn Alaska when more balloons were likely to be en route. If the exact locations of probable landings could not be pinpointed, meteorologists could at least surmise the general area toward which the prevailing winds blew on any given day.[18]

## WASHINGTON AND OTTAWA

By mid-February 1945 at least half a dozen balloons had landed or been observed in Canada. American authorities had professed themselves pleased with the handling of the Minton and Fort Simpson investigations, and assuming the Japanese offensive was unlikely to be scaled back anytime soon, they decided to formalize operating

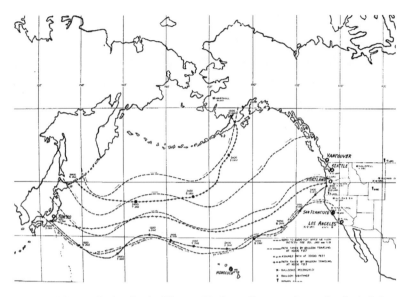

FIG. 19. Meteorologists in the Western Defense Command examined wind data from over the Pacific in a mostly unsuccessful attempt to plot possible future balloon trajectories. "Chart Showing Air Currents Over Pacific Ocean," Box 11, Series 2, Japanese Balloons, Record Group 160, Army Service Forces, Intelligence Division, NARA

procedures with Canada to better coordinate their joint efforts. (On the chance that a balloon might land in Mexico, the War Department informed the U.S. military attaché in Mexico City only that any such incident should be kept out of the newspapers.[19] Only two landings occurred in Mexico, both just across the border in Baja and Sonora.)

As with every meeting concerning the Japanese balloons, the U.S.-Canada conference at the Pentagon on February 23 opened with a statement on the confidential nature of it all. "This is a secret session and the information that you get here should be used only for official purposes," stated Colonel James M. Roamer. Invited to the meeting were liaison officers of the respective American and Canadian commands, as well as BW personnel from both Ottawa and Washington. The meeting was called, according to Lieutenant General Wilhelm

D. Styer, chief of staff of the Army Service Forces, "in order that we might get together and acquaint each other with our organizational set up, with our means and methods of procedures so as to secure better coordination between our two countries."[20] Styer made specific mention of the balloons' capacity as biological weapons: "It is a threat that merits our utmost consideration."

Colonel Roamer outlined the organizational structure that had evolved, sometimes by design and sometimes by chance, in the United States to that date. The Western Defense Command in San Francisco oversaw all operational activities with the exception of those related to BW, which were in the purview of the Chemical Warfare Service (research and analysis) and the Army Service Forces (defensive measures). The WDC G-2 office handled all intelligence and information activities. The Western Sea Frontier maintained a joint command with the WDC, although in practice the latter department had assumed nearly all operational control of the campaign. Balloons and related material were sent to the Air Intelligence Center in Anacostia, while all explosive material, everything from the incendiary devices to the blowout plugs, went to the Aberdeen Proving Ground in Maryland.

"I am not exactly sure . . . what our Canadian friends would like to know," said Roamer, "but I can assure you we will give you such information as we have available to us at the present time."[21] The Canadians had not studied the Japanese balloons to the degree as had the Americans—with the exception of the BW study of the Minton and Fort Simpson devices—and they expressed thanks at being given copies of all reports. One Canadian body, the Chemical Warfare Inter-Service Board, had prepared a comprehensive review of the balloon threat and found the devices "well suited" for transporting and dispersing organic agents that might cause damage to people, crops, or livestock.[22]

Canada faced many of the same challenges in its western provinces as did the War Department in the western states. The Royal Canadian Mounted Police had instructions to guard any landing sites and inform the nearest military authority, but any balloons landing in the mountainous, forested, sparsely populated region would likely be found by unknowing citizens if discovered at all. Colonel J. H. Jenkins, Canada's director of military operations, reported that bomb disposal officers at military installations in the West had been placed on alert and that it was the intent to have all evidence recovered in the most sterile manner possible and shipped to Ottawa immediately. As in the United States, however, the unpredictable nature of the balloon offensive proved vexing.

Otto Maass reported that in Canada each province had its own autonomous health department, all of which were coordinated (but not regulated) by the Dominion Department of Pensions and Health. "How far can we bring in our civilian agencies and still keep security," questioned Dr. Maass. "That is our problem."[23] Maass learned that in the United States the surgeon general's office had instructed the civilian agriculture, forestry, and public health agencies to immediately report any outbreaks of disease or suspicious incidents involving animals and plants—but had done so with a generic bulletin "without indicating anything about the balloon incidents."[24] Although the national and some regional directors of those agencies had been fully briefed on the Japanese balloons, the information release stopped there. The War Department justified this strict compartmentalization of information on the grounds that anything short of a breaking epidemic of disease did not require full knowledge on the part of every doctor and veterinarian in the western half of North America, and should such an epidemic occur, the subject would become widely known in short order anyway.

"Such a letter might be outlined in advance. It ought to be ready," offered Cole in reference to a bulletin that could be withheld until the proper moment and then disseminated widely. "We should be prepared with such a list."[25] A news release could go out in response to an isolated disease outbreak or in the event a large number of balloons suddenly appeared over the continent.

Colonel Jenkins then questioned whether the information restrictions might actually hinder the reporting of balloon incidents, not to mention result in civilian casualties. "We depend on the Royal Canadian Mounted Police . . . in isolated parts of Canada," he stated. "They feel there should be some form of publicity given so that trappers, rangers, et cetera, will report findings to the police and leave these strange objects alone."[26] Jenkins relayed the alarming story of a balloon that got tangled in telephone lines the week before. A group of boys who not surprisingly were first on the scene found and removed the demolition block from the carriage. They put a red hot poker to the device to melt the solder that held it together, then touched the poker to its inner contents (known to authorities to be picric acid) resulting in a bright, intense flame. "The police feel if those boys had blown themselves up there would have been hell to pay because they had not been warned," Jenkins reported.

"I can't say G-2 is going to change its policy, but I will bring to [its] attention the suggestion made by our Canadian friend that some type of directive go out," replied an American colonel. "I have a feeling, however, that because of our desire to keep from the Japanese any information on these balloons that it is unlikely the policy will be changed at this time."[27] Attendees agreed that should any information be made public in the future the issue of biological weapons was to be omitted altogether. "You will create a panic by the mere inference," stated General Styer. One participant suggested leaving the Japanese angle out altogether by simply calling them domestic weather balloons. (In the end, no public information release would be made in either the United States or Canada for another three months.)

The two-hour meeting closed with no recommendations for further action, only an agreement that the respective American and

FIG. 20. Balloon recovered in Newcastle, Wyoming on 9 February 1945. Untitled photograph, Box 42, Japanese Balloon Sightings, Record Group 499, Western Defense Command, NARA

Canadian liaisons continue to share information in the manner both commands assessed thus far as excellent.

What the men could not have known was that the balloon campaign was at that very moment entering its most active phase. From mid-February to early April, over 150 balloons would be sighted or recovered. Only eight days in that seven-week span would pass without news of a new incident. Twelve balloons landed on February 22 alone, including North Dakota's first at a small town named Ashley.[28] Ten balloons landed on March 10, including four within fifty miles of one another in central Washington. Three days later sixteen balloons fell—the highest single-day total during the war—in eight western states and provinces.

In Japan, launch personnel sent balloons aloft as quickly as possible. Production had reached its zenith that winter, leading to stockpiles of completed devices, and the launch commanders knew the window of strong winter winds was quickly closing. April would bring a marked reduction in wind velocities and with it the likely end of successful transoceanic flights. (Acting on meteorological data that suggested strong summer winds might exist at higher altitudes, engineers at Noborito had begun designing an even larger balloon envelope fifteen meters in diameter. Only two prototypes were produced and tested, however.[29])

The furious pace of paper production that winter had brought the factory schoolgirls well past the brink of exhaustion. The factory supervisors admonished the girls daily to work harder to meet the ever-increasing production quota. Girls who failed to keep up had to remain at the paper-drying boards until they finished; then they were punished by being forced to stand outside barefoot in the snow. Those on the night shift received two white pills with their dinner—ostensibly vitamins, but actually pep pills identical to those taken by pilots who needed to stay awake for long periods. Producing paper was all that mattered.

Sunday was the only day families were allowed to visit. Mothers brought dried fish, boiled eggs, sweet bean cakes, and other comfort foods. Some girls got sick from eating too much following a whole week of undernourishment. Travel proved very difficult for the families as the trains were often full of soldiers whose transport had priority. One mother traveled during the day, but her daughter worked the night shift, so she watched her daughter sleep, lightly touched her face, then left. The hard labor and isolation of the factory exacted a toll, according to Tetsuko Tanaka:

> We did our best. Our spirit was in it, but whenever we got messages or packages from home, we always broke down. In the beginning, we shared things which came from the families, but gradually, even when you thought you ought to share, you just couldn't.

There were closets on both sides of the room. Girls would put their heads into the closet and start eating. You just stopped caring about other people.[30]

All across Japan, field laborers continued to harvest *kozo* trees and *konnyaku* bulbs. Shipments arrived at the paper factories around the clock.

# 5

..............

## *Alaska*

It was late in the afternoon, almost dusk, on December 23, 1944, when Charlie Fitka looked up and saw what appeared to be a large balloon a half mile in the sky and a half mile away from where he stood. It was warm for December, about 34 degrees, but a steady rain and breeze from the east made it seem much colder. Fitka, a trapper from the small village of Marshall in western Alaska, was fourteen miles down the Yukon River near a fish camp the locals called Tukchuk. Once a village in its own right, Tukchuk was on its way to being abandoned. A sequence of epidemics over the years had taken the lives of nearly all the inhabitants. The rest were moving away. Most in the area avoided it. The place was said to have a "bad feeling."[1]

Fitka stared at the balloon and guessed it to be very large and white in color. No object appeared to be hanging underneath, but in the fading twilight he couldn't be sure. He watched the balloon descend for a few minutes until it drifted out of sight in a faraway grove of cottonwood trees. Fitka hunted in that area often, and over the next two weeks he kept an eye out for the downed balloon. Finally on January 5, 1945, while returning home on a trail that ran along the north bank of the river, he discovered large swaths of white fabric hanging from the upper branches of a tall tree. Quarter-inch manila ropes led down to some kind of apparatus—the balloon had a carriage after all—that lay suspended just off the ground in a tangle of willows. A clear plastic box set inside an iron-post frame was bolted to a metal ring about a foot across, which in turn was set atop another four-spoke metal ring twice as large. Two paper bags filled with sand (one had torn open and spilled some of its contents) hung from the rim of this bottommost ring. Wires and cables stuck out everywhere. Fitka had the presence of mind to note the smooth cover of snow showed no footprints or tracks leading either to or away from the area.

The next day he reported the find to Deputy U.S. Marshal Al Bahls, who, it turns out, was already aware of the incident. Two men had earlier reported seeing a large balloon flying low over Ohogamiut, a small camp upriver from Marshall. Bahls guessed the men had been celebrating the Christmas season with a bottle of whiskey, and he dismissed the sighting as a probable hallucination. Now Fitka stood in his office with hard evidence—two swatches of fabric he had cut from the balloon's envelope. Both looked to be factory tags of some kind. Although the writing was smeared and illegible, it looked Japanese.

Both Fitka and Bahls were members of the Alaska Territorial Guard, a reconnaissance and defense force organized in 1942 against a possible Japanese invasion of mainland Alaska. Most of its six thousand members were Alaska Natives in rural villages throughout the territory.[2] Bahls, who held the rank of captain and commanded the Marshall detachment, dutifully reported the incident to the Alaskan Department of the U.S. Army at Fort Richardson. He was told to sit tight and await further instructions.

Within days an FBI agent and a captain in Army Intelligence landed

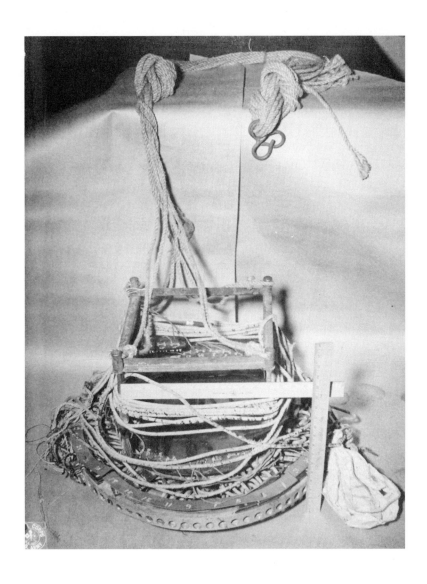

FIG. 21. The altitude-control mechanism of the Japanese balloon that landed in Marshall, Alaska, on 23 December 1944. Note the empty sandbags attached to the bottom of the device. "Attachment to balloon landed in vicinity of Marshall, Alaska, 23 December 1944, General view of time-fuse device," No. 7-4, Box 42, Japanese Balloons, Record Group 499, Western Defense Command, NARA

a small plane on a frozen lake a mile from the balloon's landing site. They went the rest of the way by dogsled. They were there to conduct an investigation and take possession of the device. Everything, the men told the villagers, was to remain confidential.[3]

What the army and the FBI knew, but the people of Marshall did not yet know, was that Charlie Fitka's discovery was the eighth in a series of unusual balloon incidents in the western states. Or the tenth. Perhaps the twelfth. It was getting harder for G-2 to keep track of the exact sequence now that balloon reports were coming in almost daily. This would prove especially true in Alaska, where a single balloon drifting over the wide-open tundra might result in numerous eyewitness reports over the course of a day or two. Was this a single balloon? Or multiple balloons that rode the same wind currents and arrived in Alaska together but in scattered formation? Much later investigators learned the Marshall balloon had been observed by no fewer than sixteen people in six different locations over a range of hundreds of miles. The mystery in identifying balloons only deepened when the devices disappeared in the backcountry, never to be recovered. In fact, based on the December 23 eyewitness account in Marshall, investigators would later designate that balloon number six, ahead of Sebastopol, Alturas, and a handful of others.[4]

Shortly after the agents retrieved the Marshall balloon word of another incident arrived from Paimiut, a small fish camp on the Bering coast whose name in Yup'ik means "people of the stream's mouth." Nicoli Savage, an Alaska Native hunter and trapper, had earlier reported seeing a balloon drifting to the east at a low but steady altitude. Although Savage was now out checking his traplines and could not be reached by radio, G-2 officials interviewed his daughter and learned the incident occurred on Christmas Eve, one day after Charlie Fitka first observed the Marshall balloon in flight.[5]

Bad weather on the coast prevented the chartered G-2 plane from reaching Paimiut, so the pilot turned to the east and flew low in the

FIG. 22. Tattered remnants of Japanese balloon in trees near Holy Cross, Alaska, 24 December 1944. "General view of balloon landing area 8 miles west of Holy Cross, Alaska, 21 January 1945," No. 18-6, Box 42, Japanese Balloons, Record Group 499, Western Defense Command, NARA

direction the balloon was thought to have traveled. By remarkable luck he spotted the tattered envelope atop some cottonwood trees eight miles southwest of Holy Cross, a village on the Yukon River one hundred fifty miles from the coast. Investigators retrieved the balloon, again with assistance from villagers who took them to the site by dogsled. The largely intact device contained a single sandbag (but no ordnance) and a large mass of blue-green ice on the ground below the suspended carriage.

Both the Marshall and Holy Cross devices were placed in crates and shipped under guard to the Technical Air Intelligence Center in Anacostia. Agents took care to place the blue-green ice, now partially thawed, into a watertight container for later laboratory analysis that revealed it was an inert water mixture with trace organic material and likely did not come from the balloon. Technicians at Anacostia eagerly awaited both packages. Of the half-dozen ballast devices already in their possession, the Alaska balloons were the first with sandbags still attached to the bottom ring.

Colonel Sidman Poole, a topographic mapmaker with administrative skills liaising the brass of the War Department with the scientists of Military Intelligence, arranged to have the U.S. Geological Survey (USGS) take the lead in the study. "Poole came in with a couple little bags of sand," a USGS micropaleontologist recalled years later. "Very much hush-hush. People who weren't classified couldn't even get into the place. Poole wanted to know where the damned sand came from."[6] Both sets of bags were made of the same paper as the balloon envelope and were secured with low-grade twine. The two bags from Marshall contained coarse, salt-and-pepper sand and weighed seven pounds apiece. The Holy Cross bag weighed only two pounds and was partially filled with fine yellow sand.

The USGS team placed the samples under a microscope and found hundreds of species of diatoms (microscopic algae), including fossils from the Pliocene era, and foraminiferal fauna, an order of marine protozoa (single-celled organisms) with perforated shells. It was clearly beach sand, but the absence of coral indicated it came from an area of cold water incapable of supporting coral growth. By comparing the mineral and organic composition of the sand to known characteristics of Japanese beaches, volcanoes, and seabeds, the analysts narrowed down the search:

> Extrusive igneous rocks exposed in the area immediately north and west of Sendai [a city on the Pacific coast northeast of Tokyo] provide an adequate source for the uncommon assemblage of heavy minerals occurring in the sand. The foraminiferal fauna . . . has been reported in the beach sands of this area. One species has

never been reported outside this immediate region. The diatom flora found in the sand has been reported . . . around Sendai and many of the species found are known from no other locality.[7]

Confident in its conclusions, the USGS named two beaches as the probable sources of the sand—the first at Shiogama near Sendai, and the second at Ichinomiya, a small town east of Tokyo. Dozens of sandbags from an equal number of balloons would continue to arrive at the USGS office over the succeeding months, all of which confirmed their earlier conclusions.

The preliminary inspection of the Holy Cross balloon conducted at Fort Richardson in Anchorage revealed several slips of paper wedged between the fuses of the altitude-control mechanism. The paper likely acted as shims to reduce vibration and prevent contact and electrical shorting of the system. Hiromu Wada, a Nisei (second generation Japanese American) translator at Fort Richardson, examined the papers and found they were sales receipts belonging to a "Mr. Kagemasu," dated in June, year unknown. Another appeared to be a page torn from a construction materials catalog. The papers proved useless from an intelligence perspective. That April a sandbag recovered in Bethel, Alaska, was found to contain a postcard, its address and postmark intact and legible. A schoolboy named Yoshiharu Shinada had mailed the card to his father, Kazuo Shinada, in Ichinomiya, Chiba Prefecture—the very coastal town the USGS believed was a likely source of the sand. Army Intelligence officials were at a loss to explain how and why the postcard ended up inside the bag. The best explanation was that Shinada, probably a soldier working at one of the launch sites, received the card from his son and placed it there as a talisman of sorts. The practice was not uncommon, investigators would discover in time, despite Noborito's rule prohibiting the use of any factory stamps or markings that might identify the balloons' place of origin.[8]

Further study of the Marshall balloon revealed a mistake in the arrangement of fuses. The fuse from the number 24 set of blowout plugs should have led to the number 25 set, but instead it skipped ahead to number 27. This explained why two sandbags, those held by the unfired number 25 and number 26 blowout plugs, remained attached to the device.[9] Investigators also discovered the Marshall balloon had the most sophisticated battery assembly of any device recovered to date. The one-cell battery sat inside a small plastic box, which in turn was nested inside a slightly larger plastic box. The narrow space between them contained a 10 percent solution of calcium chloride believed to function as a heat reservoir intended to keep the battery at operating temperature even in the subzero nighttime temperatures of the upper atmosphere. A third plastic box and large wooden box provided additional insulation in the form of a double air space around the inner boxes. The find was significant for a couple of reasons. First, it represented one more piece of evidence in the already solid case that the balloons were making a multiday, transoceanic voyage all the way from Japan. Second, the calcium chloride antifreeze solution now helped explain why some responders noticed a chemical smell on the balloons. The sheriff in Kalispell, Montana, for example, had reported the slushy liquid inside the envelope caused a sting to the eyes. From the beginning the War Department feared the presence of biological agents; now it seemed only the battery's antifreeze was to blame.[10]

THE TUNDRA ARMY

Following the Marshall and Holy Cross incidents, only a handful of balloon sightings occurred in Alaska in January and February 1945. Shifting wind currents over the Pacific those months sent most of the balloons to Washington, Oregon, Idaho, Montana, and Wyoming. But on March 13, Otto Geist, a major in the Alaska Territorial Guard (ATG), was at the detachment headquarters in Bethel when a guardsman from Nunapitchuk walked in. "Allen Stone came to Bethel," Geist wrote in his log book that night, "to report about a large balloon, black (as big as a house!), flying low between Nunachuk and Kasigluk."[11] In his role as quartermaster for the ATG, Geist traveled from village to village across the western half of the territory. Few knew the area better, and no one was more in tune with the scuttlebutt on the ground. Geist chartered a plane and flew over the area with Stone and the local marshal. They saw nothing. Six days later two ATG men from Nunachuk recovered the circular pressure-relief valve that had separated from the bottom of the envelope. Geist sent the part to Fort Richardson and recommended the men be paid fifteen dollars each for their two days of work.

Thus began a month-long odyssey where Geist and dozens of ATG servicemen criss-crossed the territory investigating one sighting after another. The winds had clearly turned north once again, as no fewer than thirty balloons arrived in Alaska over a six-week period in March and April 1945. The number may have exceeded fifty; no one knew for sure. Although the Alaska balloons were no different from those that landed across the western states, the response to their landings most certainly was. If the information blackout imposed by the War Department meant that few Americans knew of the balloons and the danger they posed, in Alaska the situation was quite different. Early on nearly every able-bodied man (and more than a few women) in the western villages had enlisted in the ATG. Information, even on a confidential basis, could be disseminated quickly along the unified chain of command. Downed balloons were guarded and reported quickly. ATG members tracked the balloons by airplane, dogsled, and on foot, a service for which they would later receive commendations.

The Alaskan Department at Fort Richardson, the headquarters of which was actually based in Seattle, identified early on the challenges of balloon recovery in Alaska and acknowledged the inestimable role the ATG would have to play:

Landings have been in isolated areas and transportation is at best crude. Planes are used to get as near the balloon landing site as possible; in the winter time dogteams are used, and in the summer the distance from plane to balloon will have to be covered on foot. Since there have been no military installations near the landings, we must depend on natives to help us out.[12]

The ATG detachments in western Alaska had been organized by Major Marvin "Muktuk" Marston, a veteran of the First World War who eagerly reenlisted in order to serve his country once again. Marston had earned his distinctive nickname in a *muktuk* (whale blubber) eating contest with an Inuit elder. Although he didn't win, the major ate enough of the chewy flesh to earn the admiration of the Inuit. Ever respectful of local culture and traditions, Marston had the trust of Alaska Natives in a way few government or military officials ever had before. In March 1941, the garrulous Marston was escorting entertainer Joe E. Brown on a tour of Alaska military bases when the duty took him to St. Lawrence Island, a treeless sliver of windswept rock off Alaska's western shore just forty miles from Siberia. He found the Eskimo population jittery and fearful. "All the white people, missionaries and teachers, had left or were leaving except one," Marston later wrote. "This one said he hesitated to run away and leave the Eskimos but that he had no guns to fight with and unless something were done, he also would have to leave." Marston learned that a Japanese naval vessel had been spotted the year before, and the Natives feared an invasion. He told the schoolteacher he would be back with guns and ammunition. "We would organize and fight the Japs on the shores of St. Lawrence Island."[13]

With the help of Ernest Gruening, the territory's governor, Marston organized the ATG in spring 1942. The Japanese occupation of Attu and Kiska, two small islands at the far western end of the Aleutians, and the bombing of Dutch Harbor that June helped to

FIG. 23. Major Marvin "Muktuk" Marston and his dog Panda on St. Lawrence Island during World War II. Marston Foundation

convince the Alaskan Department of the need for a rural reconnaissance force. Marston traveled by airplane and dogsled from village to village, signing up recruits at each stop. Gruening joined Marston in Barrow, the first time a governor had ever left Juneau to visit the rural villages. Gruening knew only one word in the Inupiaq language, *Quyanaq* (thank you), which he repeated to every enlistee as he shook his hand. Within three years Marston had enlisted 2,700 troops in over sixty rural villages, men and women ages sixteen to seventy, in what he called the "Tundra Army." He was quick to boast that every able-bodied person eagerly signed up, proud to carry the WWI-era Springfield rifles and wear the blue ATG patch that were given to all recruits.

"We were a strange looking outfit as first," admitted one ATG member. "Tall men, short men, snowshirts of all colors and descriptions. The only distinguishing mark was the cobalt blue and gold starts insignia patch of the ATG worn on the left shoulder."[14] Marston proved a popular and respected leader. He fought the racist attitudes of many Alaskan Department officers who believed the Native savages were incapable of military discipline. During the war and even afterward, the major submitted numerous memos that went well beyond his military purview. Marston recommended the construction of village hospitals to stop the spread of tuberculosis, the reintroduction of commercial reindeer herds, the supplying of fuel to the villages for nonmilitary uses, and other actions he called "humanitarian undertakings."[15] The Alaskan Department ignored virtually all of Marston's missives, but he kept sending them in one after another. One admiring ATG member said of Marston: "He's an ornery cuss . . . worse than I am. I like him."[16]

On March 10, 1945, Marston issued a bulletin to all detachments. "I want every company to be on the alert, to observe and report any strangers who may be in your area"—it was still suspected the balloons might be transporting enemy agents to America—"or any strange object you may encounter." The War Department's strict information policy prevented Marston from being more specific. "When restrictions are off," he wrote, "I will give you the story."[17]

A sequence of telegrams between Marston, Geist, and Sergeant Frank Budaj is representative of the cryptic communication style forced upon the men. Budaj wrote to Geist, "I sent a message to you through the marshal [in Bethel] so keep checking with him. It may be very important."

Geist then wired Marston in Nome: "Seventy miles from Bethel found another specimen but practically destroyed by fire. If desirable I can go and bring same to Bethel before new snow fall. Please advise."

Marston's reply: "Go and get it." But moments later, after he had consulted with Fort Richardson, the ATG commander wrote back, "Hold up action until further instructions. We may want to see it in place. Do not disturb." Geist received two G-2 men in Bethel and directed them to the location of what in his daily log he called "Specimen B." Although the uncoded telegrams sent within Alaska contained this type of obscure language, Fort Richardson was able to communicate securely with the War Department and the Western Defense Command, keeping both commands apprised of the ongoing investigations.[18]

The Alaskan Department eventually developed a secret code for radio communications:

| REPORT PHRASE | CODE WORD |
| --- | --- |
| Balloon sighted | White |
| Balloon grounded | Yellow |
| Balloon drifting toward | Orange |
| Balloon parts located at | Gold |
| Investigate balloon incident at | Scarlet |
| Rumor of balloon grounded | Pink |
| Request technical experts | Red |

| | |
|---|---|
| Search the area | Green |
| Balloon shot down at | Brown |
| Explosions heard at | Black |
| Altitude of balloon about ___ feet | Purple |

Altitude was to be expressed on a scale of 1:1,000, thus "Balloon at 10,000 feet drifting toward Nome" would be encoded as "Purple 10, Orange Nome." The code, prominently stamped "CONFIDEN-TIAL," was distributed to ATG commanders, Bureau of Indian Affairs offices, Alaska Fire Control Service offices, Forest Service employees, marshals, and radio operators around the territory. A few churches even received the code, as they housed the village radio. The wide distribution list for such sensitive information was justified on the grounds that nearly everyone in western Alaska already knew about the balloons anyway, and without the code they might transmit radio reports in clear voice. The Alaskan Department elected not to supply the code to fishing vessels in the Gulf of Alaska, however.[19]

Alaskans were long acquainted with the War Department's views on secrecy. As an officially declared military combat area, the territory was subject to what one resident called a "curtain of silence."[20] Both military and civilian communications passed through a censorship office in Seattle, where clerks monitored mail, telegrams, radio broadcasts, and even telephone conversations for prohibited material. Issues of *Time, Newsweek,* and the *Washington Post* routinely arrived in Alaskans' mailboxes with whole pages cut out. Personal letters with innocent remarks about the weather were opened by recipients who found whole passages blacked out. An example of the censors' fervor widely mocked by Alaskans was that of a schoolteacher whose volume of poetry was confiscated because it contained information about geographic locations in the North. The offending article? "The Spell of the Yukon," a gold rush–era poem by Robert Service.[21] Despite chafing against the absurd and seemingly arbitrary restrictions, ATG members and the Alaska press accepted the balloon bomb information blackout in stride.

Some two dozen officers from every military branch and detachments across Alaska gathered at Fort Richardson on April 16–17 for an intelligence briefing and conference on balloon defense procedures. Lieutenant Colonel Robert A. Matter opened the meeting with a brief history of incidents to date, then identified "biological or chemical warfare" as the most serious threat posed by the balloon offensive. "We are charged with making a plan which can be put into effect immediately, in the event the Japanese use the balloons for biological warfare," he stated.[22] Matter had attended the January conference at the Western Defense Command where officials developed preliminary procedures for specimen collection, analysis, and containment/decontamination. He now brought the same mission to Alaska.

Health officials with Army Intelligence believed any bacteriological agents would be contained in the sandbags or the clear plastic box that sat atop the carriage and contained the wet-cell battery and antifreeze solution. The list of possible agents, infections, and diseases was long: melioidosis, Japanese B encephalitis, Rift Valley fever, Aoki's disease (acute tularemia), anthrax, typhus, dysentery, psittacosis, variolla, and many others. Livestock diseases (e.g., foot-and-mouth disease, virus pleural pneumonia) also received mention. "All the material which has been received in Washington to date has been negative," Lieutenant Colonel Harold T. Little, a surgeon with the Alaskan Department, told the Fort Richardson attendees. "But this may be part of the plan, and about the time we are convinced that biological warfare is not being practiced, the Japanese will put a little payload in the sand."[23]

The draft plan recommended by Little (later adopted by the conference participants) covered three phases of balloon recovery: custody, handling, and transport of specimens; laboratory testing and analysis; and information control. Personnel, especially ATG members who were most likely to be the first responders to balloon landings, were to guard the site until a two-man team (bomb disposal officer and bacteriologist) arrived to take possession of the device. Long underwear made of wool was to be worn by all responders, as the material provided the best filtration capacity of any fabric (silk and herringbone twill, fortunately not common in rural Alaska, were named as the least effective). The bacteriologist was to place all potentially contaminated specimens into containers, which would then be sealed with paraffin, packed with dry ice, and shipped by air to Fort Richardson for forwarding on to Washington, DC. The landing site was then to be decontaminated with a solution of either 20 percent bleach or 10 percent sodium hydroxide. All laboratory testing, according to the plan, was to be performed by expert technicians in Washington. With an emphasis on speedy diagnosis, however, the War Department authorized Fort Richardson to conduct preliminary analyses. Approved techniques included microscopic examination and inoculation of guinea pigs, white mice, and chickens with samples recovered from the balloons.

Lieutenant Colonel Little stamped the plan "SECRET" (one step up from "CONFIDENTIAL") and warned against unauthorized release, which he noted might lead to "unrest or panic among the civilian populace."[24] The conference closed with a short report by Major Marston on the seventy ATG divisions under his command. He issued a positive assessment of their ability to implement the plan's first response directive.

At the conclusion of the conference, Marston finally obtained approval to give his men detailed information of the ongoing attack. "Several enemy balloons have been sighted and a couple recovered in the Yukon and Kuskokwim River area," he wrote in an April 17 memorandum to every commanding officer of the ATG. Reports of explosions had been coming in from different parts of western Alaska, though no bomb fragments or other physical evidence had been found to date. (The territory's first recovered bomb, an unexploded incendiary device of standard design, would be found eleven miles southwest of Bethel just days after Marston's memorandum.) The major issued specific instructions:

> If one should come your way, shoot it down; or, if it is found on the ground, post a guard and let no one go near it. Remember, it is contact with the enemy and anything might happen. All personnel in your organizations should be instructed to report dates and locations of balloon sightings and landings to you at the earliest possible time. . . . In case of fire in your area, put the fire out; also notify the nearest army post of its location and extent. This is a confidential matter and if it is published it will aid the enemy.[25]

The Tundra Army had been doing these things all along anyway. The memo established two zones within the ATG for the purposes of information dissemination and incident reporting. Unalakleet, a coastal village on Norton Sound, acted as the divide point. Units located north of the village would report to Nome, while Unalakleet itself and all villages to the south were to report to Fort Richardson.

One of the more incredible balloon reports reached Marston via Archie Ferguson of Kotzebue. "You had better get up there," Marston recalled him saying. "Your men have all gone crazy." According to an account Marston kept confidential during the war but published in his memoir years later, Ferguson told him about a woman in Selawik who claimed to have seen a balloon in the middle of the night from which "Little Men came down a ladder to the earth." The local ATG detachment searched the area but found nothing. "It can easily be imagined," Marston wrote, "that she saw those long ropes and the gondola, and Little Men coming down from that balloon—after all, the Japanese are little men, and we were constantly expecting an attack." Although he vouched for the credibility of the witness, Marston also surmised the report may have reflected local folklore that held the woods were populated with small human-like creatures with claws who hung from the branches of willow trees and menaced wayward travelers.[26] Although Army Intelligence had thoroughly debunked the idea the balloons carried enemy soldiers, Marston ordered the area searched and instructed ATG units in the Selawik area to remain on high alert.

# 6

............

*Defense*

By spring 1945 U.S. authorities had a solid understanding of the balloons themselves, even if the strategic objectives of the larger campaign remained unknown or at least open enough to preclude definite conclusions. Under the directorship of Vannevar Bush, the Office of Scientific Research and Development (OSRD) accordingly formed a special committee to compile a strategic overview of the offensive and its practical capabilities.[1] While the defense agencies rightly concerned themselves with each and every balloon sighting on a day-to-day basis, the OSRD took a broader view. What level of damage might actually result from ten thousand balloons? Twenty thousand, or even thirty thousand? What would be the value in dollars of the possible destruction to buildings, livestock, and forests? How much would it cost to defend against the balloons — a course the Western Defense Command was naturally pursuing — and what impact, positive or negative, might deploying those resources have on the larger war effort? It was exactly this type of long-range view for which Bush, an engineer and policymaker with high-level influence in U.S. government on scientific matters including the Manhattan Project, was well known within both military and public circles.

The OSRD balloon committee used statistical analysis to estimate the number of balloons that would likely survive the transoceanic crossing. Drawing on G-2 research into production rates of the envelopes, valves, and other components, OSRD put the number of North American balloon landings by late spring 1945 at between seven hundred and two thousand. (The number of *confirmed* landings at this time was under three hundred, but it seemed probable that many grounded balloons remained undiscovered in the sparsely populated West.) The team assumed a transoceanic success rate of roughly 7 percent—one balloon landing for every fifteen launched, a figure that took into account the landings to date, numerical distribution of serial numbers and other markings, and the likely production capacity of hydrogen by Japanese chemical plants. The committee then mapped known landing sites, detected a general northward shift in distribution from the start of the offensive (for unknown reasons), and projected the total landings on different land cover types, including forest, cropland, and livestock pasture.

The OSRD loaded its report with caveats. "Anything in the nature of a precise estimate of the extent of damage . . . seems hopeless," its authors wrote.[2] Too many assumptions concerning the scale and timing of balloon launches and distribution of landings rendered the report's findings "so largely arbitrary as to warrant very little confidence." The authors could nevertheless theorize a worst-case scenario from which more realistic outcomes could be deduced. If the worst case proved to be relatively benign, or at least to encompass acceptable risks from a strategic perspective, it would have a profound impact on Bush's policy recommendations.

This worst-case analysis assumed a total of ten thousand balloon landings in the United States and that each landing in a forested area caused one fire, resulting in the destruction of 247,100 total acres in twelve western states (Alaska was excluded from the study). Under this scenario, Oregon would bear the greatest fire burden with 1,333 separate conflagrations. Washington, Idaho, California, Utah, and Montana all stood to experience hundreds of fires each. Despite the seemingly dire forecast, the OSRD calculated the total cost of the damage at just $788,400. By comparison, naturally occurring wildfires in those twelve states in 1943 caused over $4.4 million in damage. "The fact that our estimate of damage is well below the actual damage from fire is further encouraging, in that it indicates that a balloon attack is not likely to swamp the fire protection services," the report noted.[3]

In the section of the report on transoceanic wind currents, the authors concluded the use of incendiary bombs would remain "particularly ineffective" because the westerly winds that brought them to North America also carried clouds, water vapor, and precipitation from over the Pacific Ocean. "Winter conditions are markedly unfavorable to incendiary attack, yet it is only during that season that the balloons have much chance of carrying so far eastward," the report stated.[4] The WDC had similarly recognized the shortcomings of incendiary bombs in the winter months and therefore insisted close attention be paid to any modifications in the payload of the balloons. It was particularly feared that Japan might unleash biological weapons as a last resort when defeat seemed imminent.

Turning its attention to bacteriological attack against livestock, the OSRD first assumed a uniform distribution of both animals and balloon landings in pasture acreage in the given states; then, once more assuming the worst-case perspective, it supposed that each and every balloon resulted in "contact" with livestock. Despite the huge populations of cattle, sheep, horses, and pigs, the wide-open acreage of the western states and comparatively small number of scattered balloon landings translated to miniscule contact rates. Washington and Oregon, the states with the highest number of projected landings, would experience contact rates of just 45 and 113 animals, respectively. California could expect 23 head of cattle to encounter a balloon, and Idaho 14. The numbers fell sharply farther east. Just 3 cows and 2 sheep were apparently at risk in North Dakota. Although contact between just one animal and one balloon might be sufficient to instigate an outbreak of disease in densely packed herds, the OSRD discounted the possibility of mass infection or epidemics. Furthermore, the conclusion was based on the worst-case criteria that every balloon would be weaponized with bacteriological agents, a statistical assumption backed up by no real-world evidence.

"Unless the payloads should be changed to something far more sinister than the incendiaries and explosives presently carried, the damage to be expected is far less than the cost of defensive measures," the OSRD concluded. "Only if extensive resources are diverted to defensive measures will the balloon incendiary campaign be of profit to the enemy."[5] Bush's report basically stated that the U.S. defense agencies could theoretically do nothing—perhaps even *should* do nothing considering the cost of defense procedures—and the resultant impact of the balloon campaign would be well within acceptable limits.

The U.S. Navy's Western Sea Frontier, though still officially in a joint command on the balloon investigation, had by the spring taken a back seat to the army. Once it had been established the balloons were not being released from Japanese submarines, the navy had little input while the army's Western Defense Command oversaw the U.S. response and spearheaded nearly every proactive defensive measure. One key exception was a training film produced by the navy in early 1945 with the straightforward title, "Japanese Paper Balloons." Classified "SECRET" like every other document in the balloon investigation, the film was shown to select military audiences at installations where recoveries were likely to occur.

"The film you are about to see is a Navy film on the Japanese paper balloons that have been arriving in this country," began the supplemental lecture that was to precede each screening of the twenty-two minute film.[6] "The purpose of showing you this film is to acquaint you with the appearance and functioning of the balloon, the balloon carriage, the munitions it carries, and other objects associated with the balloon." For the film's opening shot, the navy inflated and sent aloft a recovered balloon on a free, low-altitude flight. (No documentation exists on which recovered device was used for the film, but the Alturas balloon seems the likeliest candidate, given the date of the film's production.) An unidentified technician then points to every part of the carriage while the film's narrator describes each component and its function. Previously unexploded blowout plugs are fired to demonstrate the workings of the ballast release mechanism.

"Keep in mind as you see this film," the script concludes, "that your primary concern is one of recognition." The instructions made explicitly clear the film was not intended to teach anyone how to recover a balloon or disable its explosive devices, but to enable a positive identification so that the proper first responders could be contacted.

SUNSET

The Army Air Force Weather Division in San Francisco had long been compiling meteorological data over the Pacific in an attempt to trace possible balloon flight trajectories from the confirmed landing locations in the western states back to Japan. The meteorologists also hoped to be able to predict where any balloons currently airborne might come down. The north by northeast meridional shift in the high altitude winds continued as March turned to April, and the weather office warned Fort Richardson in Alaska that many balloons, perhaps hundreds, could be on the way.[7] On April 12 a fighter plane intercepted and shot down a balloon west of Attu Island, a 345-square mile rock at the far western end of the Aleutians that a large Japanese

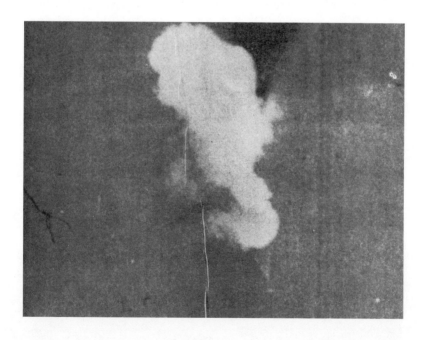

invasion force had actually held for nearly a year in 1942–43. The next day, the Eleventh Air Force detected approximately two dozen balloons grouped together in random formation over Attu's Massacre Bay.[8] Twenty-seven P-38 aircraft and four P-40N aircraft broke through heavy clouds and intercepted ten balloons between 30,000 and 37,000 feet. After taking numerous photographs, pilots of the P-38s shot nine of them down. For the next couple of days, fighter, patrol, and utility aircraft engaged numerous balloons over a wide area. The crew of a C-45 intercepted one south of Tanaga Island, roughly four hundred miles east of Attu, and attempted (unsuccessfully) to bring it down with a .45-caliber pistol. The shooting gallery was the only real action the fighter squadrons had seen in nearly a year and a half since U.S. forces had retaken Attu. One squadron, the 54th, had established a pool of money to be given to the first pilot to shoot down a Japanese balloon. The pot was subsequently divided among all those who had brought one down.[9]

The P-38s had fired 3,892 rounds of ammunition in the balloon engagement. At the request of the War Department, the pilots provided detailed information on the type, number, and effectiveness of ammunition expended in destroying each balloon. The experience led to the conclusion that a single .50-caliber round was clearly sufficient to rupture the paper envelope, but that producing such a hit required short bursts of up to two hundred rounds within the tracer limit of six hundred yards. With the balloon defense in mind, the War

FIG. 24. (*opposite*) Gun camera photographs of a Japanese balloon shot down by an Eleventh Air Force fighter plane near Attu Island on 13 April 1945. "Gun camera photograph of one of the balloons later shot down near Attu, Aleutian Is., on 13 April 1945," Nos. 4-5, Box 783, File 141, Record Group 330, Records of the Secretary of Defense, Office of the Administrative Secretary, Correspondence Control Section, Naval Combat Narratives, Dec 1941-1945, NARA

Department called for the development of a tracer with an effective range of a thousand yards.[10]

The Eleventh Air Force also reported it intercepted numerous radio transmissions thought to have come from the balloons. The unique and easily identifiable sound signature of the transmissions suggested some balloons carried meteorological instruments and radiosondes in order to send data back to Japan. Air force radar operators in the Aleutians also made contact with the April 13 balloons at a range of eighty-five miles. The return echoes on the radar screen had the appearance of aircraft, they reported, but with a markedly different signal-to-noise ratio. The report shocked the Naval Research Laboratory as its extensive testing program two months earlier found the balloons were too small and contained too little reflective metal to be reliably detected by radar at any distance. The Attu incident supplied valuable real-world data for the War Department, which was then formulating defense plans that featured fighter squadrons to be dispatched quickly to shoot down airborne balloons.[11]

The presence of radio devices on some Japanese balloons had been known since the very start of the campaign. The first recovered device, the rubber balloon pulled from the ocean off San Pedro, California, in early November 1944, featured a two-watt transmitter with a six-megacycle pulse-type signal. Technicians at the Arlington Hall Station, the army's cryptography and signal intelligence agency, examined the device and on December 30 recommended round-the-clock radio monitoring by the 115th Signal Radio Intelligence Company at Fort Lewis, Washington, and by the wdc in San Francisco.[12]

The listening operation paid off on January 19, 1945, when a wdc radio operator picked up a signal over the Pacific approximately 2,700 miles west of San Francisco. He was able to track the signal continuously for the next nine hours and nine minutes. From the moment the operator locked onto the transmission he continuously recorded its bearing as the balloon drifted slightly to the north and steadily to the east. Both the frequency and pulse rate varied slightly over time, leading the WDC to hypothesize the former was designed to reflect changes in altitude and the latter changes in temperature. It seemed reasonable to assume the Japanese were continually striving to obtain more and better meteorological data. By the time the signal was lost (for unknown reasons), the balloon was just 800 miles from the Oregon coast. It had traveled an average of 174 miles per hour in the nine hours the WDC had tracked it.[13]

The experience demonstrated that a series of radio stations along the Pacific Coast might indeed be able to provide advance warning of incoming balloons (albeit only that small percentage that carried radio transmitters) while a network of radar installations might detect at least a few of the rest. The Fourth Air Force initiated the Sunset Project in April 1945, establishing six stations along the Washington coast. Intercept aircraft, including P-38s and P-61 Black Widows, would be on alert (withheld from training exercises) at a number of airfields.[14] At the Presidio conference in January where defense authorities met and discussed the balloon attack for the first time, the Army Air Corps named the major weakness of West Coast air defense as "the almost complete lack of any means of identifying and tracking enemy aircraft which may approach vital targets within the Western Defense Command."[15] Radar systems were being utilized primarily for training purposes and emergency rescue missions, while the ground observer corps had been inactivated. Sunset might now prove a worthy effort at reactivating the mission.

Sunset became fully operational by the first week of June, yet radio operators detected only a few signals they could identify as airborne balloons. The pilots spent more time waiting on the tarmac than they did in the air. Air force meteorologists had informed the WDC the winds of the upper atmosphere would slow dramatically in the summer months; Hammond wondered if the Japanese had perhaps suspended the campaign until the winds picked up again in the fall. If so, was the attack to date only a reconnaissance phase, a series of performance tests for something bigger to come?

Meteorologists with the U.S. Forest Service knew a direct relationship existed between the amount of winter precipitation in the western states and the severity of the fire season the following summer. A forester in Butte, Montana, reported precipitation in the winter of 1944–45 was just 64 percent of normal in his region, suggesting a likely fire designation of "critical" that summer. Dry conditions throughout the other western states were certain to leave forests and grasslands in an extremely flammable condition. The importance of the information was not lost on William Hammond. A continuation of the Japanese balloon assault into June, July, and August could have devastating effects, not merely to forests but also roads, railroads, and telephone and power lines.[16]

In late April the WDC requested a legal opinion from the judge advocate general (JAG) as to whether assigning German prisoners of war to firefighting duty would violate the Geneva Convention of 1929. Presently confined in ten camps in the western states, the POWs would be placed with the Forest Service for front-line duty in the suppression of fires. The JAG replied that since not all wild-fires would originate from Japanese balloons—many would no doubt result from natural causes such as lightning strikes—the proposal did not violate the convention's prohibition on using prisoner labor for war operations. That the duty would require German prisoners to engage in "unhealthful or dangerous work," however, was problematic. According to the JAG opinion, "It is concluded that the employment of [POWs] to fight forest fires involves a high degree of hazard to life, that it is a dangerous occupation, and that the employment of prisoners [for firefighting] would be in contravention of

Article 32 of the Geneva Convention."[17] The JAG did suggest that a waiver to this article might be negotiated in the imminent terms of surrender with the recently defeated Germany.

Military officials believed the primary responsibility for the prevention and control of wildfires rested with federal, state, and civilian forest protection agencies.[18] Recognizing that civilian departments had been impaired by manpower shortages during the war, however, the Ninth Service Command agreed to supply troops when available. (Such an allocation of resources had been a primary goal of the Japanese, who hoped the balloons would start fires the Americans would be forced to fight by diverting troops and resources that might otherwise have been used in the Pacific theater.) The command's official plan acknowledged the right of civilian agencies to call directly on the nearest military installation for assistance and the authority of that commander to comply with the request when reasonable. The policy took into account the fact the territory was so large that requiring all requests be channeled through central headquarters would likely result in dangerous delays. The U.S. Forest Service, for its part, agreed to provide firefighting training to military personnel.

The Fourth Air Force staged a number of Stinson L-5 and Douglas C-47 aircraft at bases throughout the Pacific Northwest and assigned two hundred paratroopers to be on alert for firefighting missions.[19] Like the crews assembled for the Sunset Project, however, most spent a significant amount of time on the ground. Those wildfires to which they did respond invariably resulted from a cause other than a Japanese balloon.

LIGHTNING

Among all its defense strategies, the WDC placed the highest priority on the one code named "Lightning." It was the plan for defense against BW. "While no evidence has been discovered to date that the Japanese have employed [bacteriological warfare], the fact remains that such action is a possibility and plans for combating same must be formulated," the WDC wrote.[20] The development of such plans had been an ongoing concern from the arrival of the very first balloons. Still, the WDC did not formalize BW procedures until July 1945 with its "Plan for Defense against Bacteriological Warfare in Connection with Japanese Free Balloons," a report that despite being highly classified received wide distribution among commands throughout the country.

The plan contained little new information but was instead a compilation of policies and procedures that had been developed piecemeal over the previous six months. Responders holding appropriate qualifications were to detect bacteriological specimens, recover and transport such agents for identification and study, and decontaminate landing sites to prevent infection among humans, animals, and vegetation. The plan's new and most useful contribution was that it clarified the chain of command in all western sectors and granted authority to commanding officers to direct personnel in various areas of balloon response. In order to obtain prompt information on the appearance of any unusual diseases, area commanders were directed to maintain contact with local doctors, health officials, and representatives of federal agencies including Agriculture, Interior, and the Forest Service. In most cases requests were to be made quietly and through routine channels with no mention of Japanese balloons.

A subsection of the BW plan code named "Arrow" provided for the rapid air transportation of all balloon evidence to the Anacostia laboratory in Washington. Packages stamped with that label and in the custody of an intelligence officer would receive "Class A" priority on eastbound military flights.[21]

The development of Lightning, Arrow, Firefly, Sunset, and other unnamed defense strategies took place in a mostly ad hoc manner. Conferences were held, committees were formed, plans were devised—yet the overall response evolved in tandem with the growing understanding of the balloons. As late as July 1945, just a month before the end of the war, WDC officials were still speculating on the true purpose of the Japanese balloons. Were they only ranging shots, test flights to generate data for some future aerial campaign? Would enemy saboteurs begin infiltrating the United States? When would a chemical weapon be dropped from a balloon? Or was this it, just incendiary and high-explosive devices? Because the nature of the attack was never fully understood, the defense plans were predicated on hypothetical scenarios that would be difficult to identify if and when they occurred. Because no balloon contained bacteriological agents, for example, responders had to treat *every* balloon as though it might. Such sustained preparedness would be difficult to achieve even if authorities had months or even years to plan and could depend on a fully informed public able to report every incident. But the WDC had to develop its plan today in anticipation of tomorrow's balloon, and with a censorship policy that kept the populace in the dark, no less.

In fact, formulating the defense procedures did take months, and none were fully in place before summer 1945. Only after the war would the WDC discover how late they really were.

## TOPPENISH AND TOKYO

At 3:20 p.m. on March 10, 1945, a civilian pilot bringing his aircraft in for a landing at a private airfield near Toppenish, Washington, looked down and observed a large balloon skipping across the ground. At that same moment the farmer over whose land the balloon was traveling watched it slowly rise from a spot where it had been temporarily grounded. Both men had a clear view as the balloon next struck high-tension wires of the Bonneville Power Administration resulting in a shower of sparks and a fireball that completely incinerated the envelope.

The wires were part of a widespread network of power lines that delivered power from the Bonneville Dam on the Columbia River to thousands of customers in the Pacific Northwest. One customer directly affected by the explosion in Toppenish—in fact the single largest consumer of electricity on the entire grid—was the Hanford Engineer Works, an industrial facility operated by the federal government. The electrical disturbance tripped breakers in the plant's substation, which momentarily cut power to the entire facility until a back-up intertie activated automatically. An inspection by staff engineers revealed operations in three different buildings had to be suspended for between ten minutes and one hour.

It was not the first time Hanford had been visited by a Japanese balloon. On two separate occasions in February personnel observed what they described as yellow or white oblong balloons drifting high over the facility. The day after the Toppenish incident military police and civilian security guards shot down another balloon at a checkpoint on Hanford's western boundary. The Toppenish explosion had a direct impact on operations at the site, but the top-secret nature of the Hanford facility meant no one in the area, including many Hanford personnel, knew of the power outage and the buildings affected. Code-named 100-B, 100-D, and 100-F, the three structures were nuclear reactors producing plutonium for the equally top-secret Manhattan Project then taking place in the New Mexico desert. The electrical problem at Hanford necessitated a partial shutdown of the reactors. Not until three days later did engineers bring the piles back to full capacity. Plutonium produced at Hanford would later be used in a bomb code-named "Fat Man" that was dropped on Nagasaki.[22]

At the very moment the Hanford facility experienced its relatively minor airborne bomb attack, residents of Tokyo suffered a night of firebombing whose devastation compared only to that inflicted on Berlin and Dresden on the other side of the world. On March 9–10, 1945, in a raid code named "Meetinghouse," over three hundred American B-29s dropped 1,665 tons of incendiary bombs resulting in a sweeping firestorm that killed an estimated 90,000 people and incinerated sixteen square miles of the city. Flames and superheated air tore through buildings and whipped down streets and alleyways. Steel and glass melted. Rivers and canals boiled, providing no refuge to countless thousands who sought relief from the conflagration. The B-29 crews returned to bases on the Mariana Islands haunted by the sight of humans set aflame and the stench of burning flesh that hung on their clothes and person.

Although targeted primarily at factories, railroad yards, and other industrial areas, the bombing also leveled residential districts, including a densely populated section of the city called Asakusa. Major General Curtis LeMay, a hard-nosed officer known to his men as "Iron Ass" and who initiated the firebombing campaign after being placed in charge of the Pacific bomber command in January 1945, disclaimed the notion the Tokyo attack was directed at civilians. What the major general called Japan's "dispersal of industry," however, meant that many small factories were located in residential neighborhoods and that a great deal of materiel production took place in private homes. Said LeMay, "All you had to do was visit one of those targets after we'd roasted it, and see the ruins of a multitude of tiny houses, with a drill press sticking up through the wreckage of every home."[23] Firebombing tests on "Little Tokios" constructed at Elgin Field in Florida the year before had demonstrated to LeMay the brutal effectiveness of incendiaries. The resultant flames easily jumped walls, streets, rivers, and every other type of firebreak and spread quickly among the many structures the Japanese built with wood and paper. Unlike conventional precision bombing, saturation incendiary bombing ensured that every large factory and residential drill press in a wide area would be destroyed.

LeMay boasted that in addition to crippling Japan's military and industrial capacity the firebombing was an attack on civilian morale. Anxiety over the bombing caused millions of Japanese to flee urban areas for the countryside, causing disruptions to the workforce and congestion along transportation corridors. American planes dropped countless flyers that named twelve cities as possible targets for future firebombing raids and encouraged residents to evacuate for their own safety. "You are not the enemy of America," the blue-and-white flyers read. "Our enemy is the Japanese militarist who has dragged you into the war. We believe that peace will make you free . . . and a better Japan will then be born anew."[24] The Army Air Force hoped to capitalize on the fear created by the incendiary campaign to undermine civilian confidence in Japan's military leaders. Following the bombing of Tokyo, equally devastating air raids took place on Osaka, Nagoya, Yokohama, Kobe, and several other cities. Although the scale and devastation of the American firebombing attack render absurd any comparison with the Japanese balloon bombs, it bears noting that both campaigns used incendiaries as weapons of terror. For whatever material destruction might be caused by canisters packed with either thermite or jellied gasoline, the raining of fire from the sky appealed to war planners on both sides of the Pacific as a means of social disruption.[25]

John Dower writes that even before the surprise attack on Pearl Harbor in December 1941, Americans saw the Japanese as "a race apart, even a species apart."[26] Invariably referred to as "Japs" or "Nips," code words that signified racial inferiority, the Japanese were seen as mental primitives, subhuman creatures lacking in reason and driven by base aggression. Unlike the war in Europe, where a distinction between the "good German" and the Nazis could be found in the consciousness of the Western Allies, ethnic nationalist stereotypes of the Japanese led many Americans to conceive of the Pacific war as a struggle to exterminate the subhuman race. Simple vengeance for Pearl Harbor also played a part. Dower notes that while American war planners gave some moral consideration to the firebombing of civilian populations in Germany, little discussion took place regarding the Japanese campaign. The Asian imperialists had merely reaped what they had sown, according to the thinking of men like LeMay.[27]

The Japanese had their own racial formulations that underpinned the purity, righteousness, and the goals of the war. To them, Americans were monsters, barbarians whose own society (and segregated military) was rife with racial injustice. Pan-Asianism ostensibly represented a means to liberate oppressed peoples from the political, economic, and cultural subjugation of the Western colonial powers, thus the Pacific war was characterized by racial hatred, intensity of conflict, and atrocities committed against soldiers and civilians alike to a far greater degree than in any other theater of the global war. "Kill or be killed," writes Dower in describing how racial and ethnic formulations of "the Other" contributed to the merciless fighting. "No quarter, no surrender. Take no prisoners. Fight to the bitter end. These were everyday words in the combat areas, and in the final year of the war such attitudes contributed to an orgy of bloodletting that neither side could conceive of avoiding."[28]

If the firebombing of Japan took place in this context of total war, so, too, did the *fu-go* offensive. The balloon campaign might have had little effect in terms of Japan's military strategy, yet it had been carried out within the larger goal of terrorizing American civilians and weakening their will to fight. Setting ablaze the cities and forests of the western states was seen by the balloon commanders as a legitimate tactic of war. In this sense, the thousands who participated on both sides, from military planners in Washington and Tokyo to the pilots and bombardiers of the B-29s, from the Kokura schoolgirls who pasted paper to the launch personnel who released the ropes and freed the balloons, all found themselves in a conflict that demanded total destruction of the enemy.

# 7

............

*Canada*

On January 20, 1945, shortly after the third confirmed balloon incident in Canada, Brigadier General Maurice Pope sent a priority
memorandum to William Lyon Mackenzie King, the nation's prime
minister. "With regard to . . . the discovery of Japanese balloon-bombs
over western Canada," the staff officer wrote, "the object in releasing these balloons [has] more to do with a study of meteorological
conditions than anything else."[1] Pope had recently spoken to General Andrew McNaughton, Canada's national defense minister, who
believed the bombs' main purpose was not destructive but simply
to generate press reports that would help the Japanese understand
Pacific weather patterns, perhaps for some future aerial campaign.
McNaughton and Pope accordingly recommended that no publicity be given to incidents. The men did acknowledge the possibility
of bacteriological warfare and assured the prime minister that close
coordination with U.S. authorities would continue.

There is no evidence the Japanese balloon offensive occupied

any significant amount of Prime Minister King's attention thereafter—just as American presidents Franklin D. Roosevelt and Harry
S. Truman had no direct involvement with the U.S. response. The
nations' respective defense agencies collaborated from the very beginning of the balloon attack, though not without a few false starts. The
first incongruity that had to be resolved was a minor one. The Canadian Armed Forces had initially assigned the code name "Crabapple"
to the Japanese balloons but quickly replaced it with "Paper," the
U.S. War Department's preferred appellation.[2]

Next came Minton. In mid-January, following the landing of the
Saskatchewan balloon and recovery of its battery box, sandbags, and
other detritus, U.S. officials from the Western Defense Command
traveled to Vancouver on the understanding the evidence had been
shipped there and was available for inspection. Everything from
Minton had already been sent to laboratories in Ontario, however.
"It seems necessary to coordinate our efforts on the subject with the
United States authorities," wrote a frustrated Canadian army officer
to his superiors at the Department of National Defence on January
24. "Efforts so far appear to be circumscribed by the lack of definite
directives to the three services [army, navy, air force] and to the RCMP
[Royal Canadian Mounted Police]."[3]

That very day, representatives from the three service branches and
officers of the RCMP gathered at the National Defence Building in
Ottawa for a meeting of the newly formed Joint Service Committee
on Japanese Balloons (JSCJB).[4] Chaired by Colonel J. H. Jenkins,
the committee established an interservice command structure that
closely resembled that in the United States in that the army assumed
primary responsibility for recovering balloons, investigating all incidents, and dispatching bomb disposal personnel to every landing
site. Lieutenant Colonel E. L. Borradaile was accordingly directed
to establish a bomb disposal (BD) task force in the western provinces.
Where BD officers typically destroyed ordnance on site, the unique

FIG. 25. Envelope recovered at Manyberries, Alberta on 22 February 1945. "Many-berries (Wild Horse) balloon," Library and Archives Canada, Department of National Defence fonds, PA-203224

circumstances of the Japanese balloons made the collection of intelligence a high priority. Borradaile's team was therefore ordered not to blow everything up but instead to "secure for research purposes all objects connected with balloons."[5] The JSCJB charged the Royal Canadian Air Force (RCAF) with bringing down airborne balloons when possible and supplying air transport, first for bomb disposal officers to the landing sites and later for balloon evidence back to the appropriate research laboratories in Ottawa. Like its counterpart the U.S. Western Sea Frontier, the Royal Canadian Navy (Pacific Coast) assumed jurisdiction for all balloon sightings and recoveries at sea. Recognizing that most balloon landings would occur in rural areas in the western provinces, the committee assigned the RCMP the responsibility of coordinating with local law enforcement to identify, guard, and report incidents to the nearest military base.

After the conference Colonel Jenkins forwarded a copy of the meeting minutes to Francis J. Graling, a U.S. army colonel and military attaché at the American embassy in Ottawa. "The procedure which you have set up for processing enemy balloons or equipment recovered in Canada is entirely agreeable to U.S. War Department," Graling replied to Jenkins on January 29.[6] In particular, Graling had no quarrel with the JSCJB's decision to have all balloon evidence recovered in Canada sent to the National Research Council in Ottawa, not to U.S. military labs in Washington. The colonel did mention that once the initial round of tests on each balloon was completed the Anacostia laboratory would be happy to receive any Canadian evidence "for comparison and possible further investigation," but he made no such demands. Graling also asked that copies of all reports be sent to the U.S. Western Defense Command with priority status given to any report that described a modification or heretofore unknown aspect of the device in question. Graling's letter appears to underscore that while Canada's response was modeled on and nearly identical to America's, it was nevertheless established with autonomy.

The close collaboration on balloon defense occurred in the latter stages of the war, by which time relations between Ottawa and Washington had become "highly institutionalized," according to historian Galen Roger Perras.[7] Even before the war, in 1938, Franklin Roosevelt had delivered a speech in Kingston, Ontario, in which he assured Canadians he "will not stand idly by" should the northern neighbor be threatened by an aggressive foe.[8] The security alliance took more formal shape in 1940, with the establishment of the Permanent Joint Board on Defense (PJBD), a body composed of four service members and one civilian from each country. Prime Minister King was especially pleased with the word "permanent" in the board's title, which suggested an alignment of military interests that would last beyond the present war. It would be a mistake, however, to infer that Canada only passively allowed the United States to set and implement its own unilateral agenda for continental defense. A U.S. proposal to establish a naval base in Nova Scotia and lease existing Commonwealth facilities in the Western Hemisphere—part of a larger "unity-of-command" plan that would place the United States in a primary leadership role—met with strong resistance from Canada and led to a sputtering start to the PJBD. This template was in evidence on the balloon defense as well: close coordination but independent policymaking in certain areas.

One aspect in which the Canadian program differed from the American response was in the discretion given to military personnel to release balloon details to the public in sparsely populated rural areas. "Due to the extremely wide area which the balloons cover," the JSCJB wrote in March 1945, "it has been decided that military authorities . . . are now at liberty to disclose a limited amount of information on this subject to civilians, such as rural postmasters." The information was to be passed by word of mouth only and restricted to the most general balloon description that might facilitate detection and reporting. Although the circumstances of certain balloon incidents in the United States left American authorities with little choice but to inform civilian witnesses, it was never explicit policy to allow such preemptive warnings as now authorized in Canada. The policy's only real shortcoming was that it led to an abundance of false balloon reports by Canadian civilians, an unusually large number of which turned out to be sightings of the planet Venus.[9]

"Three scrambles today, two of them chasing planets again," commented a pilot in the RCAF 133 Squadron on July 2.[10] The uncommonly bright Venus, often visible even in daytime, so resembled a high-altitude balloon that it was not uncommon for a dozen P-40 Kittyhawks or DH-98 Mosquitos to be dispatched in a single day to investigate. By early summer, in an attempt to reduce the number of false reports, the RCAF began distributing charts showing the position of Venus in the sky each day. Still the scrambles continued.

As historian Mathias Joost has pointed out, since false reports could not be debunked without investigation, the controllers had no real choice: "To not scramble an aircraft against a suspected sighting of Venus could have let an actual balloon slip through the defenses. To the frustration of the fighter pilots, WAC had to scramble them against all sightings with a potential for a successful interception."[11] The prevalence of false sightings well into summer eventually prompted the JSCJB to review all previous reports for reclassification. Citations of several supposedly airborne balloons were subsequently scrubbed from the record.

At the first meeting of the JSCJB on January 24, the RCAF had been assigned the responsibility of bringing down balloons (where doing so posed no risk to people or infrastructure on the ground) and providing transportation for men, supplies, and recovered balloons. In fact, the RCAF had met internally on the subject two weeks earlier, well before the nature of the balloon attack was fully understood. At that meeting the Western Air Command (WAC) elected to place on alert one aircraft at each western base for possible reconnaissance and interception. The duty was ill-defined as the WAC was by necessity figuring out its defense strategy on its own with little input from Ottawa. At the time exactly one balloon incident had occurred in Canada. The JSCJB eventually formalized the branch's responsibilities and resolved the chain of command issues, and over the course of the spring the WAC developed what Joost has called "a maturing response."[12] The WAC held meetings with civilian pilots who were asked to report sightings to the military while remaining silent to the general public. The WAC also developed procedures for monitoring domestic balloon launches (e.g., weather balloons).

In addition to chasing Venus almost daily, RCAF pilots brought down three airborne balloons during the war, all in British Columbia. The 133 Squadron was credited with two kills. P-40 Kittyhawks shot the first down on February 21 at Sumas Mountain (the device actually came down across the border in Washington and was recorded as a U.S. incident). The second kill came on March 10 near Galiano Island. The third, an already low-altitude balloon, was forced down by a Canso (Consolidated PBY Catalina) flying boat near Coal Harbour on March 12.

The bomb disposal unit established by Lieutenant Colonel Borradaile, what defense officials in Ottawa would later admit was "one of the most hastily planned yet efficient organizations of the war,"[13] featured detachments in seven western cities: Vancouver, Prince Rupert, Prince George, Esquimalt, Calgary, Regina, and Winnipeg. Borradaile kept on his office wall a large map of western Canada and placed flag-pins on each confirmed balloon landing. He similarly tracked the daily location of his bomb disposal teams with pushpins, one for each detachment.

One of the more active pushpins on Borradaile's map was that assigned to Captain Charles A. East. As the bomb disposal officer stationed at Prince George, British Columbia, East was responsible for some of the most isolated country in Canada, from the forests of BC north to the Yukon and Northwest Territories. In March, while awaiting the arrival of a bomb disposal trainee who was to be his assistant, East received a report of a balloon landing near Fort Babine in central BC. He couldn't wait for the trainee, so he turned to a mechanic and driver in the base's motor pool, Corporal W. V. L. Smith, and asked if he was game for a trip to the bush. There would be a lot of arduous travel, East warned, including trail-breaking in deep snow and sleeping outdoors without a tent. Corporal Smith, or "Smitty" as he was known to everyone at the base, had no bomb disposal experience but great energy and enthusiasm for any duty that took him into the woods. Before the war he had been a trapper in northern BC and had worked for a logging operation. He quickly accepted East's invitation, and the men became partners for the duration of the war, often traveling by plane and dogsled around western Canada. On the Fort Babine trip they took a chartered plane to the landing site, easily secured the downed balloon, and that very night were received by the manager of the local Hudson's Bay Company outpost, who fed them a home-cooked dinner and provided lodging in separate, carpeted rooms. "Captain," Smitty joked as the men turned in, "a fellow's sure got to be tough to go on a trip with you."[14]

One of the duo's more challenging recoveries took place near Cedarvale, a whistle-stop on the Grand Trunk Pacific Railway, where passengers had noticed a billowing canvas in the trees high up a mountain slope. East's assistant had arrived in Prince George days earlier, but the man, although "game as a bird dog" according to the captain, was fifty years old, was overweight, and had never used a pair of snowshoes in his life. Smitty was therefore still on the job. Following a multiday snowshoe trek through miles of thick forest, the men, guided by a local railroad worker, located the device suspended eighty feet off the ground. Only the shroud lines had become entangled, leaving the envelope to heave outward in the shape of what East described as a "monstrous form of mushroom." So knotted were the lines in the forest canopy that not even chopping down the trees brought the balloon down. Smitty climbed another tree and managed to shake the device free, its payload of at least two visible bombs swinging ominously above.

Once East had secured the explosives from the downed chandelier, he knelt in the snow and began the disarming process:

I attached a magnetic mike and put on earphones. I checked everything again thoroughly and then taped the arming vanes to the fuse to prevent movement. Then the very thing I was trying to prevent happened. The spring-loaded striker pin that had been driven in snapped out, exposing several threads. The arming vanes had spun off four turns. Five would have caused it to detonate. While

I was working a small branch fell from high up where Smitty was working. It hit the bomb. Through the mike and earphone it was like a blast. I jumped ten feet and dodged behind a tree.[15]

It took most of the day for East and Smitty to box up the defused bombs and other evidence, which they carted down the mountain with assistance from their guide and a horse he retrieved from his nearby cabin. At war's end, East arranged for Smitty a promotion to sergeant.

Because defense officials expected the greatest number of balloon incidents to occur in British Columbia, Canada's most western and most densely forested province, Ottawa issued special instructions to the BC Provincial Police (BCPP). Although their duties were so straightforward as to be pedestrian—report sightings to nearest military installation, guard all grounded balloons, and assist bomb disposal personnel—that an official strategy integrating the hundreds of civilian police stations had been established at all marked another divergence with the U.S. response that included no such formal policy with any state police force. Canada's Security Intelligence Bureau feared that keeping the BCPP out of the response program would "hamper the prompt dispatch of information" regarding sightings and landings:

> While it was realized that all information regarding balloons must be kept from the enemy, it was considered necessary that all who might have to deal with balloons or members of organizations or services who might be in a position to supply information should be given necessary advice and instructions.[16]

The commissioner of BCPP was accordingly authorized to inform, on a confidential basis, naturally, all fire departments, civilian defense agencies, and provincial game wardens and foresters. As in Alaska, the BCPP developed a secret radio code that used colors to represent different aspects of balloon observation. BLUE meant a balloon had been sighted, BLACK grounded, GREEN drifting toward, and so on.

Springtime in the snowy forests of British Columbia was second only to the dead of winter as the season least likely to see wildfires catch—not a single naturally occurring fire had been recorded in the province in the months of January, February, and March over the previous two decades—yet one of the few actual conflagrations caused by a Japanese balloon anywhere in North America occurred at Kelly Lake on April 16. A trackwalker for the Pacific Crest Railway witnessed a series of three powerful blasts on a nearby mountaintop. Two tree stumps still smoldered when the BCPP arrived at the site the next day. "The fire had been in a rock slide," the local constable later wrote. "There was very little to burn in the slide, yet the rocks had been apparently in a very intense fire. Four trees . . . had been scorched, one as high as thirty feet up."[17] Although the recovery team found no physical evidence of a balloon, the strong chemical odor in the air and lack of any alternative explanation for the white-hot fire led the BCPP to conclude a Japanese balloon was to blame.

THE BCPP and provincial health officials responded to a different type of emergency that same month in Ardi Lake, a First Nations village in the northern reaches of the province. Of the thirty-four residents in the Alaska Highway community, fourteen were suffering from diarrhea and vomiting. Four children had already died of pneumonia by the time the responders arrived, and a fifth would soon perish from severe intestinal distress. The Natives lived a semi-nomadic, subsistence lifestyle, hunting animals and generally living from the land, and an outbreak of disease among the local deer population led health officials to wonder about a connection to the recent deaths. No balloon reports had been made in the area, but in the wide-open wilderness of northern BC it was entirely possible that at least a few balloons had arrived unseen. Investigators soon discovered, however, that the residents had salvaged and consumed canned food from a

U.S. Army dump, likely disposed of during construction of the Alaska Highway three years before and now turned rotten. The cause of the fatal illness was now clear, but a commissioner with the government of the Northwest Territories remained troubled by the balloon risk and complained to the Joint Service Committee in Ottawa that the NWT and Yukon could not be neglected. Many people in the isolated northern territories lived the same subsistence lifestyle as the Natives at Ardi Lake, according to the official, and any outbreak of disease to humans or animals could turn the territories into an "incubator region." The NWT government and chief of forestry for the region asked that a detailed information release about the balloons be made throughout the territories to doctors and select others whose stamina for the rural country should attest to their quality of character. "They are responsible men accustomed to and having to make decisions and could be relied on for what is required," the JSCJB wrote in agreeing to the proposal.[18] (Muktuk Marston was then making much the same argument to the Alaska command with regard to informing his rural troops.)

With the exception of the rigorous chemical and biological analyses conducted in Ottawa, Canadian defense officials largely deferred to their counterparts in the United States on matters of technical balloon research. The basic mechanics of each device had long been understood by the Anacostia laboratories by the time landings began occurring north of the border, thus all evidence transported to Ottawa was examined primarily for irregularities or modifications to the known balloon design. Investigators with the Canadian Army Operational Research Group (CAORG) did discover an abnormality in the altitude control mechanism on the balloon forced down in Coal Harbour, British Columbia. The number 2 blowout plugs had failed to ignite, which should have blocked the sequence of ballast release for every pair of blowout plugs thereafter. Indeed, numbers 3 through 17 remained intact. The number 18 blowout plugs, however, fired as designed and reinitiated the sequence for every remaining set. It was discovered that a wiring error in the number 2 set caused an intermittent short circuit that prevented its firing, while a corresponding short in the number 18 set created a bypass circuit that restarted the sequence. What made the find significant was that the very same wiring error between the number 2 and number 18 sets of blowout plugs had been found on three previously recovered devices: Porcupine Plains, Saskatchewan; Nanaimo, British Columbia; and Hays, Montana. This could be no coincidence. It seemed clear that a Japanese technician at one of the launch sites was inadvertently making the same wiring mistake on every chandelier he assembled.[19]

Investigators in both the United States and Canada kept detailed records on such abnormalities, fully aware that these types of patterns might hold the key to understanding the operational nature of the campaign (e.g., production rates). Recognizing that each balloon recovered in North America contained at least one component or operational failure—otherwise it would have self-destructed as designed—CAORG investigators theorized that tracking the frequency of each failure type might reveal a useful pattern. They named four broad categories: too rapid loss of hydrogen from the envelope, battery failure, barometer failure, and blowout plug failure. The first two categories were dismissed as irrelevant to the study since either a significant loss of hydrogen or battery failure would likely send the balloon into the Pacific Ocean its first day out. Barometer failure was also ruled out. The system's redundancy—each device featured four barometers—suggested a total failure of all four instruments was highly unlikely.

That left only blowout plug failure as the cause most worthy of analysis. A failure rate of just 4 to 8 percent was observed on chandeliers recovered to date. Since the T-bar mechanism supporting each ballast weight would release even if only one of the two blowout plugs in each set actually fired, however, the rate of total balloon failure was estimated at barely 1 percent of the total launched. Any single balloon could theoretically experience a blowout plug failure rate of 50 percent, and the device would still work so long as the failures were evenly distributed (i.e., one blowout plug in each set fired while the other remained intact). After acknowledging its findings were highly speculative, the CAORG wrote, "Calculations based on the meager data available show that the number of balloons reaching this country may be 30 to 1,000 times the number falling intact."[20] The CAORG would later retract this estimate after numerous subsequent recoveries revealed no statistically relevant relationship between blowout plug failures and the probability of other system failures, such as electrical shorts, loose fuse connections, and the failure of the demolition block and/or the flash bomb. The Nanaimo Lakes recovery in early March proved so anomalous as to cast additional doubt on the usefulness of every statistical projection. Only eighteen blowout plugs on that device fired, a failure rate of 75 percent. In addition, sixteen of those appeared to have blown at the same time due to an electrical short. That the balloon experienced such ostensibly catastrophic failures and still arrived in North America suggested such randomness to the flight prospects of any single balloon as to defy prediction for the overall campaign.[21]

Across the Pacific, schoolgirls at the Yamaguchi paper factory completed their shifts on February 16, 1945, and were told to gather their meager belongings and prepare to board trains for home. The plant was shutting down. *Kozo* and *konnyaku*, the two plants from which the paper and glue were made, had been overharvested in the region. The hillsides were stripped bare. Japan attempted for a time to import paper-making supplies from its annexed colonies in Southeast Asia, but other desperately needed resources, especially petroleum, took priority in the holds of the nation's cargo ships.[22] Those schoolgirls who assembled the balloons still had much work to do—huge rolls of completed sheets of paper awaited the cutting, pasting, and sewing that would turn them into spherical envelopes—but the sacrifice and service of the girls who made paper was now over. They went home, too exhausted to care or wonder about the paper they made and how precisely it contributed to the promised devastating attack on the United States. They just went home.

# 8

............

## *Censorship*

"It is suggested the time is drawing near when it will be necessary
to issue a controlled release of some sort regarding the Japanese
balloons."[1]

So wrote Lieutenant Colonel James F. Perry, a domestic specialist with the U.S. Military Intelligence Service (MIS), on March 6,
1945. The balloon offensive was entering its fifth month, each having
experienced an increase in the number of balloon landings over the
month before. Following the slow pace of recoveries in November
and December 1944, January witnessed an uptick to 18 balloons.
February saw 54, most in the Pacific Northwest but a handful as
far east as North Dakota, Nebraska, and Iowa. The easternmost
landing occurred in Farmington, Michigan, when a man found a
single incendiary device, what he first believed to be a tin can, in his
backyard garden. Fortunately for the Michigander, the bomb did
not detonate when he picked it up with a shovel and tossed it aside.
Although Lieutenant Colonel Perry could not have known it at the

time he wrote his memo, March would experience the most balloon landings by far with 113, an average of more than 3 per day. By Perry's estimation, the ever-increasing numbers justified an announcement in the name of public safety.

The MIS, a unit that included Japanese-American Nisei trained as linguists, translators, and even interrogators, had been monitoring communications from Japan for any information on the *fu-go* campaign. In his capacity as domestic specialist, Perry evaluated the effect of the War Department's censorship policy in the United States. In a confidential memo to the MIS chief he concluded the continued silence and lack of publicity was increasingly putting American civilians at risk. "If such an episode occurs [civilians being injured by balloon-borne bombs] an outcry may well be raised of such proportions that it will be impossible to maintain any censorship and the War Department will be subjected to severe criticism for its policy in the matter," Perry wrote. Although the lieutenant colonel went so far as to draft a press release, he limited his recommendation to making the advisory only "a matter of discussion" for the relevant defense agencies.

The cable made its way to the office of the G-2 chief of policy. "It appears that MIS is not fully aware of what has been done in the matter," an intelligence officer wrote in recommending against any release of information to the general public.[2] G-2 noted that all service commands, defense commands, naval installations, FBI field offices, law enforcement agencies west of the Mississippi River, and even newspaper editors and broadcasters had been made aware of the Japanese balloons. The rebuttal neatly sidestepped the MIS's primary concern that civilians in the western states knew nothing about the balloons and were therefore unaware of the danger that might be found in their backyards. Nevertheless, Major General Clayton Bissell, assistant chief of staff for intelligence, concluded that no policy change was warranted.

Responsibility for enforcing censorship rested with Byron Price and the Office of Censorship. Created by executive order of President Franklin Roosevelt just days after the Pearl Harbor attack of December 7, 1941, the office had the authority to censor international communications with "absolute discretion."[3] Such power could have easily been abused—by federalizing all radio stations, for example—yet Price held that asking journalists to censor themselves in the name of patriotic duty would prove more effective than clamping down by fiat. "The voice of a dove" was Price's motto. He believed in a quiet and credible request as opposed to angry coercion.[4]

A newsman through and through, Price had delivered papers as a boy, edited his high school newspaper, and worked his entire career in journalism. At the start of the war he left the Associated Press editor's desk, a job he loved, to take the directorship of the censorship office only after being satisfied that the president would allow him to pursue a policy of voluntary, not mandatory, censorship. The order establishing the Office of Censorship explicitly named international communications as being within its purview, but it intentionally left vague the director's powers with regard to domestic communications. Price felt the direct monitoring of all print and broadcast copy would not only needlessly alienate reporters but also require such an abundance of offices and personnel as to be next to impossible to achieve. He favored voluntary censorship as a general approach, bringing down the heavy hand of his office only when particular circumstances required he do so. As a career journalist, Price had friendships and professional dealings with editors, reporters, and broadcasters from numerous media outlets, and his accommodating nature proved a tremendous asset to the mission. "You could censor me any time and I would know you were right," former president Herbert Hoover privately told Price.[5]

In the case of the Japanese balloons, Price had employed the voluntary model to the same degree of success as in every other area of the war. On January 4, following the short articles that turned up in *Time* and *Newsweek*, the director issued a confidential memo asking reporters to withhold all information about the balloons in the name of military security. All who received the bulletin complied. In the handful of cases where the balloons received mention in a news story over the next few months, the leak invariably resulted from a lack of knowledge about the policy, not a deliberate violation.

In late February Congressman Arthur Lewis Miller, a Republican representing the fourth district of Nebraska, submitted his weekly column to all 91 newspapers in his district. He did so regularly, even though most papers ran his column only on occasion if at all. The weekly *Gordon Journal*, however, picked up the congressman's missive that week, which stated, in part, "As a final act of desperation it is believed that the Japs may release fire balloons aimed at our great forests in the northwest." Miller likely obtained the information from a congressional colleague or War Department briefing. He noted the Japanese had a stockpile of 300,000 balloons, a claim for which there was no evidence, and stated that while the balloon attack "would not affect the outcome of the war, it would have a certain nuisance value."[6]

After seeing the report in print, intelligence officers at the Seventh Service Command in Omaha began calling editors at all 91 papers. All reported receiving the congressman's column, but since most were weeklies not scheduled to go to press for another day or so, they hadn't yet run it. In the end, just two papers actually printed the column. Although the leak had been contained quickly and Representative Miller suitably chastised — "I was wondering if somebody couldn't muzzle the congressman a little bit on that," one G-2 officer queried — the incident more importantly revealed a weakness in the censorship policy. Price's memos had gone to the wire services and media outlets in every large metropolitan area in the nation, but there existed thousands of small, local newspapers and radio stations in the part of the country where balloon landings now occurred daily. Representative Miller had 91 papers in his district alone, while Nebraska as a whole had 350. How many of those papers knew of the censorship policy? Could the Office of Censorship possibly ensure its mandate reached every single one?

Major Charles D. Frierson, an intelligence officer at Omaha's Seventh Service Command, kept detailed notes on the matter as he worked to kill the Miller column. He then traveled across Nebraska and neighboring South Dakota to make contact with news outlets and assess whether they were aware of the policy. In a report submitted to his commanding officer, the major reported that only 5 of 86 newspapers and 1 of 22 radio stations had knowledge of Price's entreaty to withhold all balloon details from publication or broadcast. "Two more [radio stations] faintly remembered hearing something to that effect," the major wrote, "but admitted that they would have probably put information regarding a balloon on the air without remembering that such an incident should not be publicized."[7]

Frierson went on to note that many small, county newspapers across the West often relied on local freelancers to furnish stories of particular interest to those communities. The articles typically received no editing but went to print exactly as submitted. He determined almost none of these local stringers had heard of the balloons. Although the weeklies had small print runs, their geographic reach might be wide as local subscribers moved to other parts of the country, either with the military or for war work. One paper claimed subscribers in all forty-eight states and numerous oversea military installations. Mention of the Japanese balloons might thereby achieve great word-of-mouth distribution despite being published only in a small rural paper. Frierson closed his report by recommending intelligence officers make in-person visits to as many news outlets as possible. "The effort of seeing the newspapers is felt to be more than justified by the procuring of an excellent source of information as well as an absolutely essential security measure."[8]

TIM TYLER'S LUCK

In April 1945 intelligence officers found themselves monitoring the Sunday comics.

"We wondered whether you read the funny papers?" asked a colonel at the Fifth Service Command in Columbus, Ohio, to an intelligence officer in the Army Service Forces. "The comic strip called 'Tim Tyler's Luck' by Lyman Young, this is in the *Columbus Dispatch* of Sunday, 22 April. . . . [T]hey're in a submarine and he sights something . . . "[9]

Created by Lyman Young, brother of *Blondie* creator Chic Young, *Tim Tyler's Luck* was an adventure comic that followed the strapping Tim and his sidekick Spud on their worldwide travels and escapades. During the war, Tim and Spud found themselves in the navy, a duty that did not stop them from chasing spies and saboteurs across the globe. On this particular day the young men were serving on a submarine in the Pacific when the periscope operator observed something in the sky: "Unidentified object drifting at low altitude above the water! Definitely not a plane."[10]

"It's some kind of free balloon," said Captain Barker after the sub surfaced and they got a closer look. He ordered the gunners, "Rip enough holes through the upper part of that balloon to bring 'er down quick, men!" They recovered the downed balloon—"Jap markings on it!"—and discovered its payload was only a small box. "Let's see what's inside, Tim," said the captain. "Seed! Nothing but a mess of funny-looking little plant seeds!" A note reading "To be continued" appeared at the bottom of this last frame.

FIG. 26. (*opposite*) Two frames from "Tim Tyler's Luck" by Lyman Young, a Sunday comic that ran in newspapers throughout the United States on 22 April 1945. Tim Tyler's Luck © 1945 King Features Syndicate, World Rights Reserved

"I'll take it up with G-2 and let them get in touch with Censorship," replied the intelligence officer. Syndicated nationally by King Features, the comic appeared that Sunday in newspapers across the United States and Canada, resulting in numerous calls to G-2 from in-the-know defense officials. Although none knew at that moment what the next edition of *Tim Tyler's Luck* had in store for the submarine crew, the Office of Censorship subsequently found out and still declined to halt publication. The following Sunday, Tim, Spud, and Captain Barker appeared in the funny papers fighting the monster vines that sprang from the seeds and strangled the sub. The trio escaped to a nearby island where they encountered Dr. Matsu Unkanni, the evil Japanese horticulturist who had developed the voracious, fast-growing plant and was now air-lifting the seeds to the United States as part of a devious plot to choke the entire continent. Over the next three Sundays the men freed themselves from Unkanni's jail cell, followed him to his underground laboratory, and then escaped from the cave using one of the free balloons. The three jumped to safety and were picked up by the submarine (how it got untangled from the strangler vine was not explained) just before Unkanni's plane collided with the balloon and crashed into the ocean. Whether the fantastic storyline had been the cartoonist's intent all along or government censors convinced him to alter the story following the first strip is not known.

Zack Mosley, creator of the aviation strip *Smilin' Jack*, published a series of comics a few weeks later that also featured a Japanese balloon. Student-pilot Wickie took Jack's son Jungle Jolly on an unauthorized flight, whereupon they collided with a Japanese balloon and were forced to make an emergency landing. (A G-2 officer noted the cartoonist's depiction of the balloon was "fairly accurate."[11]) The balloon exploded after falling to the ground, forcing Wickie and Jolly to jump into a nearby river to escape the inferno. The storyline included nothing about the balloon from that point forward, revolving instead around Wickie lying about being alone at the time of the incident, worrying about Jungle Jolly giving up her secret, and losing her chance to marry Jack.[12] It remained unclear how and from where the cartoonists learned about the Japanese balloons, but with over two hundred landings at the time the comics appeared, there was certainly a great deal of word-of-mouth news. Newspaper editors in particular were well informed, and Young and Mosley may have independently received tips from a friendly reporter.

Although the Office of Censorship evidently saw no need to clamp down on the Sunday comics, an incident in late March resulted in a furious rush to keep the balloon story out of the papers. Colonel H. B. White of the service command in Omaha, Nebraska, obtained a copy of a United Press (UP) release, then pending distribution to its nationwide network of subscribers, and telephoned the Intelligence Division of the Army Service Forces. "Now what follows is the release," the colonel informed the duty officer who took the call, "and you'll find it has great deal of detail, a lot of mechanical detail on the thing, in addition to being a hell of a scare story."[13] Colonel White asked the officer to switch on his recorder and get the copy transcribed and delivered to G-2 immediately.

"Denver, Colorado, March 26, 1945," the colonel began.

Since last December the Japanese have been bombing the Rocky Mountain region in the middle west. They have been doing this bombing with bombs that come straight from Japan, from launching sites just outside of Tokyo. It takes one hundred hours for the bombs to sail across the Pacific Ocean and land somewhere in the United States and the Japs can shorten the range or lengthen it merely by turning a little screw on the weird device that carries the bombs. . . . The first indication that Americans had that Japanese bombs are being dropped in the United States came about

Christmas time, when it was announced that a strange balloon with Japanese markings had been found near Kalispell, Montana.[14]

The thousand-word article went on to state that more than one hundred balloons had been discovered in several western states. It also described, in precise detail, the altitude control mechanism, meteorological conditions over the Pacific, several of the landings, and the balloons' payload including bombs and poison gas containers.

"I don't know whether any army officer has talked on this thing or not but if he has, goddam him, he ought to be tried," barked Colonel White. The dispatch contained so much detailed information it clearly could not have been composed without a knowledgeable source. The story made mention of a defense conference held in Salt Lake City a few days earlier, and the colonel suspected the leak had come from someone at that meeting. "Our suspicion is that it probably came from some of the state defense civilian officials."[15]

The public relations officer at White's service command was at that very moment in contact with the UP office in Denver, from whom he learned the story originated at a secret briefing to the Colorado State Legislature. An official with the state defense council, who indeed had just returned from the Salt Lake City conference, presented a report and screened the navy training film. While the official dutifully prefaced his comments with the standard warning on confidentiality, a discussion of the balloons next occurred in an open hearing in the state senate where legislators were considering an appropriation to the state defense council. An eager wire service reporter in the gallery jotted down every word.

G-2 immediately feared the copy had already been transmitted to newspapers and radio stations across the country. Although the heading clearly stated "For release only after clearance," it was all but certain that at least a few outlets would jump the gun and run the story immediately. Fortunately, the editor in Denver informed

G–2 the story had not yet been teletyped but existed in only five copies—one in his possession, one each in the UP bureaus in Washington and New York, and two copies in the bureau in Dallas. All five copies were quickly retrieved and destroyed.[16]

On March 28, just after the close call in Denver, the Office of Censorship sent a confidential memo to editors and broadcasters reiterating its policy. Price called reporters' cooperation with the balloon policy to date "excellent" and noted, "There is no question that your refusal to publish or broadcast information about these balloons has baffled the Japs, annoyed and hindered them, and has been an important contribution to security." He continued:

> So far the balloons and their bombs have caused no loss of life or serious damage. It may be that sooner or later serious damage may occur. If that should happen, it is most important that published or broadcast accounts mention no connection between Japanese balloons and the damage caused by them. In any such case you are urgently requested to withhold all specific information as to the cause of the death, injury or damage, and to avoid linking the incident with enemy action.[17]

Price's note differed from all previous communications in that he now cautioned against reporting not only the balloons' existence but any "death, injury or damage" that might occur. March had seen the highest number of balloon landings, over one hundred so far that month alone as compared to just eighty-two in November through February combined. The memo seemed to acknowledge that, by the law of averages alone, some kind of incident was bound to occur.

One month later, after an additional fifty balloons had been sighted or recovered, Colonel William Hammond drafted a letter for the governors of eight western states. The letters began, "You are aware of the fact that a considerable number of free balloons dispatched by the Japanese have arrived over the West Coast of the United States during recent months."[18] Hammond went on to explain the necessity of keeping information out of the press, but also noted it was "desirable that intelligent, loyal Americans understand the existence of and the possibilities of this new threat." Hammond, the one man in the U.S. Armed Forces who likely knew more about the Japanese balloons than anyone, felt strongly by this point that the public should be warned of the danger. His letters, subsequently approved for distribution and sent to the governors, announced no policy change, only that state officials were to be kept informed and act on a confidential basis to ensure public safety.

As April turned to May, G-2 officials again debated whether the time had arrived for a controlled release of information to the public. On Wednesday, May 2, a colonel on the staff of General Clayton Bissell, who had previously refused to consider a change to the information policy, informed the Western Defense Command he was in agreement that "we should be formulating our ideas on the type of news release we would like to make to let the people, civilians especially, on the West Coast know that these balloons can be expected."[19] In addition to providing for the public safety, G-2 suggested an information campaign might be useful in generating additional intelligence from previously unreported incidents. Hammond offered the navy film be shown to the public, a suggestion that met with strong resistance at the higher levels. Screening the film publicly, according to the War Department, would make it impossible to control the story any longer in the press.

On Thursday, May 3, Hammond spoke by telephone to a major in Bissell's office. "The Commanding General [of the Western Defense Command] is very anxious that some method be worked out to enlighten more of the populace without running the risk of getting the information directly to the enemy," stated Hammond. The major proved sympathetic to the viewpoint but informed Hammond that Bissell's office was willing only to discuss the issue, not act on it. It still did not yet believe the threat justified any publicity. "What we will have to do," replied the major, "is get additional examples of where somebody took the [bombs] or incendiaries home with them."[20]

Two days later, a number of Canadian defense officials met in Ottawa to discuss the same issue. On the question of balloon publicity the Canadian censorship bureau had from the beginning taken its lead from its counterpart office in Washington. Colonel J. H. Jenkins informed attendees that draft press releases had been prepared and could be distributed "in the event of an emergency occurring that would necessitate the public being advised" of the danger.[21] The meeting adjourned at 11:40 a.m., Saturday, May 5, with no firm decision having been made on the press releases or the larger question of when to inform the public.

### SATURDAY, MAY 5

That very morning, a young woman named Cora Conner sat at the telephone switchboard in Bly, Oregon. It was the weekend, and the phone lines of Bly, population just seven hundred, would likely remain quiet most of the day. About noon, a Lake County sheriff's deputy entered the office. Lake was the next county over, but he'd driven west to Bly since it was closer to where he'd come from on Gearhart Mountain than the sheriff's office in Lakeview to the east. The deputy sat next to Conner and had her connect him on a series of phone calls to his Lakeview office, the forest ranger station, Weyerhaeuser Timber Company, and Fort Lewis in Washington. The young Conner sat stunned as the deputy reported an explosion up the Dairy Creek Road. An adult woman and children severely injured, possibly killed. The woman's husband, a pastor named Mitchell, had apparently witnessed the whole thing.

Word spread quickly through the small town, and by afternoon a large group of residents crowded outside the telephone station. Sheriff's deputies and forest rangers came and went, saying nothing, and people began to shout to Conner. "Everyone was angry," she later recalled. "They were getting very violent. They knew something had happened to the kids."[22] Conner had been ordered to say nothing, not even to worried parents. She kept quiet all day, a duty that would cause her to suffer nightmares for many years.

Ed Patzke went to the telephone office that afternoon looking for information about his younger siblings, Dick and Joan, who had left that morning for a fishing trip with the pastor of their church. No one would tell him anything. The only information he or anyone else received was that "something awful happened."[23] The parents of Jay Gifford and Sherman Shoemaker drove forty miles to the hospital in Lakeview, but no one there knew anything either. Rumors of an explosion spread through the crowd. An area rancher recalled an incident the previous winter when, while feeding cattle one day, he looked up and saw "this kind of thing drifting over . . . going from the south to the north." Thinking nothing of it at the time, he later suspected the flying object might have been the source of the explosion.

Finally, at 9:00 p.m. that evening, the Patzke, Gifford, Engen, and Shoemaker families were told the children had been killed by a bomb, one that had arrived in Bly on a Japanese balloon some time before. Archie Mitchell was still being interviewed by authorities that evening; the body of his wife Elsie has been taken with the others to the morgue in Lakeview. "I was scoutmaster of Bly troop," Einar Engen, father of Edward, later vented. "I should have been warned that balloon bombs had been coming into this territory, but I never heard a word about them."[24]

The following day, Sunday, the editor of the Klamath Falls *Herald and News* sent a priority cable to the War Department: "Earnestly urge lifting restrictions enough to permit warning to thousands of people who go into the woods of this area in spring and summer and are ignorant of the bomb danger."[25] The bright sunny days of spring and coming snowmelt on Gearhart Mountain meant many people

FIG. 27. Shrapnel from incendiary and high-explosive bombs at Bly. Untitled photograph, Box 43, Japanese Balloon Sightings, Record Group 499, Western Defense Command, NARA

would soon be fishing the same creeks as the Mitchell party. The local lumber mills shut down that day so that all employees could search the woods, in itself a risky proposition since no one really knew what they were looking for. Malcolm Epley, the Klamath Falls editor, received a reply from the censorship office stating he could report on the deaths but was not to mention anything about a balloon or even a bomb, only that the origin of the explosion was unknown.

That the bomb was Japanese and had been delivered to Bly via a hydrogen balloon was known to every editor and broadcaster in the western states. Calls for revising the policy increased significantly after Bly. Harold Cassill, a newspaper editor in Spokane, Washington, wrote to the WDC's public relations officer: "This question naturally comes to mind: How will it be possible to acquaint the public as to the danger in connection with unidentified objects without revealing at least something of the supposed source of the mysterious objects?"[26] Whatever the answer, Cassill pleaded with the WDC to authorize some sort of information release. He noted an incident in Pullman the week before where a deputy fire marshal spoke to the chamber of commerce in a cryptic manner that no doubt frightened people more than would have the plain truth. "Military censorship prevents the Army and fire officials from telling all they know about this threat," Cassill reported the man as saying, "but I can tell you that the Japs have a secret weapon which can be more destructive than the robot bombs used by the Germans." The editor noted such "half-cocked" and "half-baked" tales would continue to spread until authorities cleared the air.

Orval Thompson, editor of the *Eastern Oregon Observer* in Ontario, a town on the state's border with Idaho three hundred miles northeast of Bly, recorded his objections in a letter to Senator Wayne Morse. "It seems to me that a government which will restrain its newspapers from printing security information and helping to protect the citizens from possible danger from enemy action is definitely on the wrong track."[27] The editor of the *Pendleton East Oregonian* complained to the state's other senator, Guy Cordon, who called the War Department, which then ordered Colonel William Hammond of G-2 to visit the newspaper in person immediately. "Let people know what to do when they find these things so that they don't get killed," the editor told Hammond on the telephone four days after the Bly incident. The colonel replied his office was working on a revision to the press policy. "In fact," he said, "by the time I get up there to see you the plan will probably be in operation."[28]

On May 14, Major General Henry C. Pratt, WDC commanding general, authorized a "word-of-mouth" campaign in which community and civic organizations such as chambers of commerce and Lions, Kiwanis, and Rotary Clubs would be given basic information about the balloons and told to inform members on a face-to-face basis.

"You are aware of the fact that recently six persons were killed near Lakeview, Oregon, when a group of civilians discovered a balloon," Pratt's form letter to the community groups began.[29] The procedure of the new campaign "consists of reading an information bulletin . . . to small groups such as children in schools, boy scout troops and other youth organizations, civic clubs and other groups which meet periodically." The WDC prepared a document it called "Japanese Balloon Information Bulletin No. 1" to ensure uniformity in the presentations. The bulletin, Pratt made clear, was not to be posted, published, or broadcast, only spoken aloud at the gatherings and then immediately returned to military or state officials from whom it had been received.

The bulletin consisted of nine numbered paragraphs, the first of which began, "Army and Navy authorities wish to inform the public that during the past six months a considerable number of Japanese balloons have arrived over the western part of the United States and Canada." The next sections described the balloons and the bombs, their presumed dual purpose of starting fires and creating panic, and the necessity to continue denying information to the Japanese. The bulletin continued:

> You are being informed about these balloons because they are dangerous. . . . You are now in on the secret. Do not write about it in any letters and do not be unduly alarmed. Let us all shoulder this very minor war load in a way such that our fighting soldiers at the front will be proud of us. Think and act in accordance with what I have just explained to you.[30]

The bulletin's instructions called for it to be read verbatim twice. Paragraphs 6, 7, and 8—those informing citizens they were now in on the secret and requesting they report but under no circumstances touch any downed balloons—were to be repeated a third time.

If Colonel Hammond and the Western Defense Command believed

the word-of-mouth campaign would receive a positive reception by a populace eager for information, they were wrong. "Possibly the most fantastic scheme to come out of Washington," the *Tacoma News Tribune* called the effort when press restrictions were nearly fully lifted in late May. The paper ridiculed the notion that all citizens would receive the message. No matter how tightly knit the western communities might be, "hundreds of thousands of isolated farmers and their families" could be left unaware. The Tacoma paper also blasted the idea of making speeches in local schools, as young children invariably misheard, misunderstood, and then incorrectly repeated the stories to one another and their parents causing needless panic. According to one report, a young girl in Minnesota returned home from school in tears convinced the sky was filled with red balloons that were going to explode.

While granting that hindsight always had greater clarity than foresight, the paper expressed its view that "intelligent use" of the press and radio could have been achieved:

> How much better it would have been to have issued the warning months ago when the first balloons came down in Montana and Oregon. If the dangers had been fully explained then, during all the months since the Japanese could have been kept in ignorance of the fate of their balloons, and most probably six lives would have been spared.[31]

What made the incident even harder for the Tacoma journalists to accept was that they had long known about the balloons but had been enjoined by the War Department, albeit voluntarily, from issuing public warnings themselves. The *Los Angeles Times* made the same point in an editorial on May 24. Headlined "A Major News Bungle by the Army," the column noted the foolishness of asking professional news organizations to censor themselves while at the same time sending uniformed officers to schools with outlandish tales of exploding balloons. "If the papers had been permitted to make the information public in normal fashion, before childish imaginations had a chance to work it over," wrote the *Times*, "there would have been no stories of vast hordes of gas-borne Japs floating over the United States and throwing down bombs at the helpless populace."[32]

The WDC's only kudos came from Vandyce Hamren of the state of California's civil defense office, who voluntarily submitted a report on the campaign's effectiveness. In providing a county-by-county breakdown of attendance at the informational meetings, he boasted that "in excess of 1,000,000 persons have heard the message by word-of-mouth" and that his office believed the campaign "was of definite value."[33]

U.S. authorities had also done a poor job of educating Canadian media outlets, as evidenced by a May 24 editorial in the *Ottawa Citizen*, a paper that apparently lacked even the most basic information about the Japanese offensive. "Another puzzling aspect of the balloons is where they come from and how they are launched," the *Citizen* wrote. Noting that Japan was 7,000 miles from Vancouver and the nearest enemy–held Pacific base, Wake Island, was 5,000 miles distant, the paper stated, "They could scarcely come from these places. Are they liberated from submarines?"[34] Although these questions had been definitively answered months earlier, the paper's editors, and thus its readers, remained in the dark.

Byron Price and the Office of Censorship proved no less agitated by the word-of-mouth campaign. The WDC had launched the effort without informing Price, and he quickly realized that maintaining the information blackout, still technically official policy, would be impossible in the face of such widespread public discussion. Price went to General Bissell the day after the WDC announced its program and informed him the War Department had no choice but to go public. A descriptive but not overly detailed public statement might actually go a long way toward clearing up whatever confusion the schoolhouse chatter had created. Bissell, who had great confidence in the censorship director, authorized Price to draft a news release and send it to the army and navy chiefs of staff for approval. After several days of negotiation, the statement was ready to be released at 3:00 p.m. on May 22.[35]

So sensitive was the issue, Price sent a separate confidential memo to editors and broadcasters on the morning of the 22nd, a few hours before the scheduled release, to remind them the information they were about to receive was to be handled carefully. "There is no occasion for anyone to spread panic," he wrote. "The facts call for caution rather than alarm."[36] Price asked that any public mention of the balloons remain vague. Reporters were to name "some balloons" as opposed to a specific number. Exact locations of sightings and landings were to be avoided, substituted by more general phrases such as "western United States" or "west of the Mississippi." Under no circumstances were exact times and dates to be revealed, only "during the past few months" or some similarly indeterminate phrase.

The release, when it finally went out, contained essentially the same information as the word-of-mouth bulletin. The lifting of press restrictions, however slightly, proved to be the most dramatic aspect of the statement. Media organizations now had the green light to run stories giving "general information" about the balloons "provided no information is released concerning specific incidents."[37] Some restrictions still held. No press accounts were to mention times, dates, locations, or effects, nor should any publication feature photographs or drawings of the balloons. "The War Department remains the only appropriate authority for release of any information," read the statement's last line.

These two communications, the War Department release of May 22 and Price's confidential note to the press that same day, came into existence only because Colonel Hammond, G-2, and the Western Defense Command launched the word-of-mouth campaign a week earlier. But now it was Hammond's turn to feel blindsided, and he complained Price had gone a step too far. The colonel telephoned the G-2 office in the War Department the night of May 23 and reached the night duty officer. "Do you have your recorder on?" Hammond asked. Assured the tape was running, he let fly:

> The Commanding General, Western Defense Command is desirous of receiving information concerning the policy of the War Department and the Office of Censorship with respect to the matter of releasing technical information to the public, both by word-of-mouth and to the press and radio concerning the Japanese balloons. The confidential note from the Director of Censorship to the press and radio is not too clear on that subject and it is a matter of considerable concern to this command. . . . [I]t is considered highly advisable that appropriate steps be taken to ensure that no technical information relative to recovered balloon materiel be disseminated to the public, particularly to the press and radio.[38]

For Hammond and General Pratt, informing the public in general terms at town meetings made sense, but a wholesale revision to the press policy could possibly result in "technical information" going into print and over the airwaves. When Hammond's late-night complaint was transcribed and delivered to Price and Bissell, the latter assured WDC the policy change pertained only to information already in general circulation and that the instructions Price issued to the press represented only a guide for handling the information, not a blanket authorization for full publication or broadcast.[39] The distinction may have made sense on paper, but Hammond feared it would be misinterpreted by numerous reporters as a sign the policy had been lifted altogether.

In the days and weeks that followed, stories about the Japanese balloons appeared in dozens of newspapers and magazines all over the country. Mention even occurred in weeklies at a few Japanese

American relocation camps, including the *Rohwer* (Arkansas) *Outpost* and the *Minidoka Irrigator* in Hunt, Idaho.[40] Not surprisingly, many stories in the mainstream press overstepped the censorship office's regulations just as Hammond had feared they would. The contradictory nature of the word-of-mouth campaign and the May 22 memos cleared up confusion in some areas but created it in others.

Robert Everest, the head of the journalism department at University of Washington, obtained a mimeographed copy of notes made by a Seattle police captain during a confidential briefing (in itself a violation as no information from such meetings was to be printed and distributed). Following the relaxing of restrictions by the Office of Censorship, he telephoned a friend in the state office of civilian defense and received permission to publish a story. "Explosive-Laden Balloons Sail to U.S. from Japan," announced the headline in the May 23 issue of the *University of Washington Daily*.[41] Essentially a journalistic rewrite of the WDC bulletin, the article contained one offending paragraph in particular, listing the number of balloons sighted on the West Coast and in the immediate Seattle area. Although the numbers were incorrect—the article listed 650 total balloons when the actual number by that date was just 238—what mattered was that any number had been given at all. Everest willingly returned the mimeographed copy of the bulletin to the FBI agent who interviewed him, but the editor remained confused as to how the article violated the censorship policy he believed was no longer in effect.[42]

In Canada military censors had been enforcing a blackout policy identical to that in the United States. In mid-May the *Vancouver Sun*, *Edmonton Journal*, and other papers ran long-withheld photos of the balloons on the authority of defense officials who desired citizens be made aware of the danger. The *Toronto Daily Star* ran a series of photos under the alarming headline, "Don't play with Jap balloon bomb like this. It might kill you."[43] The clearance angered the U.S. censorship office, though the Canadian censors could have been forgiven for similarly misunderstanding the confusing signals from Washington.[44] The Defense Headquarters subsequently issued a statement informing residents of the western provinces to be on the alert for any balloons that might be buried beneath melting snow. Farmers were asked to report any suspicious material discovered in their fields while going about spring planting.[45]

Pressure was mounting on the Office of Censorship to allow the publication of details of the Bly incident. By the end of May, nearly a month after the deaths, the office still forced the withholding of all specific information such as the origin and exact location of the blast. Finally, on May 31, Price determined the dozens of newspaper articles over the past few weeks had rendered pointless any further censorship of this one event, and he lifted the restriction. A United Press wire story picked up by several papers named the victims and described the tragedy in Lakeview (the wire service report was date-lined Lakeview, the location of the sheriff's office and morgue, instead of Bly). Upon discovering the balloon, the news report stated, the church group had assembled around the grounded device, and one of the kids had touched something that set off the explosion. The bodies, according to a report filed later by one of the foresters on scene, lay on the ground like spokes of a wheel with the smoldering crater at the hub.

Most significantly, the wire story featured a firsthand account from Archie Mitchell. "As I got out of my car to bring the lunch, the others were not far away and called to me they had found something that looked like a balloon," stated Mitchell. "I had heard of Japanese balloons so I shouted a warning not to touch it. But just then there was a big explosion. I ran up there, and they were all dead."[46] Mitchell explained how the group had ventured to the woods that morning for a day of fishing and a picnic lunch. After having tried one fishing spot farther down the mountain without success, he suggested they continue up the road and have a quick lunch. It was at that point the children bolted from the car, Elsie Mitchell following behind, while Archie removed the picnic basket from the automobile's trunk. Several large trees stood between Mitchell and the others, and he wondered whether they saved him from the debris from the blast.

The interview with Mitchell had evidently been conducted some days before it appeared in the newspaper. At the time the article ran he was in Port Angeles, Washington, Elsie's hometown, burying her body.

# 9

...............

## *Summer*

Almost from the moment the first balloons began arriving in North America in late 1944, Brigadier General P. E. Peabody of the Military Intelligence Service closely monitored reports of intercepted radio transmissions over the Pacific. He guessed that at least some of the signals came from airborne balloons. In March, the month when the number of balloons landings spiked, he noted thirty-four radio transmissions had been detected by radio operators on the Pacific coast. The recorded frequencies and pulse rates matched the known sound signatures of other confirmed balloons, leading Peabody to conclude the Japanese were still outfitting dozens of the vehicles with transmitters in order to track their flights. Of the thirty-four detected in March, operators obtained directional fixes on seventeen. Peabody plotted the locations where each device went silent—either because the transmitter failed, its battery went dead, the balloon dropped into the ocean, or some other unknown cause for failure—and found an average range of 3,900 miles east-northeast of Tokyo, well within range of the West Coast of the United States.

In June, on the other hand, radio operators locked onto only eleven signals, nearly all of which went silent just 1,900 miles east of Tokyo, less than half the distance traveled by the March balloons. The winds of the upper atmosphere, so strong in the winter months, had slowed to a breeze and now brought the balloons not even halfway across the Pacific before dumping them into the sea. "Assuming that the same type of radio-carrying balloon[s] were used in June as in March, the results obtained should indicate to the Japanese that recent wind conditions were not favorable for launching," Peabody wrote. "As far as is known, no such balloons landed in the United States during June."[1] The War Department's intelligence division had been disseminating a daily "Balloon Report" to affiliated defense agencies, but it now announced the updates would be published monthly instead. There were so few new incidents to report.

The decline in balloon sightings had been obvious to William Hammond as early as April. He requested the G-2 science office prepare a memorandum and offer a few theories for the downturn. Army Air Force meteorologists continued to detect meridional wind shifts that turned sharply north, leading the G-2 scientists to conclude "the number of balloons released [in April] was probably as great as any other time, but the wind currents . . . took them northward to Alaska and the Bering Sea, where, because of the sparse population, very few have been reported."[2] Although the hypothesis may have had some basis in fact, troops in the Alaska Territorial Guard similarly noted fewer balloons seemed to be arriving. Those they did recover were found on the ground; by late April none were observed in the air. A single weathered sandbag weighing two pounds, four ounces was found on Adak Island, no doubt once part of a balloon passing overhead and dropped in the prescribed manner. Its worn condition suggested the flight had occurred some time before, however. On

April 27, as the coming spring continued to relax winter's frozen grip on the territory, an ATG unit stationed at Platinum found and chipped from the snow a balloon carriage that had obviously been on the ground for some time. (The site of a rich platinum deposit, the eponymous village on the Bering Sea coast and its valuable mines had been guarded by an ATG detachment on high-alert status throughout the war.)

By May, the winds had turned again and now pointed directly toward Washington, Oregon, and California, but fewer and fewer recoveries occurred on land, and there were no reports of balloons observed in flight. Hammond speculated that the ongoing bombing of Japan by American B-29s might have damaged launch sites or balloon manufacturing centers, thereby disrupting the offensive. "Although there is no positive evidence that such locations have been the targets for bombing attacks, it is possible that they were hit in raids on other targets," he noted.[3] The firebombing of Tokyo and other Japanese cities that spring and summer had caused a near total disruption in the nation's manufacturing and transportation systems. It occurred to Hammond that perhaps the widespread destruction of roads, bridges, and railways prevented the transport of balloon supplies or hydrogen tanks.

At some point that spring, the exact date remains unknown, an American plane, possibly a B-29 bomber, flew high above the east coast of Honshu near Sendai and snapped dozens of photographs of the terrain below. On May 25, an analysis of those photographs revealed what looked like five partially inflated balloons in a barracks area and a circular pad near the beach that might have been used for launching. The intelligence analyst who wrote up the report on the photographs reminded readers of the U.S. Geological Survey's sand analysis that suggested it had been collected from a beach in that very area of the Sendai region.[4] Hammond collected the accumulated evidence in a secret report entitled "Possible Launching and Manufacturing Sites of Japanese Free Balloons." He made no recommendations for military action in the report, and no evidence exists the air force ever intended to attack the supposed launch stations. (Indeed, after the war U.S. troops would discover the launch sites abandoned, not destroyed.)

In early June a rancher and former army captain named Charles Ragsdale contacted authorities to report a balloon landing on his property near Yerington, Nevada. The landing had occurred the previous November, he told them, but when he called the local sheriff at that time the lawman told him to forget about it. Ragsdale got the same answer from someone at the nearby Hawthorne Army Depot, so he assembled his family in front of the huge billowing envelope, snapped a photograph, then cut apart the envelope to use as tarpaulins to cover bales of hay. He was only calling now, eight months later, because he'd heard the warning to be on the lookout for Japanese balloons. He showed the photo to authorities, who noticed it strongly resembled the rubberized silk specimen from San Pedro, the very first balloon that had been fished out of the Pacific in November 1944. The Eleventh Naval District at San Diego dispatched an intelligence officer to Yerington. "From his [Ragsdale's] testimony and the physical examination of the envelope and valve," the officer wrote, "it appears obvious that the two balloons—San Pedro and Yerington—were of identical construction and . . . probably were launched at the same time."[5] The device came down on November 9, as far as Ragsdale could remember. He discovered it tangled in a cottonwood tree one morning and spent the next several hours wrestling it free and tying its shroud lines to the trailer hitch of his pickup truck. The balloon's cargo had apparently broken free, leaving only a wooden platform from which dangled a narrow tube made of glass and rubber (likely an aneroid connection). The WDC later arranged to have Ragsdale interviewed by the same intelligence officer who inspected the San Pedro balloon. He concluded the two were indeed the same type of device. Authorities had long assumed the first Japanese balloons to make landfall, at Thermopolis and Kalispell, arrived in late November or early December. Now it appeared the Yerington balloon had landed weeks earlier.[6]

At around 6:00 p.m. on July 19, 1945, an aircraft from the Las Vegas Army Air Base flew north of the field over the small town of Indian Springs. Thirty-five miles northeast of the town the crew spotted what looked like a white parachute on the ground. A rescue team sent into the desert the next day wrote the word "JAP" in large letters in the sand, a message the pilots flying overhead had no trouble decoding and delivering to an intelligence officer in Las Vegas. "The envelope was torn," wrote the lead investigator when the device had been retrieved a few days later. "Indications were that it been dragged [and] caught in the brush. Valve bearing No. 17083 was in good shape; shroud lines were 1/4 inch manila rope."[7] No explosives, not even a flash bomb on the weathered but intact envelope, were found.

The response crew discovered hundreds of dead insects and one dead lizard tucked in a fold of the envelope, leading the epidemiology unit of the Eleventh Naval District to call for a survey of animal life and any recent disease outbreaks in the area. An oily substance coating sections of the envelope was later tested for the presence of chemical agents, but the responders unfortunately botched the recovery when they placed the stained paper sample in an orange juice can that had not been rinsed out. Laboratory analysis later revealed the presence of diesel oil and, of course, orange juice.

Although no one knew it at the time, the Indian Springs balloon would be the last recovered in North America during the war.

THE COMPTON REPORT

Alan Waterman arrived in New Guinea in May 1945 for an important meeting with General Douglas MacArthur, commander of U.S. forces in the South Pacific. The physicist from Yale had been dispatched

FIG. 28. The Yerington balloon recovered and photographed by Charles Ragsdale. Although not reported until June 1945, investigators believed the B–Type rubberized silk balloon was one of the first to arrive in North America the previous November. Untitled photograph, Box 43, Japanese Balloon Sightings, Record Group 499, Western Defense Command, NARA

by Karl T. Compton, the longtime president of the Massachusetts Institute of Technology and since 1943 chair of the Office of Field Service, a branch of Vannevar Bush's Office of Scientific Research and Development. Waterman's mission was quite simple: convince MacArthur to authorize the formation of an OSRD office in New Guinea in order to streamline procedures for direct communication between scientists and military officials then planning their island-hopping advance toward Japan. With the OSRD headquarters still located in Brisbane, Australia, its technical and scientific advice often failed to reach advancing forces thousands of miles away. MacArthur readily agreed to the request.

Compton had advised the U.S. government on scientific matters for over a decade. First appointed to a science advisory post by Franklin Roosevelt in 1933, Compton joined the National Defense Research Committee (precursor to the OSRD) at the outbreak of the Second World War and immediately led a research team studying the use of radio waves for detecting faraway objects, an emerging technology known as radar. For most of the war he'd been posted to Europe, but following the defeat of Germany in summer 1945 Compton transferred his attention to the Pacific. His duties there included the organization of expert technicians and the development, modification, and construction of required equipment, everything from rubber gaskets on gasmasks to scientifically enhanced weapons systems.

Once MacArthur approved Waterman's proposal to establish a forward OSRD base, Compton quickly began assembling teams of scientists, several dozen men recruited from a wide range of disciplines, to accompany troops in active theaters of the Pacific war. According to Compton, the arrangement marked "the peak in the development of technique for making scientists useful" to the war effort.[8] Joining Compton on the mission was Edward Moreland, dean of engineering at MIT and recently selected by MacArthur to directly advise his chief of staff. Both men arrived in the Philippines on Sunday, August 5, 1945.

The next day a B-29 named *Enola Gay*, piloted by Colonel Paul Tibbets, took off from a U.S. airbase on the tiny Pacific island of Tinian. The atomic bomb the aircraft dropped that morning, a uranium-235 fission weapon code named "Little Boy," wiped out over four square miles of the city of Hiroshima and killed an estimated 70,000 people instantly. An equal number of people would be dead by the end of the year from injuries sustained in the blast or radiation sickness. On August 9, an even more powerful plutonium device was dropped on Nagasaki, killing an estimated 80,000 people. The Japanese surrender would come within the week.

The end of the war obviously meant the end of Compton's Pacific forward operating base. The sixty scientists then en route from the United States to the Pacific were quickly directed to return home. As Compton noted in his official postwar reports, however, V-J Day had barely ended before every branch of the armed forces began submitting requests for research teams to investigate the state of Japan's scientific programs. "In this war of such highly developed technical character," Compton wrote, "how far had Japan gone, either in production or in development or even in conception of new methods of warfare which might prove dangerous to world peace in the future?"[9] Compton and Moreland assembled a small team composed of those scientists who had already arrived in Manila. They insisted on moving to Tokyo at the earliest practicable date, despite the fact almost no logistical arrangements had been made in Japan even for U.S. military personnel, let alone the scientists. MacArthur himself had agreed to refrain from landing in Japan until two weeks after the surrender, so as to give the Japanese people time to grow accustomed to the end of the war. Compton feared any delay in the investigators' arrival might provide Japanese personnel with enough time to destroy records and make themselves unavailable for interviews by scattering throughout the country.

In the first week of September, just one month after the Hiroshima and Nagasaki bombings, the Compton-Moreland team arrived in Tokyo and began inspecting laboratories and interviewing Japanese officials. The team had been established under U.S. military jurisdiction, not civilian, so as to allow its members to take possession of documents and arrest recalcitrant or fugitive officials, if necessary. The arrangement placed Moreland, MacArthur's scientific attaché, in charge of the team, yet Compton would oversee preparation of the official five-volume report later submitted to President Harry Truman.

"The objective of the survey," the Compton Report began, "was to make a quick, preliminary investigation to determine how the Japanese had organized for scientific war research."[10] Although they discovered many records had indeed been destroyed in the days immediately following Japan's surrender, the American scientists were able to interview approximately three hundred scientists and engineers from fifty different institutions. Compton described the Japanese officials as invariably courteous, candid, and helpful. He noted only one outright lie was discovered in the course of the interviews, that supplied by a young naval officer on a wholly inconsequential detail.

Among those interviewed were officials from Noborito who had worked on the *fu-go* program. On September 19, two American investigators (but not Compton himself) spoke with Lieutenant Colonel Terato Kunitake of the Japanese General Staff and an army major identified in the report only as Inouye. (This latter individual may have been a "Colonel Inoue" identified elsewhere as the regiment commander in charge of launch sites at Ichinomiya, Otsu, and Nakoso.[11]) The men confirmed all balloon records had been destroyed in compliance with a directive handed down on August 15, the day after the surrender. With no documents to impound, nearly every-thing the U.S. authorities were to learn about the strategic objectives of the balloon campaign was to come from this single interview.

"The Japanese report they originally planned to make 20,000 of the paper bombing balloons [but] they had actually produced and released 9,000," the investigators wrote. U.S. defense officials had long attempted to estimate the total number of balloons likely to be launched from Japan. Statistical analysis of the valve serial numbers in particular had led them to conclude tens of thousands of balloons might be produced. Here was confirmation their estimates were not far from the mark.

The investigators further learned each balloon cost 10,000 yen to produce (approximately $2,000 in 1945 U.S. dollars) and that the cam-paign had been undertaken "almost exclusively for home propaganda purposes" designed to offset the shame of the Doolittle raid three years earlier.[12] The Imperial Army did not expect the balloons to be particularly effective as an offensive weapon, Kunitake and Inouye admitted. Project leaders knew the winds of the upper atmosphere reached their highest speeds in the winter months, November to March, which was precisely the timeframe when wildfires would be the least likely to catch in the snowy western states. The winds were practically nonexistent in the dry summer months, for the Japanese an unfortunate meteorological oddity with respect to the balloon campaign. Nevertheless, the Imperial Army pursued the project for the uplift in morale it would create. When reports of actual damage and destruction in America were not forthcoming, the Japanese public received made-up news reports of raging wildfires that were sure to weaken the already fragile American resolve.

When asked about the organizational structure of Noborito, the men admitted the balloon program had taken place in direct consulta-tion with the institute's Ninth Chemical Laboratory. Kunitake and Inouye insisted this did not reflect any plan to weaponize the balloons with chemical or biological agents, only that the chemical division had a well-deserved reputation for solving complex engineering problems and that even nonchemical projects were often developed there. The Compton Report notes investigators had no reason to distrust the Japanese officials, nor was there any evidence suggesting a payload other than bombs had ever been intended for the balloons.

The balloon launches ceased in mid-April 1945, according to Kunitake and Inouye. (The news, once relayed back to America, must have given authorities pause as their carefully planned defense measures—Lightning, Firefly, Sunset, and the like—had not been fully implemented until the summer months.) The Imperial Army had terminated the balloon program in April for two main reasons. First, Japan was so resource poor by that stage of the war it simply could not continue manufacturing balloons. Not only was paper in short supply, but the army also lacked the means to produce hydrogen in sufficient quantities. In particular, the bombing of the Showa Denko factory by American B-29s the previous March had crippled Japan's chemical production efforts. The bombing raids also destroyed rail networks in and around Tokyo, so what stockpiles of hydrogen tanks did exist that spring could not be transported to the launch sites. The second factor leading to the cessation of launches was that the Japanese could obtain almost no information about whether the balloons were even reaching North America, let alone igniting wildfires or causing any damage. Apart from a few newspaper articles following the discovery of the very first balloons in December 1944, the War Department's information blackout successfully kept Noborito completely in the dark. The two Japanese officials stated that even if the war had continued into the fall of 1945, when the westerly winds were due to pick up again, the Imperial Army had no plans to resume the balloon campaign.

A review of balloon incident reports revealed that from December 1944 to April 1945, sightings of airborne balloons occurred with some frequency, but that starting in mid-April only grounded devices were recovered, many that had obviously landed weeks if not months before. A navy aircraft shot down a balloon over four hundred miles east-southeast of Tokyo in July 1945—one of the only summer aerial sightings—but the device sank to the ocean floor before it could be recovered. If part of the *fu-go* campaign, and not a barrage or weather balloon, the lost device may have come from a launch site clearing its inventory of balloons assembled prior to the April shut down. The radio transmissions detected and reported by Brigadier General Peabody as late as June almost certainly originated from the same final stock, none of which survived the Pacific crossing on the weak summer winds.

At the close of the Kunitake-Inouye interview, the Compton team learned that Major General Sueki Kusaba, the head of the *fu-go* program, had recently returned to Tokyo. In accordance with protocol and established procedure, the team requested that he be made available for a conference. Notes taken by the investigative team indicate the Kusaba interview was to take place on October 3. Whether the interview ever took place is unclear, but there is no further mention of Kusaba in the Compton Report.[13]

Turning its attention to the nation's overall wartime performance, the Compton Report identified numerous key problems that severely handicapped the Japanese scientific community's efforts. Extreme, bitter antipathy between the Imperial Army and Navy represented a significant barrier to scientific cooperation. One Compton interviewee commented that "a general and an admiral would rather lose the war than shake hands."[14] The report also cited "the failure of the Army and Navy to make effective use of university scientists in helping to solve their technical problems." Compton and his colleagues, university researchers all, had good reason to measure the Japanese failure against the markedly successful practice in the United States, the capstone for which had been the devastating atomic bomb developed by Robert Oppenheimer, James Conant, Edward Teller, Ernest Law-rence, and numerous other professors from prestigious American universities. Japanese military leaders, on the other hand, despite having many scientists who "unquestionably" (Compton's word) could have made great contributions to the war effort, viewed them with distrust and suspicion, in part because so many had received their training in Europe and the United States before the war. One example cited by the report is that of Hidetoshi Arakawa, the civilian meteorologist who prepared the atmospheric wind charts at the start of Noborito's balloon research. When interviewed by the Compton team on October 13, Arakawa could only reiterate that he produced wind charts. He provided no other details because he possessed none. According to Compton, "due to the lack of interchange of informa-tion between military and civilian agencies, he [Arakawa] was unable to learn the extent to which his predictions had been realized."[15] Like the schoolgirls who pasted paper and stitched together the balloon envelopes, even the scientists were kept out of the secret.

ALASKA

Buzz Walters, a sergeant in the U.S. Army stationed in Nome, Alaska, arrived at the local school on the evening of August 14, 1945, with a reel-to-reel tape recorder under his arm. Native dancers from King Island were scheduled to perform that evening, and Sergeant Walters wanted to record the drumming and singing. The school gymnasium was packed with three hundred people when he arrived, the crowd spilling out the doors into the foyer. He made his way to an open space on the floor near the drummers where he set up his equipment.

Walters brought more than just a tape recorder that night. He immediately sought out Muktuk Marston and delivered news of the Japanese surrender. World War II was finally over. Marston took the stage and, after informing the crowd of the war's end, delivered an impromptu speech in which he praised the Native soldiers of the ATG:

Right here let me say to the everlasting glory and credit of the Eskimo people that every able-bodied Eskimo from sixteen to sixty-five years of age that I was able to contact is a member of the Tundra Army or the regular army. . . . You have proved your loyalty and patriotism in defending the shores of Alaska and I have been proud to be your leader.[16]

With Buzz Walters's tape machine humming nearby, the major closed by saying, "I shall remember you always and think of you as one great Arctic Brotherhood." The King Island dancers then took the stage with a performance that marked both the evening's jubilation and what Marston called the "solemnity of the occasion." Marston later borrowed Walters's recording in order to have phonograph records produced and distributed to the ATG detachments across the territory. His speech appeared on one side of the disk, the King Island music on the other. The record would later be broadcast on KFAR, the radio station in Fairbanks. The ever-generous Marston produced the records at his own expense of over one hundred dollars.

The war over and information restrictions lifted in practice if not policy, Marston began noting with pride the role of the Alaska Territorial Guard in the balloon bomb defense. He named it as one of the Tundra Army's singular accomplishments, along with the repair of dozens of backcountry cabins, the blazing of hundreds of miles of new trails, construction of eighteen armories, and the search for and rescue of a pilot forced to parachute from his disabled aircraft near the village of Ruby—all services performed without regular pay. In his October 1945 status report, Marston wrote, "The Tundra Army did an excellent service in observing, shooting down, and recovering Japanese balloons carrying demolition bombs and fire incendiary bombs." Marston likely engaged in some hyperbole in his description; there is no evidence ATG troops actually *shot down* any airborne balloons with their antiquated rifles. Nevertheless, the major noted the troops' overall service to the country had lasting positive effects for Alaska's Native people:

> The act of swearing them in and giving them guns built up their loyalty and made them proud to be "Uncle Sam man," as they put it. The act of making them soldiers caused them to realize their citizenship more than anything the U.S. Government has done in the past. . . . If the Army elects to take the material (guns, helmets, parkas, shoulder patches) away from the Eskimo, it will undo a lot of the good work done in causing the Eskimo to be proud of his citizenship.[17]

Marston's memo amounted to a passionate appeal to the Alaskan Department to keep the ATG active. Although the army disbanded the regiment in 1947, the troops were allowed to keep their rifles, and the ATG's legacy as a powerful agent of change remained intact. The Guard provided a formal organizational structure that, for the first time, brought together members of every ethnic group in Alaska: Aleut, Inupiaq, Yupik, Athabaskan, Tlingit, Haida, and others. Native organizations, such as the Alaska Native Brotherhood, had existed for years, yet the ATG was the first with both a sizeable territory-wide membership and a mission that required its daily participation. Marston often called the ATG an army of 20,000, a number that included not just the soldiers but the women in the villages who prepared the food and mended clothes and old men and children who carried meat home from the hunt and cared for the dogs. Every ATG detachment built its own armory or *kashim* (traditional meeting place) that became the center of local activity as well as a training ground for Native leaders.

The later political, economic, and social gains of Alaska Natives, in particular the land claims movement of the 1960s and the development of regional and village corporations under the Alaska Native Claims Settlement Act of 1971, can in part be traced back to the

ATG and the culture of civic responsibility and self-determination it produced.[18] John Schaeffer Jr. of Kotzebue, whose father served in the ATG under Marston and who himself was adjutant general of the Alaska National Guard from 1986 to 1990, believed the Natives' WWII military experience helped to restore the cultural identity that decades of contact with missionaries and paternalistic federal bureaucrats had previously weakened. "Almost all leaders in western and northern Alaska came out of the Guard, a whole generation of leadership," stated Schaeffer.[19]

The *fu-go* campaign demonstrated that any part of North America could be attacked by weapons launched from across the oceans. The villages of Arctic and western Alaska, previously among the most isolated on the continent, found themselves positioned on the frontlines of enemy attack. Defending the territory required communication, coordination, travel, and reconnaissance activities best performed by men and women familiar with the land. The balloons proved a tactical failure in terms of Japan's strategic objectives, but this in no way diminished the ATG's efforts, undertaken in the moment when the true nature of the attack remained unknown and the threat was believed to be extreme. Although barely a footnote in the sweeping history of the Second World War, the Japanese balloon bomb offensive figured prominently in the narrative of the Alaska Territorial Guard, an all-volunteer force that existed for less than five years but established an enduring legacy.

Otto Geist, the ATG quartermaster and Marston's right-hand man, went back to the University of Alaska, where before the war he had founded the college museum. He hoped to bring one of the Japanese balloons back to Fairbanks and add it to the museum's permanent collection, but the War Department refused to release any of the still classified devices. Although most of the balloon evidence collected in the western states during the war had been shipped to Anacostia as instructed, some components remained at scattered detachments and field offices. Bulletins calling for the destruction of all balloon material went out from both Washington and Ottawa. The blowout plugs and fuses were to be soaked in water for at least four hours, according to the memo, while the incendiaries, high-explosive bombs, demolition blocks, and flash charges were to be destroyed with a well-placed stick of dynamite. All inert balloon material was to be disposed of in whatever manner the field office saw fit.[20]

In January 1955, nearly a decade after the end of the war, an Alaska bush pilot named Don Hulshizer was flying near the village of Fort Yukon when he noticed a dull white object resembling a parachute spread out on the ground near the Sheenjek River. The balloon later recovered by a U.S. Air Force helicopter crew was found to contain one unexploded incendiary device, dozens of sandbags, and a paper envelope so durable that it failed to rip easily even after weathering ten years on the Alaska tundra.[21]

The Fort Yukon balloon was one of a dozen or so to be discovered in the years immediately following the end of the war. Discoveries took place in British Columbia, Washington, Oregon, and other areas as farmers, hunters, hikers, miners, pilots, and other backcountry travelers stumbled across long-grounded devices, many with live ordnance still secured to rusty hooks. During the war Vannevar Bush's Office of Scientific Research and Development estimated that roughly 7 percent of balloons launched would survive the transoceanic voyage and arrive in North America. The validity of the estimate can be neither known nor tested, but if accurate it would mean as many as 630 balloons—7 percent of 9,000 launched—may have landed in North America between November 1944 and April 1945. With the number of confirmed landings standing at just over 300, it seems probable that a number of balloons, at least one or dozens or possibly hundreds, await discovery. The paper on any such device has almost certainly disintegrated over time. Perhaps, too, the ropes. Other components may be rusted and corroded but still intact.

THE WORLD'S FIRST INTERCONTINENTAL BALLISTIC MISSILE

*Fu-go* was a weapon intended to boost morale in Japan and incite panic in the United States. In that sense the bomb-laden balloons were qualitatively no different from the tons of napalm-filled incendiary bombs dropped by American B-29s over Tokyo and other cities across Japan. Although Major General LeMay desired targeted (but not precision) bombing that would destroy industrial facilities of strategic importance, he approved the use of incendiaries also for the fear the firebombs would create among the populace. Irrespective of the technological limitations that prevented the Japanese from such large-scale aerial bombing of U.S. targets, the strategic goals of the paper balloons were not that dissimilar. Each balloon was launched in the hopes it would bring fire and panic to the shores of America.

In 1947, two years after the Japanese surrender, Brigadier General W. H. Wilbur located Sueki Kusaba, the head of the *fu-go* program. The recently retired Wilbur was on assignment for *Reader's Digest*, and "Those Japanese Balloons," his article that appeared in the magazine in 1950, was for most Americans the first they had ever heard of the unusual weapon. Kusaba confirmed the findings of the Compton team regarding the April 1945 cancellation of the balloon program. Kusaba told Wilbur he had been summoned to the army's general staff headquarters in Tokyo that month with an order to produce concrete evidence the balloons had reached the United States. All he could scrape together was a single article from a Chinese newspaper. It was a five-month old reprint of the Kalispell, Montana, story. The dearth of evidence convinced Kusaba's superiors that none of the balloons had reached North America, and he was ordered to stop wasting Japan's ever-dwindling resources on the hopeless campaign. Kusaba recalled the officers exclaiming, "You know the Americans could not possibly keep their mouths shut for months if the balloons were really reaching their country."[22] (Cornelius Conley, a sergeant in the U.S.

Air Force working toward a history degree in the early 1960s, also located the elderly Kusaba in Tokyo and interviewed him in April 1963, just two weeks before the general's death. Conley included information from the interview with Kusaba in a 1968 article in *Air University Review*.)

Nearly every press article about the Japanese balloons published at the end of the war in 1945 emphasized the complete failure and even the absurdity of the campaign. With America triumphant and its incomprehensibly powerful nuclear weapon sure to usher in a new era in human history, the nation's press mocked the paper balloons with headlines that regularly used the words "flop" and "dud." That not a single devastating wildfire and only a handful of small, self-extinguishing conflagrations had been set by enemy balloons only proved the futility of the effort. Brigadier General Wilbur, however, admired the ingenuity behind the offensive. "Ridicule has been heaped upon this attack," he wrote,

> but the fact remains it marked a significant development in the art of war. For the first time missiles were sent overseas without human guidance, and although only a few landed and did little or no harm, yet a new era in conflict was opened. The danger of great damage, even a major catastrophe, was very real. . . . The Japanese are a capable people, no doubt of that. Any nation that can span 5,000 miles of ocean with unmanned weapons has resourcefulness and initiative.[23]

George E. Weidner, a civilian engineer commissioned by the War Department in 1946 to conduct a complete technical analysis of the balloons, agreed. He concluded the Japanese displayed "originality and ability" in solving the many problems with sustained high-altitude balloon flight. "The only deficiencies," Weidner believed, "were the shortage of materials and a lack of facilities to produce cheaper and better equipment."[24] Both Weidner and Wilbur cautioned bomb-laden balloons might yet appear on the Pacific horizon once again. The westerly winds would continue to blow, they warned, and who knew what strategic goals the Russians and Chinese might pursue in the future.

Advances in missile technology and the development of even more powerful nuclear weapons would shortly render those dire warnings moot, even quaint from a modern perspective. Yet Wilbur proved remarkably prescient in noting the balloons had opened "a new era in conflict." *Fu-go* was a failed campaign to be sure, but as a weapon of terror it also foretold the fear and anxiety of the coming Cold War and its vastly more powerful airborne weapons. As the world's first intercontinental ballistic missile, the Japanese balloons marked the humble beginning of a type of warfare the Cold War superpowers would refine and expand almost beyond imagining.

# Epilogue

Frank Patzke visited Colonel Charles Bisenius at the Western Defense Command's G-2 headquarters in San Francisco in July 1945. It had been two months since his children Dick and Joan had been killed in Bly. Patzke was then separated from his wife, Bertha Myrtle, and on his way to North Dakota where a job with the Great Northern Railway awaited him. Bisenius served in the G-2 Northwestern Sector, and he'd met Patzke the day after the tragic incident when he traveled to the small logging town. Now Patzke called on Bisenius with a question: Might the U.S. government, for nearly four years engaged in a formally declared war with Japan, pay an indemnity on civilian deaths caused as a direct result of that conflict?

Bisenius looked into the matter and, after checking with the G-2 judge advocate, found himself in the unenviable position of giving the dead children's father the bad news. "The incident does not appear to be one upon which a claim may be predicated," the colonel wrote in a letter to Patzke.[1] He cited a 1943 army regulation that disallowed any financial claims for injury to persons or destruction of property as a result of "action by the enemy." Bisenius closed the letter by saying that while the army's hands were tied by the regulation, Patzke might approach his congressman to obtain the relief he sought.

Two years later, as Congress debated such a bill to financially compensate the five surviving families, the Department of the Army wrote that it was "opposed to the enactment of . . . a bill for the relief of Frank J. Patzke, Archie Mitchell, J. L. Shoemaker, Einar Engen, and N. L. Gifford."[2] The army stated that while the events in Bly were certainly tragic, "there do not appear to be any facts or circumstances which would warrant singling out these claimants for preferential treatment over other claimants in similar circumstances." The army also maintained there could be no legal liability because the deaths did not result from any negligence on the part of military personnel.

"The committee disagrees," wrote Patrick McCarran of Nevada, chair of the Senate Judiciary Committee.[3] McCarran disputed the claim that the proposed bill singled out the survivors for preferential treatment. How could it when no such event had ever happened before in the nation's history? The six deaths in Bly were the only casualties in the mainland United States from enemy action in the entire war, thus no "other claimants in similar circumstances" would ever come forward. "[I]n this unique case," wrote the senator, "where loss of life occurred to innocent citizens . . . who were completely unaware of any danger from enemy activity, the persons who suffered because of these bombs should be compensated in a reasonable amount." McCarran also assailed the army's claim that no negligence had occurred: "This may be true. However, there is no question but what the Department of the Army [was] aware of the danger . . . and took no steps, for what may have been valid reasons, toward warning the civilian population of the danger involved."

Congress authorized payments in the amounts of $3,000 to the Shoemaker, Engen, and Gifford families, $6,000 to Patzke (who had lost two children), and $5,000 to Archie Mitchell for the loss of his pregnant wife, Elsie. "Not that any amount of money could bring her back or even begin to make up for the loss that she is to me," Mitchell wrote to William Lemke, the North Dakota congressman who introduced the bill, "but because I think that the accident could have been avoided by just a few words of warning."[4]

At the same time Congress was preparing to compensate the Bly families, the Weyerhaeuser Timber Company made plans to honor the victims with a monument at the blast site. A company forester designed a truncated pyramid, six and one-half feet high, that a local mason then constructed of native basalt stone. A bronze tablet affixed to the stone monument listed the names of the deceased.

The site was dedicated as the Mitchell Recreation Area on August 20, 1950, on a twenty-acre parcel of forested land donated by Weyerhaeuser. Oregon governor Douglas McKay spoke to the three hundred people who gathered for the ceremony. He stated the six civilians who died were casualties of war "just as surely as if they had been in uniform."[5] The monument was placed at the exact spot where the explosion occurred five years earlier.

Archie Mitchell could not attend the dedication ceremony as he was then serving as a missionary in Vietnam. He and his new wife, the former Betty Patzke (older sister of Dick and Joan), had left Bly in late 1947 for a life of Christian service at a leprosarium in Ban Me Thuot, a city in the central highlands of South Vietnam. Weyerhaeuser had invited the Mitchells to the event, but Archie replied, "Although I'm afraid it will be impossible for me to be there for the dedication of it, I would certainly have no objection to the name that you mentioned, Mitchell Recreation Area, and am glad to give you my permission to call it that if you so desire."[6]

On the evening of May 30, 1962, Archie sat in the living room of the family home at the leprosarium helping his thirteen-year-old daughter Rebecca with her stamp collection. Betty was helping the three younger children get ready for bed when a dozen Viet Cong guerillas stormed the house and accused the Mitchells of betraying the people of Vietnam. A skirmish between South Vietnamese forces and the Viet Cong had occurred three days earlier some miles away from the leprosarium, leading to American military advisers visiting Mitchell and other hospital staff to check on their safety. Mitchell

FIG. 29. Mitchell monument. Author photograph

FIG. 30. The parents of Elsie (Winters) Mitchell view the monument at its dedication in 1950. U.S. Forest Service, Fremont-Winema National Forests

assured the troops there was nothing to fear as the leprosarium operated independently of the government, and they had never been
harassed before. The visit apparently convinced the Viet Cong that
the aid workers were in collusion with the U.S. military, and now the
guerillas tied Archie's hands behind his head and hauled him away.
Also abducted that night were two other American missionaries,
Eleanor Vietti and Dan Gerber. The three were never seen again.

### THE INNOCENTS

Yuzuru Takeshita, a Japanese American teenager born to immigrant
parents in Alameda, California, sat inside the barbed-wire-enclosed
yard at the Tule Lake internment camp in northern California in early
1945 and looked skyward hoping to catch a glimpse of a balloon. "I
had heard about the balloon bombs, I didn't know it was real," he later
said. "I don't know where the rumor came from, it may be that the
radio was broadcasting some incidents involving balloon bombs, but
there was a rumor throughout the camp . . . so we stood out, almost
all day, gazing up at the sky trying to spot one of these balloons."[7]

Although an American citizen, Takeshita had spent much of his
youth living with his grandfather in Japan. He and his best friend,
a boy named Tsugio Inouye, built model airplanes and pretended
to be fighter pilots themselves, all the while dreaming of joining the
Imperial Navy one day and flying the real thing. Takeshita was fated
to spend the war years very differently, however. He returned to the
United States just before the Pearl Harbor attack of December 1941
and, like thousands of other Japanese Americans subject to President
Franklin Roosevelt's internment order, soon found himself imprisoned at Tule Lake. Whatever anger he might have felt toward the
Americans manifested in his constant skygazing, hoping a bomb-laden
balloon would pass silently overhead. He never saw one.

The young man's frustration and disillusionment eventually

abated due to the efforts of a woman named Margaret Gunderson, his history teacher at Tule Lake. Gunderson and her husband had been teaching at a public school, but after watching all of their young Japanese American students sent away to the internment camps they resigned in protest and followed their charges to Tule Lake. "I don't see how you stand being locked up all the time," she told Takeshita. "I couldn't."[8] The bold and honest words changed the young man's life. Here was an American woman who empathized with him, who disagreed with the actions of her government and now sought to make the best of a very bad situation by providing her students with lessons in freedom and democracy, subjects they could have been forgiven for dismissing as nonexistent at the barbed wire-enclosed camp. "She taught us about the U.S. Constitution and that's when she mentioned the Constitution is not to blame for what happened," Takeshita later remembered. "It's the violation of the constitutional rights of due process that every citizen is entitled to."[9] At war's end, just before being released from the camp, Takeshita asked Gunderson to give him an American name. He planned to make the United States his permanent home. She gave her prize pupil her father's name: John.

Forty years later, John Takeshita, now a professor at the University of Michigan, visited the village of his deceased grandfather where he had spent so much of his youth. He learned Tsugio Inouye, his boyhood friend, had indeed become a navy pilot but died in a kamikaze attack in 1945. He met Toshiko Inouye, his friend's widow, and learned she had worked at a paper factory during the war making the panels that were assembled into the balloons. Takeshita realized that had he remained in Japan as he wanted to at the time, he certainly would have participated in the war effort in some like manner. His life would have turned out so differently. He looked at his teenage daughter Junko, noting with some sadness that she was the same age now as the young women who pasted paper and sewed the balloons were then. He couldn't help but acknowledge Junko was also the same age as the youths killed in Bly.

Takeshita returned to Michigan and wrote letters to Inouye and Yoshiko Hisaga, a schoolteacher whose students had been conscripted to manufacture balloons. He'd seen her on television talking about the hardships of the war. In his letter, he listed the names of the six people killed in Bly. "When you talk about balloon bombs in the future," he continued, "could you please pray for these innocents?"[10]

The names affected Hisaga and her former students greatly. "Until then although I'd heard of the victims, [they] still seemed distant," stated one woman, then in her late fifties. "But once I learned their names and ages, I started to feel a sense of guilt about what we had done." Said another, "As if scales had fallen away from my eyes, I suddenly learned what I had been wondering for decades . . . the effects of our actions."[11] Hisaga gathered her students, and the women folded one thousand paper cranes, a Japanese symbol of peace, healing, and forgiveness. These Takeshita delivered to Ed Patzke and Dottie (Patzke) McGinnis in Bly in 1987. The professor translated Hisaga's letter to the families: "We participated in the building of weapons used to kill people without understanding much beyond the knowledge that America was our adversary in a war. To think that the weapon we made took your lives as you were out on a picnic! We are overwhelmed with deep sorrow."[12]

"The horror of war always comes to those who are weakest," said Toshiko Inouye. "And even if the suffering is different, everyone still suffers."[13]

Three decades after the war, Tetsuko Tanaka found a book in her parents' home. As a young girl in 1944, days before she departed for the factory in Kokura where she would work herself nearly to death assembling the balloons, she had taken a lock of her hair, clippings of her nails, and her last will and testament and pressed them into the book. "I'll go to the Kokura Arsenal and do my best for the sake of the nation," the eighteen-year-old student had written. Certain she would never return home, she asked her parents to forgive her for dying early.[14]

"Finding that will was a terrible embarrassment," the adult Tanaka admitted. She felt no sentimentality for the war. Once she learned about the children killed in Bly, dwelling on her own suffering and remembering her blind, youthful devotion seemed indecent. She threw the book away. "I made those weapons. Until then [learning about the Bly deaths], I had felt only that our youth had been stolen from us, and that I'd missed my chance to study. I thought we were victims of the war."[15]

In 1995, on the fiftieth anniversary of the tragedy, Yoshiko Hisaga arranged to have six cherry trees planted in a circle around the Mitchell monument. She hoped the gift would help make the area "a place where people could gather to contemplate the importance of peace and understanding among peoples across nations."[16] The trees were planted during a monument rededication ceremony attended by five hundred people. Betty Patzke stood near the stone monument at the spot where her brother and sister died half a century earlier and accepted the gift on behalf of the people of Bly: "I want to thank the Japanese. . . . They've showed that they are really sorry and had a desire to be forgiven."[17]

Ill-suited to the high alpine environment, the cherry trees began wilting within just a couple of years. The soil and climate of Gearhart Mountain simply couldn't sustain their growth. Just a few feet from the monument, however, stands a native ponderosa pine, well over a century old and 125 feet tall, that bears on its trunk the scars of a bomb blast from a day many years before when five unknowing children and their chaperone saw something interesting on the ground and gathered for a look. The tree thrives despite its wounds. The shrapnel has long since been removed.

FIG. 31. Ted Durment of Weyerhaeuser Timber Co. points to gouges in a ponderosa pine left by the Bly explosion. U.S. Forest Service, Fremont–Winema National Forests

# Appendix

MAPS AND TABLE OF FU-GO INCIDENTS, 1944–1945

The first attempt at creating a comprehensive list of North American balloon incidents was made by the Western Defense Command (WDC) in early 1945, while the war and the balloon attack were still going on. The WDC produced a complete list in August 1945 that included the date and location of all sightings and recoveries to the end of the war. Working from that master list in 1968, a U.S. Air Force officer named Cornelius Conley reviewed each citation and created the format used in the list below: incident number, location, date, and remarks. In the 1970s, two other historians, Robert Mikesh and Bert Webber, revised the list by examining and cross-referencing original balloon incident reports. The list that follows represents a compendium of these scholars' efforts, and the author acknowledges their contributions.

The most difficult question to answer regarding the Japanese balloon bomb attack is also the most basic: How many balloons arrived in North America? The WDC, Conley, and Mikesh lists all put the figure at 285 (or 286 if one counts the Yerington balloon listed below as incident number 1a). Webber counts 342 balloon arrivals, a number that includes unconfirmed reports, incidents that occurred during the war but apparently were not reported until afterward (and therefore did not make the official WDC list), and sightings and recoveries that may have been related to known incidents already on the official list. Conley, Mikesh, and Webber also tracked down numerous news reports of balloons discovered after the end of the war, one as late as 1968. Although the exact total will never be known, it seems certain the number of Japanese balloon arrivals equals or perhaps even surpasses 350.

Readers should note that because the maps included here are limited in geographic scope, a handful of outlying balloon incidents, such as Kailua, Hawaii, and Farmington, Michigan, for example, do not appear. Readers should also be aware that all locations are approximate. The process of identifying and recording balloon locations in 1944 and 1945 was often conducted by individuals, some trained in balloon recovery procedures and some not, and by a diverse array of organizations including the WDC, FBI, U.S. Forest Service, Royal Canadian Mounted Police, U.S. Coast Guard, Alaska Territorial Guard, and numerous local sheriff's and police departments. The lack of standardized recording procedures left discretion to local responders, so recoveries might have been named for whatever town, county, forest, mountain, island, river, lake, or other local landmark the responders felt best identified the incident location. Occasionally when adding an incident to its master list, the WDC subsequently changed the location to the nearest town, further obscuring the balloon's true point of recovery. The list that follows may be taken as the most complete possible record given the many challenges in producing an accurate census of balloons. The list does not include the approximately one dozen balloons discovered after the end of the war.

Readers will notice several locations experienced multiple balloon incidents, often in the same week or even on the same day. In certain instances—an incendiary bomb and balloon envelope discovered miles apart but in the same township, for example—the Western Defense Command typically listed such recoveries as separate events, even when the evidence pointed to a single Japanese balloon. In some cases the WDC assigned different incident numbers to an eyewitness sighting of a balloon and the later physical recovery of evidence from what was likely the same balloon. Holy Cross, Alaska (incidents number 7 and number 23) is an example of this pattern. The list included here preserves such distinctions.

In the list below, "envelope" refers to an intact paper sphere and gas relief valve, "envelope fragment" to a swatch or swatches of paper only (no valve), "shroud lines" to the manila ropes that connected the envelope's suspension skirt to the payload, "rigging" to the shroud lines, rubber shock cord, and square metal bracket that attached to payload, and "chandelier" to the altitude control mechanism including battery, altimeters, fuses, blowout plugs, aluminum ballast rings, demolition block, sandbags, and bombs. "Complete device" refers to a largely intact vehicle that includes all pertinent equipment but may be lacking previously released sandbags or bombs.

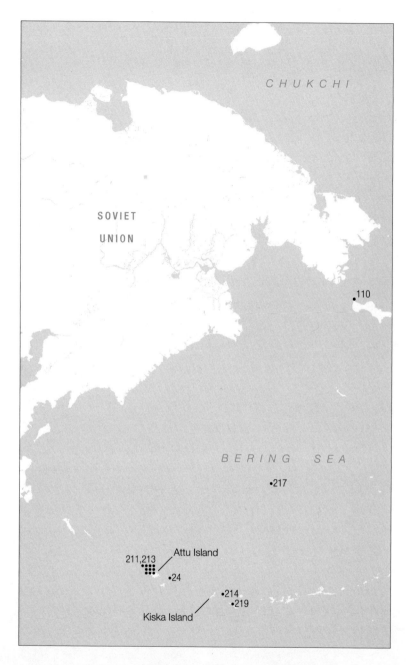

MAP 1: *Fu-go* incidents, Alaska, 1944-45. Cartographer: Dixon Jones

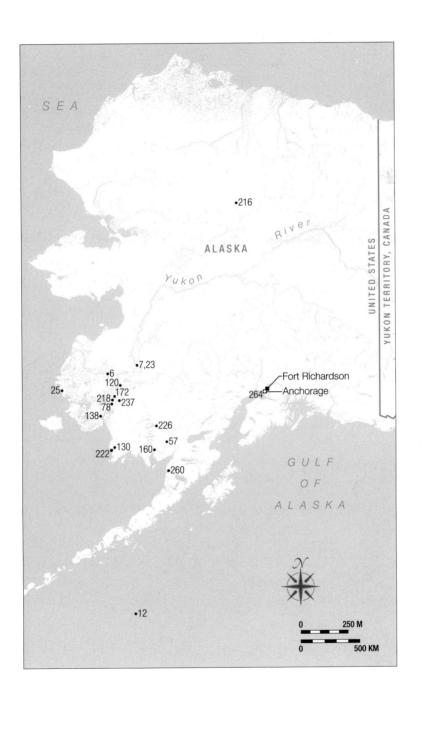

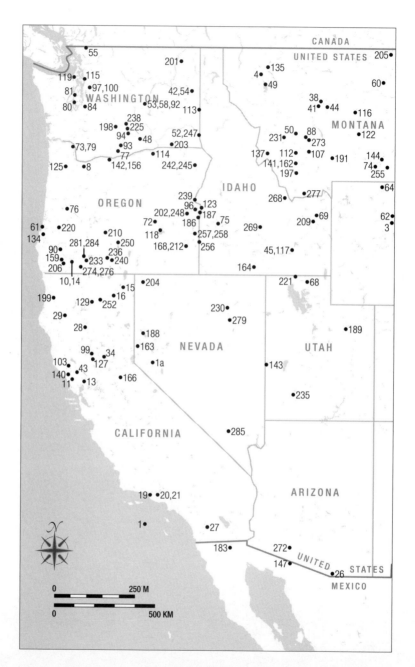

MAP 2: *Fu-go* incidents, United States, 1944–45. Cartographer: Dixon Jones

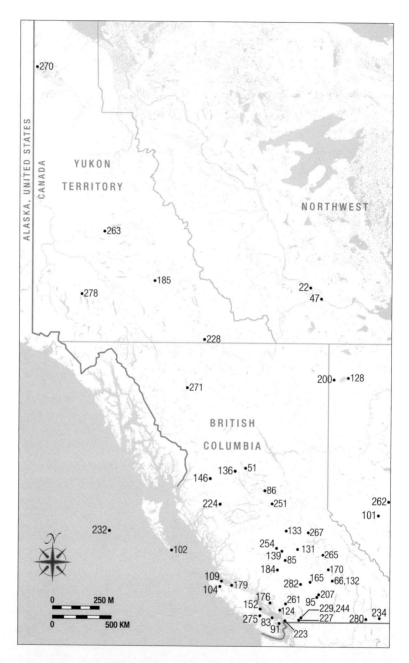

MAP 3: *Fu-go* incidents, Canada, 1944–45. Cartographer: Dixon Jones

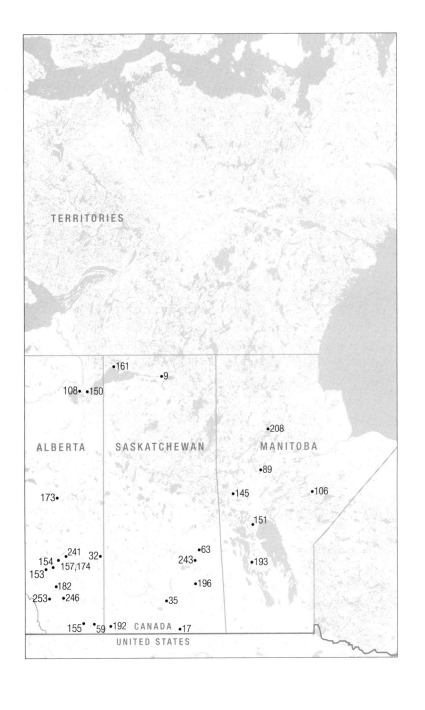

TERRITORIES

•161
•9
108• •150

•208

ALBERTA    SASKATCHEWAN    MANITOBA

•89

173•    •145    •106

•151

•63
241    32•    243•
154 •157,174
153•
•182                •196
253• •246
35

155• •59 •192 CANADA •17
UNITED STATES

## TABLE 1: *Fu-go* incidents, 1944–45

| NO. | LOCATION | DATE | REMARKS |
|---|---|---|---|
| 1 | San Pedro, California | 11/4/44 | Rubber balloon in Pacific Ocean. Envelope, rigging, and ballast mechanism recovered. |
| 1a | Yerington, Nevada | 11/9/44 | Rubber balloon identical to San Pedro device, not reported until June 1945. |
| 2 | Kailua, Hawaii | 11/14/44 | Paper envelope, rigging, and chandelier recovered at sea by U.S. Coast Guard. |
| 3 | Thermopolis, Wyoming | 12/6/44 | Fragments of 15-kg high-explosive bomb recovered. Incendiary explosions and airborne balloon observed by multiple witnesses, but not recovered. |
| 4 | Kalispell, Montana | 12/11/44 | Envelope and rigging recovered. Balloon thought to have landed in mid-November. |
| 5 | Manderson, Wyoming | 12/19/44 | Envelope fragment 3 by 4 ft. Possibly part of Thermopolis device (see incident #3). |
| 6 | Marshall, Alaska | 12/23/44 | Envelope, chandelier, and 2 sandbags. |
| 7 | Holy Cross, Alaska | 12/24/44 | Envelope sighted in trees, recovered 1/21/45. See incident #23. |

| 8 | Estacada, Oregon | 12/31/44 | Envelope, rigging, part of chandelier. |
| 9 | Stony Rapids, Saskatchewan | 1/1/45 | Several fragments of envelope. |
| 10 | Medford, Oregon | 1/4/45 | Explosion from incendiary bomb observed by 2 witnesses. Debris from device recovered. See incident #14. |
| 11 | Sebastopol, California | 1/4/45 | Tattered envelope, suspension skirt, and chandelier including 4 incendiary bombs crashed to earth in front of witnesses. See incident #13. |
| 12 | At sea: 52:5 N, 160:00 W | 1/5/45 | Balloon shot down by merchant vessel southwest of Kodiak Island, Alaska, entire apparatus lost to ocean bottom. |
| 13 | Napa, California | 1/5/45 | Envelope fragments recovered, likely from incident #11. |
| 14 | Medford, Oregon | 1/7/45 | Fragments of exploded incendiary device recovered, likely part of incident #10. |
| 15 | Alturas, California | 1/10/45 | Balloon forced down by F6F Hellcat aircraft. Intact envelope reinflated and studied for radar reflective properties. See incident #16. |

| 16 | Adin, California | 1/10/45 | Balloon reported by eyewitnesses, likely same device as incident #15. |
| 17 | Minton, Saskatchewan | 1/12/45 | Balloon impacted ground and released sandbags, incendiary bomb, and battery box, then re-ascended and drifted away, not to be recovered. |
| 18 | Lame Deer, Montana | 1/13/45 | Envelope and shroud lines. |
| 19 | Ventura, California | 1/15/45 | High-explosive bomb detonated upon contact with ground. |
| 20 | Moorpark, California | 1/15/45 | Airborne balloon observed 15 miles east of Ventura, likely same device in incident #19. |
| 21 | Moorpark, California | 1/17/45 | Envelope and rigging recovered 23 miles east of Ventura. Incidents #19, #20, and #21 likely same device. |
| 22 | Fort Simpson, Northwest Territories | 1/19/45 | Envelope, rigging, and some parts of chandelier. |
| 23 | Holy Cross, Alaska | 1/21/45 | Envelope, rigging, chandelier, and 1 sandbag recovered. Same device as incident #7. |
| 24 | Shemya, Alaska | 1/25/45 | Balloon shot down by fighter plane at 28,000 ft., landed in ocean and not recovered. |

| 25 | Kashunuk, Alaska | 1/30/45 | Envelope fragment. |
|----|----|----|----|
| 26 | Nogales, Arizona | 1/31/45 | Envelope fragment. |
| 27 | Julian, California | 1/31/45 | Complete (but badly smashed) device recovered. |
| 28 | Red Bluff, California | 2/1/45 | Envelope and rigging. |
| 29 | Hayfork, California | 2/1/45 | Complete device with both intact and detonated bombs recovered. |
| 30 | Laurens, Iowa | 2/2/45 | Envelope, rigging, and chandelier. |
| 31 | Schuyler, Nebraska | 2/2/45 | Envelope fragment with charred edges, likely from detonation of demolition block. |
| 32 | Provost, Alberta | 2/7/45 | Envelope, rigging, and chandelier. |
| 33 | Newcastle, Wyoming | 2/8/45 | Envelope and rigging. |
| 34 | Camp Beale, California | 2/8/45 | Severely damaged envelope, rigging, and parts of chandelier including 33 unexploded blowout plugs. |
| 35 | Moose Jaw, Saskatchewan | 2/9/45 | Envelope and rigging. |
| 36 | Lodge Grass, Montana | 2/9/45 | Envelope fragment. |
| 37 | Hardin, Montana | 2/12/45 | Envelope, shroud lines, and fragments of exploded bomb recovered. |

| 38 | Riverdale, Montana | 2/12/45 | 3 exploded incendiary bombs recovered. |
|---|---|---|---|
| 39 | Burwell, Nebraska | 2/12/45 | Tattered envelope, shroud lines, parts of chandelier, and 2 incendiary bombs. |
| 40 | Nowlin, South Dakota | 2/12/45 | 1 sandbag and debris from 2 detonated incendiary bombs. |
| 41 | Cascade, Montana | 2/12/45 | Bomb debris with strong scent of ammonia recovered. |
| 42 | Spokane, Washington | 2/12/45 | 2 unexploded incendiary bombs recovered. See incident #54. |
| 43 | Calistoga, California | 2/23/45 | Balloon shot down by P-38 fighter plane. Envelope fragment recovered. Listed out of sequence by WDC for unknown reason. |
| 44 | Eden, Montana | 2/13/45 | Envelope fragment and shroud lines. |
| 45 | American Falls, Idaho | 2/13/45 | Envelope fragment and shroud lines. |
| 46 | Hardin, Montana | 2/13/45 | Valve and shroud lines. |
| 47 | Marie River, Northwest Territories | 2/13/45 | Envelope fragment. |
| 48 | Prosser, Washington | 2/15/45 | Envelope, rigging, and parts of chandelier. |
| 49 | Flathead Lake, Montana | 2/17/45 | Envelope fragment 50 ft. square with blue tape over seams. |

| | | | |
|---|---|---|---|
| 50 | Deer Lodge, Montana | 2/18/45 | 2 fragments of envelope. |
| 51 | Takla Lake, British Columbia | 2/19/45 | Partially inflated envelope, rigging, and parts of chandelier. |
| 52 | Asotin, Washington | 2/20/45 | Envelope fragments and shroud lines. |
| 53 | Ephrata, Washington | 2/21/45 | 3 sandbags dropped when balloon impacted ground. Device re-ascended and was not recovered. See incident #58. |
| 54 | Spokane, Washington | 2/21/45 | 1 incendiary and 1 high-explosive bomb recovered. Possibly a duplicate report of incident #42. |
| 55 | Sumas, Washington | 2/21/45 | Balloon shot down by Canadian Air Force in British Columbia, landed on Washington side of border. |
| 56 | Ashley, North Dakota | 2/22/45 | Envelope and shroud lines. |
| 57 | Ekwok, Alaska | 2/22/45 | Envelope fragments and battery box. |
| 58 | Ephrata, Washington | 2/22/45 | 3 sandbags recovered. Likely a duplicate report of incident #53. |
| 59 | Manyberries, Alberta | 2/22/45 | Envelope, rigging, and parts of chandelier including 5 unexploded blowout plugs. |
| 60 | Hays, Montana | 2/22/45 | Complete device recovered. |

| 61 | North Bend, Oregon | 2/22/45 | Balloon shot down by fighter plane at 12,000 ft. Envelope and shroud lines recovered. |
| 62 | Kirby, Wyoming | 2/22/45 | Envelope, rigging, and parts of chandelier. |
| 63 | Porcupine Plains, Saskatchewan | 2/22/45 | Complete device recovered. |
| 64 | Powell, Wyoming | 2/22/45 | Balloon observed exploding in air. Complete device recovered. |
| 65 | Glendo, Wyoming | 2/22/45 | Complete device recovered. |
| 66 | Chase, British Columbia | 2/22/45 | Envelope fragment. |
| 67 | Ellsworth, Nebraska | 2/22/45 | Valve and shroud lines. |
| 68 | Tremonton, Utah | 2/23/45 | Complete device recovered. |
| 69 | Rigby, Idaho | 2/23/45 | Envelope and rigging. See incident #209. |
| 70 | Bigelow, Kansas | 2/23/45 | Complete device recovered. |
| 71 | Grand Rapids, Michigan | 2/23/45 | Complete device recovered. |
| 72 | Burns, Oregon | 2/23/45 | Complete device recovered. |
| 73 | Deer Island, Oregon | 2/23/45 | Airborne balloon observed exploding, envelope fragment recovered. See incident #79. |
| 74 | Boyd, Montana | 2/23/45 | Complete device recovered. |
| 75 | Boise, Idaho | 2/25/45 | Complete device recovered. |

| 76 | Eugene, Oregon | 2/26/45 | Envelope fragment and valve. |
| 77 | Goldendale, Washington | 2/27/45 | Complete device recovered. |
| 78 | Bethel, Alaska | 2/27/45 | Burned envelope recovered. |
| 79 | Deer Island, Oregon | 2/27/45 | Envelope fragment, likely from same device in incident #73. |
| 80 | Lakebay, Washington | 2/28/45 | Envelope fragment and parts of chandelier. |
| 81 | Vaughn, Washington | 2/28/45 | Envelope fragment. |
| 82 | Holstein, Iowa | 2/28/45 | Incendiary bomb debris. |
| 83 | Nanaimo, British Columbia | 3/3/45 | Complete device including 1 incendiary bomb recovered. |
| 84 | Puyallup, Washington | 3/3/45 | Envelope fragment. |
| 85 | Big Creek, British Columbia | 3/4/45 | Complete device including 1 high-explosive bomb. |
| 86 | Stuart Lake, British Columbia | 3/5/45 | Envelope fragment. |
| 87 | Buffalo, South Dakota | 3/6/45 | Envelope fragment and shroud lines. |
| 88 | Bernice, Montana | 3/10/45 | Complete device recovered. |
| 89 | Nelson House, Manitoba | 3/10/45 | Debris from detonated high-explosive bomb. |

| 90 | Wolf Creek, Oregon | 3/10/45 | Envelope fragment. |
|----|----|----|----|
| 91 | Galiano Island, British Columbia | 3/10/45 | Balloon shot down by Canadian Air Force. |
| 92 | Ephrata, Washington | 3/10/45 | Complete device including 49 unexploded blowout plugs and 1 sandbag. |
| 93 | Satus Pass, Washington | 3/10/45 | Complete device recovered. |
| 94 | Toppenish, Washington | 3/10/45 | Envelope exploded when contacting electric transmission lines, complete device recovered. Explosion temporarily cut off power to Hanford Engineer Works. |
| 95 | Nicola, British Columbia | 3/10/45 | Envelope and one high-explosive bomb. |
| 96 | Vale, Oregon | 3/10/45 | Envelope fragment and shroud lines. |
| 97 | Cold Creek, Washington | 3/10/45 | Envelope, parts of chandelier, and 2 incendiary bombs. See incident #238. |
| 98 | Hammond, Montana | 3/11/45 | Envelope and shroud lines. |
| 99 | Meridian, California | 3/11/45 | Envelope fragment. |
| 100 | Cold Creek, Washington | 3/11/45 | Balloon shot down by military police and civilian security guards just outside Hanford Engineer Works. Complete device recovered. |
| 101 | Edson, Alberta | 3/11/45 | Complete device recovered. |

| 102 | Kunghit Island, British Columbia | 3/11/45 | Complete device recovered. |
| 103 | West Cloverdale, California | 3/12/45 | Envelope fragment. See incident #140. |
| 104 | Coal Harbour, British Columbia | 3/12/45 | Balloon forced down by Canadian Air Force plane. |
| 105 | At sea: 30:18 N, 132:52 W | 3/12/45 | Complete device recovered by vessel. |
| 106 | Oxford House, Manitoba | 3/12/45 | Envelope, rigging, parts of chandelier. |
| 107 | Whitehall, Montana | 3/12/45 | Complete device including 2 incendiary bombs. |
| 108 | Baril Lake, Alberta | 3/13/45 | Balloon recovered, equipment and condition not specified in official reports. |
| 109 | Port Hardy, British Columbia | 3/13/45 | 2 balloons sighted, 1 recovered. |
| 110 | Gambell, Alaska | 3/13/45 | Envelope fragment. |
| 111 | Legg, Montana | 3/13/45 | Damaged envelope, rigging, and chandelier with 36 unexploded blowout plugs. |
| 112 | Divide, Montana | 3/13/45 | Complete device with 29 unexploded blowout plugs. |
| 113 | Farmington, Washington | 3/13/45 | Envelope, shroud lines, and parts of chandelier. |
| 114 | Echo, Oregon | 3/13/45 | Complete device with 11 sandbags and 1 incendiary bomb. Archived at Smithsonian Air and Space Museum. |

| | | | |
|---|---|---|---|
| 115 | Everett, Washington | 3/13/45 | Damaged envelope, rigging, chandelier, and 1 incendiary bomb. |
| 116 | Benchland, Montana | 3/13/45 | Complete device recovered. |
| 117 | American Falls, Idaho | 3/13/45 | Envelope fragment and shroud lines. |
| 118 | Malheur Lake, Oregon | 3/13/45 | Complete device including 1 incendiary bomb. |
| 119 | Chimacum, Washington | 3/13/45 | Complete device recovered. |
| 120 | Phillips, Alaska | 3/13/45 | Envelope fragment and shroud lines. |
| 121 | Delta, Colorado | 3/13/45 | Envelope fragment and shroud lines. |
| 122 | Harlowton, Montana | 3/13/45 | Fuses, 3 sandbags, and debris from 1 detonated high-explosive bomb. |
| 123 | Ontario, Oregon | 3/13/45 | Envelope fragment, shroud lines, and parts of chandelier. |
| 124 | Gambier Island, British Columbia | 3/14/45 | Envelope fragment. |
| 125 | Yamhill, Oregon | 3/14/45 | Envelope fragment and incendiary bomb. |
| 126 | Pocahontas, Iowa | 3/14/45 | Envelope fragment and shroud lines. |
| 127 | Grimes, California | 3/14/45 | Complete device including 17 unexploded blowout plugs, 3 sandbags, 1 incendiary bomb, and 1 high-explosive bomb. |

| 128 | Hay Lake, Alberta | 3/14/45 | Parts of chandelier and 1 sandbag. |
|-----|-------------------|---------|-----------------------------------|
| 129 | Big Bend, California | 3/14/45 | Envelope fragment, valve, and shroud lines. |
| 130 | Mumtrak, Alaska | 3/15/45 | Envelope and shroud lines. |
| 131 | Williams Lake, British Columbia | 3/15/45 | Envelope. |
| 132 | Chase, British Columbia | 3/15/45 | Damaged envelope, rigging, and parts of chandelier. |
| 133 | Baker Creek, British Columbia | 3/15/45 | 2 small envelope fragments. |
| 134 | Coquille, Oregon | 3/15/45 | Envelope fragment. |
| 135 | Coram, Montana | 3/16/45 | Envelope fragment. |
| 136 | Fort Babine, British Columbia | 3/17/45 | Envelope fragments and valve. |
| 137 | Sula, Montana | 3/17/45 | Bomb debris, type not recorded. |
| 138 | Kinak, Alaska | 3/18/45 | 2 explosions reported, envelope fragment recovered. |
| 139 | Alexis Creek, British Columbia | 3/18/45 | Envelope fragment. |
| 140 | Guerneville, California | 3/18/45 | Envelope fragment, possible part of device in incident #103. |
| 141 | Glen, Montana | 3/18/45 | 1 incendiary bomb. |
| 142 | The Dalles, Oregon | 3/18/45 | Debris from 1 incendiary bomb. See incident #156. |
| 143 | Garrison, Utah | 3/18/45 | Complete device including 56 unexploded blowout plugs and 5 sandbags. |

| 144 | Laurel, Montana | 3/18/45 | Envelope and shroud lines. |
| 145 | Marie Lake, Manitoba | 3/19/45 | Complete device recovered. |
| 146 | Cedarvale, British Columbia | 3/19/45 | Envelope. |
| 147 | Sonora, Mexico | 3/19/45 | Envelope and shroud lines, possibly shot down by U.S. fighter plane. |
| 148 | Timnath, Colorado | 3/20/45 | 1 unexploded incendiary bomb and debris from 1 detonated high-explosive bomb. |
| 149 | Chadron, Nebraska | 3/20/45 | Complete device recovered. |
| 150 | Fort Chipewyan, Alberta | 3/20/45 | Complete device recovered. |
| 151 | Williams Lake, Manitoba | 3/20/45 | Complete device including 5 sandbags. |
| 152 | Denman Island, British Columbia | 3/20/45 | Complete device including 2 unexploded incendiary bombs. |
| 153 | Olds, Alberta | 3/20/45 | Debris from 1 exploded incendiary bomb recovered. Possibly related to incidents #154, #157, and #174. |
| 154 | Wimborne, Alberta | 3/20/45 | Unidentified bomb debris. See incidents #153, #157, and #174. |
| 155 | Foremost, Alberta | 3/20/45 | Envelope, rigging, and parts of chandelier. |

| 156 | The Dalles, Oregon | 3/20/45 | Debris from at least 1 exploded incendiary bomb. Possibly related to incident #142. |
| 157 | Delburne, Alberta | 3/20/45 | Envelope, shroud lines, and 1 high-explosive bomb recovered. See incidents #153, #154, and #174. |
| 158 | Gillette, Wyoming | 3/21/45 | Envelope fragment. |
| 159 | Murphy, Oregon | 3/21/45 | Envelope fragment. See incident #206. |
| 160 | Dillingham, Alaska | 3/21/45 | Envelope and one sandbag. |
| 161 | Camsell Portage, Saskatchewan | 3/21/45 | Complete device including 1 incendiary bomb. |
| 162 | Glen, Montana | 3/21/45 | Witness reported falling object and explosion. No debris, but 1 unexploded incendiary bomb recovered. |
| 163 | Reno, Nevada | 3/22/45 | Balloon shot down by P-63 fighter plane. Complete but damaged device including 27 unexploded blowout plugs, 1 sandbag, and 2 incendiary bombs. |
| 164 | Rogerson, Idaho | 3/22/45 | Complete device recovered. |
| 165 | Ashcroft, British Columbia | 3/22/45 | Balloon reportedly found, no details listed in report. |
| 166 | Volcano, California | 3/22/45 | Complete device including 20 unexploded blowout plugs. |

| 167 | Basin, Wyoming | 3/22/45 | Envelope fragment. |
| 168 | Rome, Oregon | 3/22/45 | Complete device recovered. |
| 169 | Ree Heights, South Dakota | 3/22/45 | Complete device recovered. See incident #215. |
| 170 | Barrier Lake, British Columbia | 3/23/45 | Balloon recovered, no information recorded. |
| 171 | Desdemona, Texas | 3/23/45 | Complete device including 2 intact high-explosive bombs. Only known device to feature 2 such bombs. See incident #175. |
| 172 | Bethel, Alaska | 3/23/45 | Valve recovered. |
| 173 | Athabasca, Alberta | 3/23/45 | Balloon reported, no details available. |
| 174 | Delburne, Alberta | 3/23/45 | Envelope fragments and shroud lines. See incidents #153, #154, and #157. |
| 175 | Desdemona, Texas | 3/23/45 | Unidentified bomb debris, likely related to incident #171. |
| 176 | Britain River, British Columbia | 3/24/45 | Envelope fragment. |
| 177 | Osceola, Nebraska | 3/24/45 | Envelope and shroud lines. |
| 178 | Woodson, Texas | 3/24/45 | Envelope fragment and shroud lines. |
| 179 | Hanson Island, British Columbia | 3/25/45 | Envelope fragment. |
| 180 | Farmington, Michigan | 3/25/45 | Incendiary bomb. |
| 181 | Kadoka, South Dakota | 3/26/45 | Several small envelope fragments. |

| 182 | Strathmore, Alberta | 3/28/45 | Envelope fragment and valve. |
| 183 | Baja California, Mexico | 3/28/45 | Balloon shot down by U.S. fighter plane over Imperial Valley, California. Device landed in Mexico, no equipment recovered. |
| 184 | Whitewater, British Columbia | 3/28/45 | Envelope, 12 sandbags, and 2 incendiary bombs. |
| 185 | Canol Road, Yukon Territory | 3/29/45 | Debris from detonated high-explosive bomb. |
| 186 | Adrian, Oregon | 3/29/45 | High-explosive bomb recovered. See incident #187. |
| 187 | Nyssa, Oregon | 3/29/45 | 2 sandbags and 1 high-explosive bomb, likely a duplicate report of incident #186. |
| 188 | Pyramid Lake, Nevada | 3/29/45 | Complete device including 23 unexploded blowout plugs and 4 sandbags. |
| 189 | Duchesne, Utah | 3/30/45 | Complete device recovered. |
| 190 | Grafton, North Dakota | 3/30/45 | Complete device recovered. |
| 191 | Bozeman, Montana | 3/30/45 | Complete device including 4 damaged sandbags. |
| 192 | Consul, Saskatchewan | 3/30/45 | Envelope and 1 high-explosive bomb. |
| 193 | Waterhen Lake, Manitoba | 3/30/45 | Envelope. |
| 194 | Red Elm, South Dakota | 3/30/45 | Complete device recovered. |

| 195 | Marcus, South Dakota | 3/31/45 | Debris from high-explosive bomb. |
| 196 | Ituna, Saskatchewan | 3/31/45 | Envelope. |
| 197 | Dillon, Montana | 4/1/45 | Envelope fragments, valve, and shroud lines. |
| 198 | Tampico, Washington | 4/1/45 | Complete device including 1 incendiary bomb. |
| 199 | Hoopa Reservation, California | 4/1/45 | Complete device recovered. |
| 200 | Hay River, Alberta | 4/1/45 | Complete device including 7 sandbags and 2 incendiary bombs. |
| 201 | Colville, Washington | 4/1/45 | Envelope and shroud lines. |
| 202 | Harper, Oregon | 4/3/45 | Envelope fragments, valve, rigging, and parts of chandelier. |
| 203 | Walla Walla, Washington | 4/3/45 | Complete device including 4 unexploded blowout plugs. |
| 204 | Massacre Lake, Nevada | 4/5/45 | Complete device recovered. |
| 205 | Turner, Montana | 4/6/45 | Envelope. |
| 206 | Provolt, Oregon | 4/7/45 | Envelope fragments. Possibly related to incident #159. |
| 207 | Merritt, British Columbia | 4/8/45 | Complete device including 1 high-explosive bomb. |
| 208 | Southern Indian Lake, Manitoba | 4/10/45 | Envelope and other unspecified equipment. |

| 209 | Plane, Idaho | 4/10/45 | Sandbag and attaching hook, possibly related to incident #69. |
| 210 | Bald Mountain, Oregon | 4/10/45 | Complete device including 2 sandbags, 1 high-explosive bomb, and 4 incendiary bombs. |
| 211 | Attu Island, Alaska | 4/12/45 | Balloon shot down by fighter plane, nothing recovered. |
| 212 | Rome, Oregon | 4/12/45 | Complete device recovered. |
| 213 | Attu Island, Alaska | 4/13/45 | 9 balloons shot down over Massacre Bay by P-38 aircraft from the Eleventh Air Force. |
| 214 | Tanaga Island, Alaska | 4/13/45 | Balloon observed by C-45 aircraft. Location also listed as Little Sitkin Island, which is 150 miles east of Tanaga Island. |
| 215 | Wolsey, South Dakota | 4/13/45 | Envelope fragment, possibly related to incident #169. |
| 216 | Midas Creek, Alaska | 4/15/45 | Complete device recovered. |
| 217 | At sea: 52:46 N, 178:30 W | 4/15/45 | Balloon sank 750 miles northeast of Attu Island in Bering Sea. |
| 218 | Bethel, Alaska | 4/15/45 | 2 aneroid boxes from unknown devices recovered. |
| 219 | Amchitka Island, Alaska | 4/15/45 | Complete device recovered. |

| | | | |
|---|---|---|---|
| 220 | Tyee, Oregon | 4/15/45 | Envelope fragment. |
| 221 | Snowville, Utah | 4/16/45 | Envelope fragment. |
| 222 | Platinum, Alaska | 4/16/45 | Long-grounded complete device found covered in snow and ice. |
| 223 | Boundary Bay, British Columbia | 4/17/45 | Complete device including 1 incendiary bomb and 1 high-explosive bomb. |
| 224 | Morice Lake, British Columbia | 4/17/45 | Complete device including 22 sandbags and 2 incendiary bombs. |
| 225 | Wapato, Washington | 4/19/45 | Envelope fragment. |
| 226 | Tikchik Lake, Alaska | 4/20/45 | Complete device recovered. |
| 227 | Vedder Mountain, British Columbia | 4/20/45 | Balloon recovered, no details available. |
| 228 | Watson Lake, Yukon Territory | 4/20/45 | Unspecified balloon parts recovered. |
| 229 | Chilliwack, British Columbia | 4/20/45 | Envelope and shroud lines. |
| 230 | Elko, Nevada | 4/21/45 | Envelope fragment and valve. |
| 231 | Philipsburg, Montana | 4/21/45 | Envelope. |
| 232 | At sea: 53:3 N, 135:52 W | 4/23/45 | Envelope of rubberized silk recovered from ocean west of Queen Charlotte Islands. |
| 233 | Lake of the Woods, Oregon | 4/23/45 | Complete device recovered. See incidents #281 and #284. |

| 234 | Kitchener, British Columbia | 4/24/45 | Envelope and shroud lines. |
| 235 | Paragonah, Utah | 4/25/45 | Envelope fragment. |
| 236 | Beatty, Oregon | 4/26/45 | Envelope fragment. |
| 237 | Akiak, Alaska | 4/28/45 | Complete device including 3 unexploded blowout plugs and 2 sandbags. |
| 238 | Moxee City, Washington | 4/30/45 | Unspecified balloon parts recovered. Possibly related to incident #97. |
| 239 | Huntington, Oregon | 5/2/45 | Envelope fragments. |
| 240 | Bly, Oregon | 5/5/45 | Detonation of high-explosive bomb killed woman and 5 children on Gearhart Mountain northeast of Bly. Complete device including 8 sandbags and 4 incendiary bombs recovered. |
| 241 | Stettler, Alberta | 5/5/45 | Envelope fragments. |
| 242 | Enterprise, Oregon | 5/12/45 | Incendiary bomb. See incident #245. |
| 243 | Kelvington, Saskatchewan | 5/15/45 | Valve and parts of chandelier recovered. |
| 244 | Chilliwack, British Columbia | 5/20/45 | Complete device including 2 sandbags, 1 high-explosive bomb, and 2 incendiary bombs. |
| 245 | Enterprise, Oregon | 5/21/45 | Envelope fragments recovered. Possibly related to incident #242. |

| 246 | Milo, Alberta | 5/23/45 | Envelope fragment. |
|---|---|---|---|
| 247 | Asotin, Washington | 5/25/45 | Unspecified balloon parts recovered. |
| 248 | Harper, Oregon | 5/25/45 | Unspecified balloon parts recovered. |
| 249 | Madison, South Dakota | 5/26/45 | 1 unexploded incendiary bomb. |
| 250 | Summer Lake, Oregon | 5/26/45 | Envelope fragments, shroud lines, and parts of aluminum ballast ring. |
| 251 | Vanderhoof, British Columbia | 5/26/45 | Envelope fragment. |
| 252 | Soldier Mountain, California | 5/26/45 | Envelope fragments. |
| 253 | High River, Alberta | 5/28/45 | Damaged envelope and unspecific ballast equipment. |
| 254 | Chilanko River, British Columbia | 5/29/45 | Envelope fragments and 2 incendiary bombs recovered. |
| 255 | Pryor, Montana | 6/1/45 | Envelope fragment. |
| 256 | Jordan Valley, Oregon | 6/7/45 | Small envelope fragments. |
| 257 | Mahogany, Oregon | 6/8/45 | Parts of aluminum ballast ring and envelope fragments, 1 of which contained paper tag with Japanese characters. See incident #258. |
| 258 | Mahogany, Oregon | 6/9/45 | Envelope fragments from incident #259. |

| | | | |
|---|---|---|---|
| 259 | Collbran, Colorado | 6/12/45 | Envelope fragment. |
| 260 | Egegik, Alaska | 6/14/45 | Balloon reported grounded, no other details available. |
| 261 | Skukuma Creek, British Columbia | 6/15/45 | Envelope fragment. |
| 262 | Whitecourt, Alberta | 6/15/45 | Envelope fragments. |
| 263 | Mayo, Yukon Territory | 6/16/45 | Envelope fragments. |
| 264 | Anchorage, Alaska | 6/18/45 | Complete device including 3 sandbags, 2 incendiary bombs, and 1 high-explosive bomb. |
| 265 | Mahood Lake, British Columbia | 6/18/45 | Envelope fragments. |
| 266 | Tampico, Montana | 6/21/45 | Complete device recovered. |
| 267 | Yank, British Columbia | 6/23/45 | Envelope fragments. |
| 268 | Gilmore, Idaho | 6/24/45 | Envelope and shroud lines. |
| 269 | Hailey, Idaho | 6/24/45 | Envelope, shroud lines, and unspecified ballast equipment. |
| 270 | Old Crow, Yukon Territory | 6/24/45 | Envelope fragments. |
| 271 | Dease Lake, British Columbia | 6/27/45 | Envelope and 3 incendiary bombs, 1 intact, 2 exploded. |
| 272 | Ajo, Arizona | 7/2/45 | Damaged envelope and shroud lines. |

| 273 | Boulder, Montana | 7/4/45 | Envelope fragment. |
| 274 | Lake Hyatt, Oregon | 7/5/45 | Envelope, shroud lines, and 1 unexploded incendiary bomb. See incident #276. |
| 275 | Alberni, British Columbia | 7/5/45 | Complete device including 1 incendiary bomb and 1 high-explosive bomb. |
| 276 | Lake Hyatt, Oregon | 7/5/45 | Duplicate report of incident #274, reason for duplication unknown. |
| 277 | Monida, Montana | 7/6/45 | Envelope and shroud lines. |
| 278 | Aishihik, Yukon Territory | 7/11/45 | Complete device recovered. |
| 279 | Jiggs, Nevada | 7/12/45 | Envelope, shroud lines, aneroids, and other unspecified parts. |
| 280 | Salmo, British Columbia | 7/16/45 | Envelope fragments and shroud lines. |
| 281 | Mount Pitt, Oregon | 7/18/45 | Incendiary bomb recovered, possibly dropped by balloon in incident #233. See also incident #284. Location also known as Mount McLoughlin. |

| 282 | Lillooet, British Columbia | 7/19/45 | Envelope and shroud lines. |
| 283 | At sea: 430 miles east-southeast of Tokyo | 7/19/45 | Balloon shot down by U.S. Navy aircraft, not recovered. |
| 284 | Mount Pitt, Oregon | 7/20/45 | Incendiary bomb recovered. Possibly related to incidents #233 and #281. |
| 285 | Indian Springs, Nevada | 7/20/45 | Envelope and shroud lines. |

# Notes

INTRODUCTION

1. Juillerat, "Mitchell Monument," 109–12; Webber, *Retaliation*, 94. The accounts offered by the two eyewitnesses, Mitchell and Barnhouse, differ in places. Mitchell stated he had stepped out of the car and was collecting the lunches at the moment of the explosion, while Barnhouse remembered Mitchell had just stopped the car and hadn't yet gotten out. Any discrepancies may be explained by the traumatic nature of the incident and the fact that neither man was allowed by authorities to discuss the matter publicly until weeks later, by which time their memories certainly diverged, as is common among witnesses to the same event. Additionally, the numerous published articles on the incident, both contemporary and historical, take further liberties with the narrative, making it nearly impossible to know the exact chain of events. Some reports note Elsie (whose name is sometimes spelled Elyse) explicitly mentioned "a balloon" when calling out to her husband—this version is supported by a later statement from Mitchell himself—while others record that she did not identify the object in any way before the explosion. Other accounts state it was one of the children, not Elsie, who called out prior to the blast. Reports further state that one or more of the children alternately kicked, pulled, tugged, dragged, dropped, or otherwise disturbed the balloon, its lines, or the explosive device itself. The account provided here draws on many sources and, minute variations aside, may be assumed to be a faithful reconstruction of events. The two most complete collections of primary source material on the Bly incident are (1) Mitchell Collection, Bly Ranger District,

Fremont National Forest, Bly OR; and (2) Box 36, Record Group 95: Records of the U.S. Forest Service, Region 6, Portland OR, Historical Collection ca. 1902–85 (hereafter cited as RG 95), National Archives and Records Administration, Seattle (hereafter cited as NARA-Seattle). See, in particular, Merle S. Lowden, "Statement of Accident," 7 May 1945; F. H. Armstrong, "Memorandum for Forest Supervisor," 6 May 1945; Richard R. Barnhouse, "Statement," 5 May 1945, Box 36 RG 95, NARA-Seattle.

2. Mikesh, *Japan's World War II*, 40–54, 58–61, 69–77. Mikesh's primary source for the technical information is George E. Weidner, "Technical and Technological Survey, Japanese Bombing Balloons," report prepared for Chief of Engineers, War Department, U.S. Army, 2 January 1946, Record Group 24-C-1, File 8872-1, Library and Archives Canada (hereafter cited as LAC). Although the Weidner report is a primary document and Mikesh secondary, the latter will be more accessible to readers, and therefore this book cites that work wherever possible.

3. "Blast Kills 6," *Klamath Falls (OR) Herald and News*, 7 May 1945, 1.

4. Elsie Mitchell death certificate, 7 May 1945, Box 14, Bert Webber Papers, Hoover Institution, Stanford University (hereafter cited as BWP).

### 1. PAPER

1. Doolittle, *I Could Never Be So Lucky*, 1-13; Glines, *Doolittle Raid*, 49-78.

2. Glines, *Doolittle Raid*, 144.

3. Mercado, "Japanese Army's Noborito Research Institute," 287–89.

4. Mikesh, *Japan's World War II*, 3.

5. Lewis, "Ooishi's Observation," 362.

6. In 2003 the American Meteorological Society evaluated Ooishi's raw data using modern scientific methods. Although the study revealed several minor errors in his original analysis, many due to the limitations of the single-theodolite observing technique, the AMS largely confirmed Ooishi's overall findings. See Lewis, "Ooishi's Observation," 364–66.

7. Mikesh, *Japan's World War II*, 7.

8. Cook and Cook, *Japan at War*, 188.

9. Cook and Cook, *Japan at War*.

10. Teiji Takada, [Balloon Bomb], 46. The Takada article that appeared in *Shizen*, a popular Japanese magazine, was the first Japanese-language account of the *fu-go* campaign. Takada was a lead technician on the balloon research program at Noborito Research Institute, and his article is an invaluable firsthand source of technical information. An English translation of the article, made by Ken Suda of the Central Meteorological Observatory in Tokyo, can be found in the Bert Webber Papers at Stanford University's Hoover Institution Archives.

11. Mikesh, *Japan's World War II*, 13.

12. Cook and Cook, *Japan at War*, 188–89.

13. Mikesh, *Japan's World War II*, 11.

14. Cook and Cook, *Japan at War*, 188.

15. Eidai, *Onnatachi no Fusen Bakudan*, 100–103.

16. Eidai, *Onnatachi no Fusen Bakudan*, 104.

17. Eidai, *Onnatachi no Fusen Bakudan*, 112–13.

18. Mikesh, *Japan's World War II*, 13–15, 40.

19. Cook and Cook, *Japan at War*, 191.

20. Mikesh, *Japan's World War II*, 9–11; Webber, *Retaliation*, 102–3, 168–71.

21. R. H. Bullard, "Kalispell Paper Balloon," 8 January 1945, Box 9, Reports and Studies re: Japanese Balloons, Record Group 160: Army Service Forces, Intelligence Division, Topical File 1942–45 (hereafter cited as RG 160), National Archives and Records Administration, College Park, MD (hereafter cited as NARA).

22. R. H. Bullard, "Balloon, Japanese Paper, from Marshall, Alaska, CEE 22179," 1 February 1945, Box 6 RG 160, NARA.

23. Mikesh, *Japan's World War II*, 8–9, 14.

24. Takada, [Balloon Bomb], 68–69.

25. Takada, [Balloon Bomb], 60.

26. Webber, *Retaliation*, 171. Four former Japanese navy officers interviewed by Webber in 1974 positively identified balloon B-32 as the one

discovered off the California coast. By comparing Japanese records of the B-type launches to U.S. Navy reports (including photographs), the men concluded only this one balloon matched both sets of records.

27. Transcript of decoded telegram, 19 December 1944, Box 41, Japanese Balloons 1945, Record Group 499, Records of U.S. Army Defense Commands, World War II (hereafter cited as RG 499), NARA.

28. "AAFPOA Weekly Intelligence Summary No. 312," 18 November 1944, Box 40 RG 499, NARA. Both Yawata and Okayama are located in southern Japan, hundreds of miles from Ichinomiya and the other east coast launching sites. If these were experimental paper balloons, they may have been launched from the nearby Kokura Arsenal or another paper factory in the region.

29. "Japanese Navy Weather Service, U.S. Pacific Fleet Weekly Intelligence Report No. 2760," 10 November 1944, Box 40 RG 499, NARA.

30. Forrest Sherman to Commander Western Sea Frontier, 21 January 1945, Box 36 RG 499, NARA; R. H. Bullard, "Balloon and Appurtenances, Japanese, from Kailua, Hawaii," 15 January 1945, Box 6 RG 160, NARA.

31. Mikesh, *Japan's World War II,* 23.

2. THERMOPOLIS

1. Wade Pipkin, "Memorandum for the Officer In Charge," 5 January 1945, Box 36 RG 499, NARA; H.B. White to Commanding General, Western Defense Command, 4 January 1945, Box 41 RG 499, NARA.

2. Eldon W. Lucy, "Discovery of Japanese Balloon, Kalispell," 27 December 1944, Box 35 RG 499, NARA.

3. William H. Hammond, "Air Information," 16 December 1944, Box 35 RG 499, NARA.

4. Lucy, "Discovery of Japanese Balloon."

5. "Transcript of Telephone Conversation, Number 294," 19 December 1944, Box 35 RG 499, NARA.

6. Lucy, "Discovery of Japanese Balloon."

7. "Transcript of Telephone Conversation, Number 294."

8. "Transcript of Telephone Conversation, Number 278," 16 December 1944, Box 35 RG 499, NARA.

9. R. H. Bullard, "Kalispell Paper Balloon," 8 January 1945, Box 6 RG 160, NARA.

10. R. H. Bullard to Officer in Charge, Technical Air Intelligence Center, 9 January 1945, Box 6 RG 160, NARA.

11. R. H. Bullard to Officer in Charge, Technical Air Intelligence Center, 15 January 1945, Box 6 RG 160, NARA.

12. "Summary of Balloon Incidents," undated report, Box 37 RG 499, NARA; J. Willard Wagner to Commanding General, Western Defense Command, 6 January 1945, Box 34 RG 499, NARA; "Telephone report from Colonel Hammond, WDC," Box 7 RG 160, NARA.

13. R. H. Bullard to Officer in Charge, Technical Air Intelligence Center, 18 January 1945, Box 6 RG 160, NARA; "Parachute Found Near Sebastopol, California, January 4, 1945," Box 41 RG 499, NARA.

14. "Transcript of Telephone Conversation, Number 363," 5 January 1945, Box 36 RG 499, NARA.

15. "Transcript of Telephone Conversation, Number 363."

16. R. H. Bullard to Officer in Charge, 18 January 1945.

17. "Telephone conversation between Col. Hammond, WDC and Col. Hosterman," 6 January 1945, Box 7 RG 160, NARA.

18. R. H. Bullard to Officer in Charge, 18 January 1945.

### 3. ALTURAS

1. "Jap Balloon Found in Timber," *Libby (MT) Western News*, 14 December 1944, 1.

2. Webber, *Retaliation*, 111.

3. "Balloon Mystery," *Newsweek*, 1 January 1945, 36.

4. "What Next, Please?" *Time*, 1 January 1945, 4.

5. "Transcript of Telephone Conversation, Number 294," 19 December 1945, Box 35 RG 499, NARA.

6. William Hammond, "Publicity Given Estacada Balloon Incident," 2 January 1945, Box 34 RG 499, NARA.

7. Byron Price, "Confidential Note to Editors and Broadcasters," 4 January 1945, Box 11 RG 160, NARA.

8. W. P. Fischer to Commanding General, 2 May 1945, Box 8 RG 160, NARA.

9. "Transcript of Telephone Conversation, Number 401" 13 January 1945, Box 34 RG 499, NARA.

10. "Transcript of Telephone Conversation, Number 395," 11 January 1945, Box 34 RG 499, NARA.

11. "Technical Air Intelligence Center Report #41: Japanese Balloon and Attached Devices," May 1945, Box 6 RG 160, NARA.

12. "Technical Air Intelligence Center Report #41."

13. "Japanese Balloons: Detection, Destruction," OPD Special Supplement no. 1, 3 April 1945, Box 8 RG 160, NARA.

14. William H. Hammond, "Japanese Free Balloon Report," 26 February 1945, Box 7 RG 160, NARA.

15. "Technical Air Intelligence Center Report #41."

16. P. E. Peabody, "Japanese Aircraft Makers' Plates and Markings," Military Intelligence Report no. 78, 16 May 1945, 3, Box 40 RG 499, NARA.

17. "Japanese Balloon and Attached Devices, Report #41," report of Technical Air Intelligence Center, Anacostia, May 1945, Box 6 RG 160, NARA.

18. "Proceedings of Conference of Interested Commands and Agencies Relative to Balloon Borne Attacks against the West Coast," 17 January 1945, 1, Box 11 RG 160, NARA.

19. "Proceedings of Conference," 1.

20. "Proceedings of Conference," 3.

21. "Proceedings of Conference," 17.

22. "Proceedings of Conference," 7.

23. "Proceedings of Conference," 8.

24. "Proceedings of Conference," 40.

25. "Proceedings of Conference," 41.

26. "Proceedings of Conference," 46.

27. Eidai, *Onnatachi no Fusen Bakudan,* 220–22; Webber, *Retaliation,* 112.

28. "Tokyo Radio," transcript of radio broadcast, 17 February 1945, Box 37 RG 499, NARA.

29. "Daily Report, Foreign Radio Broadcasts," 17 November 1944, Box 7 RG 160, NARA.

30. De Mendelssohn, *Japan's Political Warfare*, 111.

31. William H. Hammond, "Japanese Propaganda concerning Secret Weapons for Use against America," 19 February 1945, Box 37 RG 499, NARA.

32. J. C. King, "Japanese Paper Balloon Bombs," Military Attache (Argentina) Report no. R-431-45, 31 May 1945, Box 8 RG 160, NARA.

4. BW

1. Avery, "Canadian Scientists, CBW Weapons," 229.

2. Avery, "Canadian Scientists, CBW Weapons," 236.

3. G. B. Reed, "Bacteriological Report on Two Japanese Balloons Recovered in Canada," Directorate of Chemical Warfare Report no. 15, 8 February 1945, Box 7 RG 160, NARA.

4. James Craigie, "Material from Japanese Balloons Discovered at Minton, Sask., and Fort Simpson, N.W.T.," Connaught Laboratories Report to C.1 Committee, 7 February 1945, 4, Box 7 RG 160, NARA.

5. Reed, "Bacteriological Report," 2.

6. Reed, "Bacteriological Report," 6.

7. Reed, "Bacteriological Report," 11.

8. "Proceedings of Conference of Interested Commands and Agencies," 43.

9. Albert Paul Krueger, "B.W. Aspects of West Coast Balloon Incidents," 31 January 1945, Box 36 RG 499, NARA.

10. O. J. Golub to W. H. Hammond, 26 January 1945, Box 36 RG 499, NARA.

11. "Japanese Balloon Exploded at Hayfork, California, 2-1-45," FBI Report 65-3734, 2 March 1945, Box 41 RG 499, NARA.

12. "Japanese Balloon Exploded at Hayfork, California."

13. Sanford Elberg to Assistant Chief of Staff, G-2, 6 February 1945, Box 36 RG 499, NARA.

14. Charles I. Lutz to Assistant Chief of Staff, G-2, 20 April 1945, Box 35 RG 499, NARA.

15. Hewlett Thebaud et al., "Coordination of Intelligence Activities in Connection with Japanese Balloons," memorandum, 6 January 1945, Box 11 RG 160, NARA.

16. "Collection and Shipment of Specimens," 21 April 1945, Box 10 RG 160, NARA.

17. Robert S. Fleming to H. I. Cole, 13 April 1945, Box 8 RG 160, NARA.

18. Charles L. Dubose to Commanding Officer, 9 January 1945, Box 37 RG 499, NARA.

19. Clayton Bissell, "Japanese Free Balloons in Mexico," memorandum, 2 February 1945, Box 11 RG 160, NARA.

20. "Resume of the Minutes of the Conference," 23 February 1945, Box 10 RG 160, NARA.

21. "Resume of the Minutes," 4.

22. Avery, "Canadian Scientists, CBW Weapons," 242.

23. "Resume of the Minutes of the Conference," 15.

24. "Resume of the Minutes," 16.

25. "Resume of the Minutes," 19.

26. "Resume of the Minutes," 21.

27. "Resume of the Minutes," 23.

28. Unsworth, "Japanese Balloon Bomb Campaign," 21-26.

29. Takada, [Balloon Bomb], 1.

30. Cook and Cook, *Japan at War*, 191.

5. ALASKA

1. Robert A. Matter to Deputy Commander, Alaskan Department, 16 January 1945, Box 38 RG 499, NARA; Frank Keim to author, e-mail communication, 21 December 2009. Keim was a schoolteacher in Marshall in the 1980s and 1990s and heard firsthand accounts of these events from Charlie Fitka and others.

2. For a comprehensive account of the formation of the ATG and the circumstances that led to its eventual disbanding, see Hendricks, "Eskimos and the Defense of Alaska," 271–95.

3. Robert A. Matter to Deputy Commander, 16 January 1945.

4. Commanding General, Alaskan Department to War Department, 17 January 1945, Box 9 RG 160, NARA.

5. "CIC Monthly Information Report, 467th CIC Detachment," 14 March 1945, Box 8 RG 160, NARA; Robert A. Matter to Deputy Commander, Alaskan Department, 8 February 1945, Box 7 RG 160, NARA.

6. McPhee, "Balloons of War," 55.

7. Chas. B. Hunt to Sidman Poole, 28 April 1945, Box 40 RG 499, NARA.

8. P. E. Peabody, "Japanese Balloon Report," 19 May 1945, Box 8 RG 160, NARA; P. E. Peabody, "Japanese Balloon Report," 2 June 1945, Box 8 RG 160, NARA; Robert A. Matter to Assistant Chief of Staff, G-2," 9 May 1945, Box 7 RG 499, NARA.

9. "Technical Air Intelligence Center Report #41," May 1945, 58, Box 6 RG 160, NARA.

10. "Technical Air Intelligence Center Report #41."

11. Log Book 1945, Series 16, Box 6, Folder 119, ATG Papers, Otto Geist Collection, Alaska and Polar Regions, Rasmuson Library, University of Alaska Fairbanks (hereafter cited as Geist Collection).

12. "Condensed Minutes of Alaskan Department Balloon Defense Meeting at Fort Richardson, Alaska, 16-17 April 1945," 2, Series 16, Box 17, Folder 265, Geist Collection.

13. Marvin R. Marston, "Report on Tundra Army," 11 October 1945, Box 18, Folder 294, Geist Collection.

14. Quoted in Wooley and Martz, "Tundra Army," 158.

15. M. R. Marston, "A Five Point Plan for the Eskimo," undated memo-randum (circa 1945), Box 17, Folder 269, Geist Collection.

16. Wooley and Martz, "Tundra Army," 157.

17. M. R. Marston to ATG Commanders, 10 March 1945, Series 16, Box 15, Folder 248, Geist Collection.

18. Frank Budaj to Geist, undated telegram, Series 16, Box 18, Folder 287, Geist to Marston, undated telegram, Marston to Geist, undated telegrams, Series 16, Box 15, Folder 244, Geist Collection; Log Book 1945; "WDC G-2 Section, Balloon Sightings and Related Incidents in Alaska & Unalaska," Box 40 RG 499, NARA.

19. Marston to Commanding Officers, 17 April 1945, Series 16, Box 17, Folder 265, Geist Collection; "Condensed Minutes," 26–28.

20. Hays, "Silent Years in Alaska," 142.

21. Naske, *Ernest Gruening*, 73–79.

22. "Condensed Minutes," 3.

23. "Condensed Minutes," 5–9; Robert S. Fleming to H. I. Cole, 13 April 1945, Series 2, Box 8 RG 160, NARA.

24. "Condensed Minutes," 3, 8–12.

25. Marston to Commanding Officers, 17 April 1945.

26. Marston, *Men of the Tundra*, 159–61.

6. DEFENSE

1. Joseph C. Boyce, "Report to V. Bush on the Japanese Balloon Problem," June 1945, Box 6 RG 160, NARA.

2. Boyce, "Report to V. Bush," 18.

3. Boyce, "Report to V. Bush."

4. Boyce, "Report to V. Bush," 32.

5. Boyce, "Report to V. Bush," 1.

6. F. A. Kreidel to Commanding General, 8 June 1945, Box 8 RG 160, NARA.

7. Charles A. Carlson, "Meteorological Study in Connection with Japanese Balloons," 20 May 1945, Box 37 RG 499, NARA; William H. Hammond, "A Study of Japanese Free Balloons and Related Incidents, Western Defense Command Intelligence Study No. 1," 38–42, Series 2, Box 6 RG 160, NARA; P. E. Peabody, "Japanese Balloon Report," 28 April 1945, Box 8 RG 160, NARA.

8. A detailed account of the Aleutian campaign can be found in Garfield, *Thousand-Mile War*.

9. John Cloe to author, e-mail communication, 18 April 2012.

10. "Japanese Balloons: Detection, Destruction," OPD Special Supplement no. 1, 3 April 1945, Box 8 RG 160, NARA.

11. Technical Air Intelligence Center, "Japanese Balloon and Attached Devices, Report #41," 86–93, May 1945, Box 6 RG 160, NARA; Samuel

R. Peterson to Commanding General, Eleventh Army Air Force, 30 April 1945, Everett M. Fazioli to Commanding General, Alaskan Department, 3 May 1945, Box 8 RG 160, NARA.

12. "Summary of Suspected Balloon Transmission, 30 December 1944 to 28 March 1945," 29 March 1945, Box 39 RG 499, NARA.

13. M. J. Marshall to Major Walker, 22 January 1945, Box 39 RG 499, NARA.

14. Mikesh, *Japan's World War II*, 34.

15. Proceedings of Conference, 24.

16. P. E. Peabody, "Japanese Balloon Report," n.d., Box 8 RG 160, NARA.

17. Thomas H. Green, "Use of Prisoners of War to Combat Forest Fires," memorandum, 17 May 1945, Box 2903, Record Group 407: Army-AG Classified Decimal File, 1943–45, 452.26 to 452.4, NARA.

18. "Ninth Service Command, Forest Fire Fighting Plan, 1945," undated memorandum, Box 10 RG 160, NARA.

19. Mikesh, *Japan's World War II*, 29.

20. "Plan for Defense against Bacteriological Warfare in Connection with Japanese Balloons," 20 July 1945, Box 10 RG 160, NARA.

21. "Shipments of BW Samples Collected from Japanese Balloons," undated memorandum, Box 11 RG 160, NARA.

22. Webber, *Retaliation*, 122; Lyall E. Johnson, "Japanese Balloon, Toppenish, Washington, 10 March 1945," memorandum, 28 March 1945, Box 1, Record Group 77: U.S. Army Corps of Engineers, Manhattan Engineer District, Intelligence Office, Japanese Balloons 1945, Correspondence and Reports, NARA-Seattle.

23. LeMay and Kantor, *Mission with LeMay*, 384.

24. Quoted in Schaffer, *Wings of Judgment*, 142.

25. Schaffer, *Wings of Judgment*, 107; Crane, *Bombs, Cities, and Civilians*, 125–36.

26. Dower, *War without Mercy*, 8.

27. Dower, *War without Mercy*, 41.

28. Dower, *War without Mercy*, 10–11.

7. CANADA

1. Maurice Pope, "Memorandum for the Prime Minister," 20 January 1945 RG 25-A-3-b, Vol. 5739, File Part 1, 22-Ts, LAC.

2. "Conference Held at Western Air Command," 3 May 1945, File C-15-13-9 (Vol. 4) RG 24, Vol. 5195, LAC.

3. Orville Eadie to D.M.I., 24 January 1945 RG 24-C-1, File 8872-1, LAC.

4. "Report on Coordinating Meeting, re: Japanese Balloons," 24 January 1945 RG 24, Vol. 222, File 1400-16 part 1, LAC.

5. "General Summary: Japanese Balloons in Canada," 15 March 1945, File C-15-13-9 (Vol. 4) RG 24, Vol. 5195, LAC.

6. Francis J. Graling to J. H. Jenkins, 29 January 1945, File C-15-13-9 (Vol. 1) RG 24, Vol. 5195, LAC.

7. Perras, *Franklin Roosevelt*, 121.

8. Perras, *Franklin Roosevelt*, 43.

9. "General Summary, Japanese Balloons in Canada," 15 March 1945 RG 24, Vol. 222, File 1400-16 part 2, LAC.

10. Quoted in Joost, "Western Air Command," 65.

11. Joost, "Western Air Command," 66.

12. Joost, "Western Air Command," 62.

13. "Emergency Anti-Balloon Squad Which Countered Jap Menace Disbanded," *Toronto Globe and Mail*, 6 September 1945, 1.

14. East, *White Paper*, 15.

15. East, *White Paper*, 28.

16. "British Columbia Police: Japanese Balloons," 30 April 1945 RG 24, Vol. 2678, LAC.

17. J. D. L. Gray, "Re: Pacific Crest Eastern Railway–Complaint of," 18 April 1945 RG 24, Vol. 2678, LAC.

18. "Ardi Lake, B.C. Incident," 16 April 1945; E. G. D. Murray, "Interview with Mr. Charles Camsell," 12 April 1945 RG 24, Vol. 2678, LAC.

19. "Japanese Balloon Incidents, Summary No. 8," 4 April 1945, S.I. 9-1-72, Sub-file Vol. 2 RG 24, Vol. 11894, LAC.

20. R. W. McKay, "Memorandum No. 19," 2 February 1945, S.I. 9-1-72, Sub-file Vol. 2 RG 24, Vol. 11894, LAC.

21. "Examination of Recovered Balloons," undated report, File C-15-13-9 (Vol. 4) RG 24, Vol. 5195, LAC.
22. Eidai, *Onnatachi no Fusen Bakudan*, 168–69, 173.

8. CENSORSHIP

1. James F. Perry to Chief, MIS, 6 March 1945, Box 11 RG 160, NARA.
2. "Censorship Policy with Regard to Japanese Balloons," 9 March 1945, Box 11 RG 160, NARA.
3. Sweeney, *Secrets of Victory*, 36.
4. Sweeney, *Secrets of Victory*, 6.
5. Hoover, quoted in Sweeney, *Secrets of Victory*, 36.
6. "Tactical Conversation, Colonel Gruhn–Colonel White," 19 March 1945, Box 8 RG 160, NARA.
7. Charles D. Frierson to Commanding General, 25 March 1945, Box 8 RG 160, NARA.
8. Frierson to Commanding General, 25 March 1945.
9. "Conversation between Col. Kreidel, Fifth Service Command, and Colonel Sharp, Intelligence Division, A.S.F." 23 April 1945, Box 8 RG 160, NARA.
10. *Tim Tyler's Luck*, syndicated comic, *Columbus (OH) Dispatch*, 22 April 1945.
11. "Annex No. 1 to G-2 Periodic Report No. 188," 4 August 1945, Box 11 RG 160, NARA.
12. *Smilin' Jack*, syndicated comic, *Chicago Tribune*, 29 July 1945.
13. "Telephone Conversation," 5 April 1945, Box 8 RG 160, NARA.
14. "Telephone Conversation," 5 April 1945.
15. "Telephone Conversation," 5 April 1945.
16. H. B. White to Assistant Chief of Staff, G-2, 6 April 1945, Box 8 RG 160, NARA.
17. Byron Price, "Strictly Confidential Note to Editors and Broadcasters," 28 March 1945, Box 11 RG 160, NARA.
18. H. C. Pratt to Earl G. Warren, 5 May 1945, Box 37 RG 499, NARA.
19. "Transcript of Telephone Conversation, No. 618," 2 May 1945, Box 37 RG 499, NARA.

20. "Transcript of Telephone Conversation, No. 623," 3 May 1945, Box 37 RG 499, NARA.

21. "Special Japanese Balloon Committee, Minutes of the 3rd Meeting," 5 May 1945 RG 24, Vol. 2678, LAC.

22. Juillerat, "Mitchell Monument," 112.

23. Juillerat, "Mitchell Monument," 111.

24. Einar Engen to William Lemke, 20 September 1945, "Frank J. Patzke and Others, Report No. 360," 8, U.S. Senate, 81st Congress, 1st Session.

25. Juillerat, "Mitchell Monument," 112.

26. Harold Cassill to Paul F. Ewing, 16 May 1945, Box 39 RG 499, NARA.

27. Orval Thompson to Wayne L. Morse, 9 May 1945, Box 37 RG 499, NARA.

28. "Transcript of Telephone Conversation No. 635," 9 May 1945, Box 34 RG 499, NARA.

29. H. C. Pratt to Mr. Blank, 14 May 1945, Box 37 RG 499, NARA.

30. "Japanese Balloon Information Bulletin No. 1," 14 May 1945, Box 10 RG 160, NARA.

31. "Those Jap Balloons," *Tacoma News Tribune and Sunday Ledger*, 3 June 1945.

32. "A Major News Bungle by the Army," *Los Angeles Times*, 24 May 1945.

33. Vandyce Hamren to Commanding General, WDC, 15 June 1945 RG 24-C-1, File 8872-1, LAC.

34. "Paper Balloon Bombs," *Ottawa Citizen*, 24 May 1945.

35. Sweeney, *Secrets of Victory*, 192–93.

36. Byron Price, "Confidential Note to Editors and Broadcasters," 22 May 1945, Box 37 RG 499, NARA.

37. Edgar F. G. Swasey to The Staff, 22 May 1945, Box 11 RG 160, NARA.

38. "Telephone Conversation 0005z," 23 May 1945, Box 40 RG 499, NARA.

39. Clayton Bissell to Commanding General, 26 May 1945, Box 40 RG 499, NARA.

40. The internment camp newspapers mentioned the balloons only in passing as editors and reporters possessed no detailed information

about the devices or U.S. defense procedures. Articles noted only possible sightings by camp residents and rumors of downed balloons in the area. See *Rohwer (AR) Outpost*, 13 June 1945; *Minidoka Irrigator* (Hunt ID), 7 July 1945. One newspaper, the *Heart Mountain (WY) Sentinel*, referred to the Kalispell balloon in a January 18, 1945, article.

41. "Explosive-Laden Balloons Sail to U.S. from Japan," *University of Washington Daily* (Seattle), 23 May 1945.

42. Elmore H. Biles, "Violation of Censorship by the *University of Washington Daily*," 30 May 1945, Box 39 RG 499, NARA.

43. "Don't Play with Jap Balloon Bomb like This. It Might Kill You," *Toronto Daily Star*, 31 May 1945.

44. Bourrie, *Fog of War*, 229–30.

45. "West Warned against Unexploded Bombs Fallen with Jap Balloons," *Ottawa Citizen*, 23 May 1945; "Secrecy Well Kept," *Toronto Globe and Mail*, 23 May 1945.

46. "Saw Wife and Five Children Killed by Jap Balloon Bomb," *Seattle Times*, 1 June 1945. Mitchell's statement that he had previously heard of the Japanese balloons cannot be confirmed. It seems unlikely, however, because no other Bly resident claimed to possess such knowledge in advance of the explosion. Mitchell himself contradicted the statement in a letter written eight months after the incident: "First of all I want to say that none of us had ever heard anything about the Japanese bombs and didn't even suspect that such a thing existed." See Archie E. Mitchell to William Lemke, 18 January 1946, "Frank J. Patzke and Others, Report No. 360," 7.

## 9. SUMMER

1. P. E. Peabody, "Japanese Balloon Report, No. 128," 26 July 1945, Box 8 RG 160, NARA.

2. William H. Hammond to Chief of Staff, 24 May 1945, Box 39 RG 499, NARA.

3. Hammond to Chief of Staff, 24 May 1945.

4. P. E. Peabody, "Japanese Balloon Report, No. 82," 2 June 1945, Box 8 RG 160, NARA.

5. C. A. Perkins, "Japanese Balloon recovered near Yerington, Nevada, on or about 9 November 1944," 5 June 1945, Box 41 RG 499, NARA.

6. "Statement of Charles F. Ragsdale," 17 April 1975, Box 1, Folder 1, BWP.

7. Martin A. Campbell, "Inspection of Japanese Free Balloon Recovered near Indian Springs, Nevada, 20 July 1945," Box 35 RG 499, NARA.

8. Compton, quoted in Home and Low, "Postwar Scientific Intelligence Missions," 530.

9. Home and Low, "Postwar Scientific Intelligence Missions," 531.

10. United States Army Forces, Pacific Scientific and Technical Advisory Section, "Report on Scientific Intelligence Survey in Japan, September and October 1945," vol. 1, 1 November 1945 (hereafter cited as Compton Report), 1, Records of the War Department General and Special Staffs, Military Intelligence Division, Record Group 165, S-C Intelligence Reference Pubs ("P" File), 1940-1945, Box 2045, NARA.

11. Sueki Kusaba to Cornelius Conley, 24 November 1961, Box 13, BWP.

12. Compton Report, vol. 1, 6.

13. An Associated Press story about the balloon program dated October 2, 1945 — one day before the Kusaba interview was to take place — refers to an interview with "the staff officers' technical section, Japanese headquarters." If Kusaba was the unnamed source for the article, it seems likely a reporter located the general in Tokyo and spoke to him separately from Compton, who never would have allowed information from his highly classified interviews to be made public. The article notes the total number of balloons launched, estimated cost of the program, and reasons for its termination in April 1945. The information might also have come from Kunitake, Inouye, or another balloon official. See "Japs' Expensive V-1 Bombs Fail to Impress Victims," 2 October 1945, clipping from unknown newspaper, File 149, War Pacific 1941, Weapons, Balloon Bombs, Canadian War Museum, Ottawa.

14. Compton Report, vol. 3, 3-A-1.

15. Compton Report, Appendix 23-1, 2.
16. Marston, *Men of the Tundra*, 203–4.
17. Marvin R. Marston, "Report on the Tundra Army (ATG)," October 11, 1945, 1-3, Series 16, Box 18, Folder 294, Geist Collection. Although Marston staunchly advocated Alaska Native rights and unfailingly regarded them as equals, it must be noted his rhetoric frequently sentimentalized Natives and contained common stereotypes of the day. For example, he was given to refer to Natives as *dusky-skinned* and *simple kindly folk*, terms that today appear insensitive. Chris Wooley and Mike Martz write of cultural relativism and the ATG: "In the 1940s, even the most enlightened non-Natives generally considered Eskimos to be noble, unassuming, and happy conquerors of the forest and tundra—complete masters of the natural world but unable to comprehend or cope on their own with events in the 'modern' world. With the luxury of a historical perspective, and using an anthropological approach, we can see through these stereotypes and appreciate the men and women of the ATG within the context of their unique cultures." See Wooley and Martz, "Tundra Army," 155.
18. Wooley and Martz, "Tundra Army," 160.
19. John Schaeffer, interview by Barry Zellen, July 1992 (unpublished, personal collection of the author).
20. "Instructions for Disposing of Japanese Balloon Materiel," undated memorandum RG 24-C-1, File 8872-1, LAC (although the memo itself is undated, an accompanying document in the same file carries a date of 22 September 1945). Charles Keim, a professor of journalism at the University of Alaska, authored a biography of Otto Geist in 1969, in which he wrote, "[Geist] salvaged the paper and bottom rim of this one [a balloon recovered near the village of Kipnuk] and sent part of it to the University of Alaska Museum." In 2008 the author contacted the curator of historical collections at the museum, who found no balloon materials in the museum's collection and no written record that such materials were ever received. It is possible that Geist, an inveterate collector of Alaskana whose home and office

were both crammed full of memorabilia of every type, kept the balloon evidence but did not officially catalog the material. See Keim, *Aghvook, White Eskimo*, 252.

21. "Bush Pilot Sights Japanese Balloon North of Ft. Yukon," *Fairbanks Daily News-Miner*, 3 January 1955, 1–2.

22. W. H. Wilbur, "Japan's Balloon Raid on America," unpublished draft, William F. McDermott Papers, Box 16, Folder 163, Special Collections and University Archives, Richard J. Daley Library, Chicago, Illinois.

23. Wilbur, "Japan's Balloon Raid on America."

24. George E. Weidner, "Technical and Technological Survey, Japanese Bombing Balloons," report prepared for Chief of Engineers, War Department, U.S. Army, 2 January 1946, Record Group 24-C-1, File 8872-1, LAC.

EPILOGUE

1. Charles F. Bisenius to Frank J. Patzke, 8 August 1945, Box 34 RG 499, NARA.

2. Kenneth C. Royall to Earl C. Michener, 10 November 1947, letter included in U.S. Senate Report No. 360 (H. R. 1299), 81st Congress, 1st Session.

3. U.S. Senate Report no. 360 (H. R. 1299), 81st Congress, 1st Session.

4. U.S. Senate Report no. 360.

5. McKay, quoted in Juillerat, "Mitchell Monument," 113.

6. Archie Mitchell to T. S. Durment, 9 April 1950, Mitchell Collection, Bly Ranger District, Fremont National Forest, Bly, Oregon.

7. Sol, *On Paper Wings*, documentary.

8. Gunderson, quoted in Fincher, "On Wings of Forgiveness," 87.

9. Sol, *On Paper Wings*.

10. Fincher, "On Wings of Forgiveness," 88.

11. Sol, *On Paper Wings*.

12. Juillerat, "Mitchell Monument," 114.

13. Sol, *On Paper Wings*.

14. Cook and Cook, *Japan at War*, 192.

15. Cook and Cook, *Japan at War*, 192.
16. Hisaga, quoted in Mary Ellen Rodgers, "Mitchell Recreation Area, National Register of Historic Places Registration Form," 31 July 2001, section 7, p. 5.
17. Rodgers, "Mitchell Recreation Area," section 8, p. 8.

# Bibliography

ARCHIVAL COLLECTIONS

Alaska and Polar Regions, Rasmuson Library, University of Alaska Fairbanks
    Otto Geist Collection
Bly Ranger District, Fremont National Forest, Bly, Oregon
    Mitchell Collection
Canadian War Museum, Ottawa
    War Pacific 1941 Papers (Weapons, Balloon Bombs)
Hoover Institution, Stanford University
    Bert Webber Papers
Library and Archives Canada
    Record Group 24, Volumes 222, 2678, 5195, 11894
    Record Group 24-C-1
    Record Group 25-A-3-b, Volume 5739
National Archives and Records Administration, College Park, Maryland
    Record Group 160: Army Service Forces, Intelligence Division
    Record Group 165: War Department General and Special Staffs, Military
    Intelligence Division
    Record Group 407: Army Adjutant General's Office
    Record Group 499: Records of U.S. Army Defense Commands
National Archives and Records Administration, Seattle, Washington
    Record Group 77: U.S. Army Corps of Engineers, Manhattan Engineer District
    Record Group 95: U.S. Forest Service

Richard J. Daley Library, Chicago, Illinois
William F. McDermott Papers

BOOKS, ARTICLES, GOVERNMENT PUBLICATIONS, AND OTHER FORMS

Avery, Donald. "Canadian Scientists, CBW Weapons and Japan, 1939–1945." In *Science and the Pacific War: Science and Survival in the Pacific, 1939–1945*, edited by Roy M. MacLeod, 229–51. Dordrecht, The Netherlands: Kluwer Academic, 2000.

Bourrie, Mark. *The Fog of War: Censorship of Canada's Media in World War Two*. Vancouver: Douglas & McIntyre, 2011.

Cook, Haruko Taya, and Theodore F. Cook, eds. *Japan at War: An Oral History*. New York: New Press, 1992.

Crane, Conrad C. *Bombs, Cities, and Civilians: American Airpower Strategy in World War II*. Lawrence: University Press of Kansas, 1993.

de Mendelssohn, Peter. *Japan's Political Warfare*. London: George Allen & Unwin, 1944.

Doolittle, James H. *I Could Never Be So Lucky Again: An Autobiography*. New York: Bantam Books, 1991.

Dower, John W. *War without Mercy: Race and Power in the Pacific War*. Pantheon: New York, 1986.

East, Charles A. *White Paper: Japanese Balloons of World War Two*. Prince George, British Columbia: College of New Caledonia Press, 1993.

Eidai, Hayashi. *Onnatachi no Fusen Bakudan*. Tokyo: Aki Shobou, 1985.

Fincher, Jack. "On Wings of Forgiveness." *Reader's Digest*, March 1989, 85–90.

"Frank J. Patzke and Others, Report No. 360, H. R. 1299." U.S. Senate, 81st Congress, 1st session, 1950.

Garfield, Brian. *The Thousand-Mile War: World War II in Alaska and the Aleutians*. Fairbanks: University of Alaska Press, 1995.

Glines, Carroll V. *The Doolittle Raid: America's Daring First Strike against Japan*. New York: Orion Books, 1988.

Hays, Otis E., Jr. "The Silent Years in Alaska: The Military Blackout during World War II." *Alaska Journal* 16 (1986): 40–47.

Hendricks, Charles. "The Eskimos and the Defense of Alaska." *Pacific Historical Review* 54, no. 3 (August 1985): 271–95.

Home, R. W., and Morris F. Low. "Postwar Scientific Intelligence Missions to Japan." *Isis* 84, no. 3 (September 1993): 527–37.

Joost, Mathias. "Western Air Command and the Japanese Balloon Campaign." *Canadian Military Journal* 6, no. 2 (Summer 2005): 59–68.

Juillerat, Lee. "Mitchell Monument: A Place Remembered." *Journal of the Shaw Historical Library* 17 (2003): 109–16.

Keim, Charles J. *Aghvook, White Eskimo: Otto Geist and Alaskan Archaeology*. College: University of Alaska Press, 1969.

LeMay, Curtis E., with MacKinlay Kantor. *Mission with LeMay: My Story*. Garden City NY: Doubleday, 1965.

Lewis, John M. "Ooishi's Observation: Viewed in the Context of Jet Stream Discovery." *Bulletin of the American Meteorology Society* 84, no. 3 (March 2003): 357–69.

Marston, Muktuk. *Men of the Tundra: Alaska Eskimos at War*. New York: October House, 1969.

McPhee, John. "Balloons of War." *New Yorker*, 29 January 1996, 52–60.

Mercado, Stephen C. "The Japanese Army's Noborito Research Institute." *International Journal of Intelligence and Counterintelligence* 17, no. 2 (2004): 286–99.

Mikesh, Robert C. *Japan's World War II Balloon Bomb Attacks on North America*. Washington DC: Smithsonian Institution Press, 1973.

Naske, Claus-M. *Ernest Gruening: Alaska's Greatest Governor*. Fairbanks: University of Alaska Press, 2004.

Perras, Galen Roger. *Franklin Roosevelt and the Origins of the Canadian-American Security Alliance, 1933–1945: Necessary, but Not Necessary Enough*. Westport CT: Praeger, 1998.

Rodgers, Mary Ellen. "Mitchell Recreation Area, National Register of Historic Places Registration Form," 31 July 2001.

Schaffer, Ronald. *Wings of Judgment: American Bombing in World War II*. New York: Oxford University Press, 1985.

Sol, Ilana, dir. *On Paper Wings*. Film Is Forever Productions, 2008.

Sweeney, Michael S. *Secrets of Victory: The Office of Censorship and the American Press and Radio in World War II.* Chapel Hill: University of North Carolina Press, 2001.

Takada, Teiji. [Balloon Bomb.] *Shizen* 6, no. 1 (January 1951): 24–33.

Unsworth, Michael E. "The Japanese Balloon Bomb Campaign in North Dakota." *North Dakota History* 64, no. 1 (Winter 1997): 21–26.

Webber, Bert. *Retaliation: Japanese Attacks and Allied Countermeasures on the Pacific Coast in World War II.* Corvallis: Oregon State University Press, 1975.

Wooley, Chris, and Mike Martz. "The Tundra Army: Patriots of Arctic Alaska." In *Alaska at War, 1941–1945: The Forgotten War Remembered: Papers from the Alaska at War Symposium, Anchorage, Alaska, November 11–13, 1993,* edited by Fern Chandonnet, 155–60. Anchorage: Alaska at War Committee, 1995.

# Index

Page numbers in italic indicate illustrations.

Page numbers in bold type refer to an entry in the appendix.

Studies in War, Society, and the Military

To order or obtain more information on these or other University
of Nebraska Press titles, visit nebraskapress.unl.edu.